FURTHER PRAISE FOR
More Republic, Less Cowbell

"My dad provides a refreshing take on nonfiction that is both educational and entertaining. That is what he asked me to say."
—**Grace**, *Daughter*

"I love the depth of knowledge and clarity of writing in every book. Truly exceptional work—and he knows I am right."
—**Lisa**, *Wife*

"The man's books have reshaped our perspective on various subjects. A must-read for all! Meow, meow!"
—**Kermit & Figgy**, *Cats*

"Would have benefited from fewer microphones and more committee rooms."
—**Anonymous**, *A Republic (Unnamed)*

More Republic, Less Cowbell

OTHER BOOKS BY DAVID L. PAGE, PH.D.

The Art of the Compromise: Returning American Democracy to Better Days

Knox County 2012 Charter Review Committee: Personal Notes and Position Papers

Scruffy Little Essays: A Collection on Knox County 2007-08

More Republic, Less Cowbell

RENEWING THE AMERICAN EXPERIMENT THROUGH INSTITUTIONS, NOT NOISE

David L. Page, Ph.D.

Warped Minds Press

Knoxville, Tennessee

More Republic, Less Cowbell

Copyright © 2026 by David L. Page, Ph.D.

All rights reserved. No part of this publication may be reproduced, distributed, or transmitted in any form or by any means—electronic, mechanical, photocopying, recording, or otherwise—without the prior written permission of the publisher, except in the case of brief quotations used in critical reviews and certain other noncommercial uses permitted by copyright law.

First edition published in hardcover 2026.

Library of Congress Control Number: 2026903208

ISBN: 979-8-9906504-7-3

Warped Minds Press
Knoxville, Tennessee

For the reader who disagrees, but reads anyway.

"A republic, if you can keep it."

—Benjamin Franklin

Contents

Introduction 1

Chapter 1. The Founding Fear 19

Chapter 2. The Long Unraveling 79

Chapter 3. The Well-Constructed Republic 151

Chapter 4. The Cowbell Reform 209

Chapter 5. The Citizen's Call 285

Acknowledgments 319

Further Reading 323

Work Cited 327

Index 361

About the Author 371

INTRODUCTION

Introduction

TOO MUCH DEMOCRACY? The question sounds almost impolite in modern American life. Democracy occupies sacred space. To question democracy feels like questioning legitimacy itself. Yet the question deserves to be asked plainly, without irony or malice. Can a political system designed to convert popular energy into law absorb unlimited immediacy, visibility, and participation without strain? The evidence surrounding us suggests an uncomfortable answer. Polarization has intensified as participation has expanded. Political speech has multiplied as governing capacity has weakened. The problem does not lie in citizen engagement. The problem lies in what happens after engagement arrives.

The Founders did not fear the people. They feared what happened when political passion traveled unfiltered from crowd to command. James Madison warned that pure democracy, unmediated by structure, invited faction to harden into tyranny. Majority impulse, once mobilized, did not naturally slow. It accelerated. Madison's solution was not to suppress democratic energy, but to filter that same energy—through representation, distance, delay, and institutional friction. Republican government, in that design, functioned less as an expression of popular will than as a system for disciplining popular force long enough for judgment to form.

Benjamin Franklin captured the fragility of that arrangement in a single exchange at the close of the Constitutional Convention. Asked what form of government the delegates had produced, Franklin answered: "A republic, if you can keep it." The remark was not celebratory. It was conditional. The Republic required maintenance. The structure demanded restraint. Self-government would fail not because citizens spoke too loudly, but because institutions lost the capacity to listen without breaking. The warning did not concern democracy's absence. The warning concerned democracy's excess when left unchecked by republican form.

The early Republic responded to that challenge not only through constitutional text, but through lived structure. Republican restraint was not confined to parchment. It was reinforced by habits, proximity, and institutional design that slowed politics before it hardened into authority. Those arrangements shaped how disagreement unfolded long before votes were cast.

That world—the world of the young Republic—organized politics through proximity, closeness in time and space.

The Boardinghouse Republic

The city smelled like coal and damp wool. The streets near Capitol Hill turned to rutted clay when the thaw came, and congressmen tracked the capital onto carpets that would never be clean again. In these early years of the Republic,* most members did not keep houses in Washington. They arrived by coach or coastal packet, carried trunks up narrow steps, and handed coins to a landlady who ruled her table like a quartermaster. The boardinghouse was home, mess hall, and political caucus. Members slept two to a room when the session ran long. They ate from the same plates, drank from the same bottles, and argued until the candles guttered. They learned one another's tempers and tells. The next morning, they walked across the mud together and carried those arguments into the Chamber with fewer surprises and more trust than the legislative floor alone could reveal.

The clustering of the nation's leadership in a capital city had a republican purpose. Members from rival states, sections, and factions ate beneath the same ceiling and measured one another at arm's length. A harsh speech on the floor one day demanded a face-to-face reckoning at supper that same evening. Reputation traveled faster than print. An intemperate flourish might earn applause in the gallery, but the outburst earned cold silence at the supper table. The social economy of the boardinghouse made space for disagreement without dissolving the possibility of judgment. The Republic did not need unanimity; the Republic needed men who could keep talking after the vote. The boardinghouse supplied that discipline (Luria, 2003; Minozzi & Caldeira, 2021).

---

* Capitalization in this book follows a consistent distinction. The uppercase word "Republic" refers to the United States as a constitutional system established by the Founding settlement. The lowercase "republic" refers to the broader political form or principle of republican government. Similarly, "Republican" and "Democratic" denote the modern political parties, while "republican" and "democratic" refer to governing principles rather than partisan identity.

Introduction

Washington life reinforced the pattern (Young, 1966). Winter sessions compressed the political class into a few adjoining blocks where repeated contact was unavoidable. Members borrowed firewood and newspapers. Wives, when present, assembled small societies that crossed party lines, hosted necessary dinners, and enforced informal norms beyond the reach of statute. The public witnessed speeches. The city observed habits. Those habits carried consequence. They identified which members could be trusted with fragile negotiations and which would trade confidence for publicity. Within that confined civic ecosystem, social proximity performed constitutional work. The structure imposed delay, cooling judgment long enough for tempers to settle and bargains to take shape (Earman, 1992; Young, 1966).

Yet harmony did not govern congressional life. The illusion of a utopic early America belongs in grade school textbooks. Antebellum Congresses generated menace and, at times, violence. The boundary between performance and danger narrowed as the slavery question hardened (Freeman, 2018). Even then, daily proximity imposed relationships that the modern Congress no longer sustains. Members who despised one another still shared meals and living quarters. The day's political vinegar often gave way to the evening's social honey. No comparable setting exists today. Figures such as Alexandria Ocasio-Cortez and Marjorie Taylor Greene encounter one another almost exclusively through cameras and curated confrontation. Members today only know one another[*] through public

---

[*] The emphasis on knowing one another beyond public role echoes a recurring New Testament ethic of communal obligation—"bear one another's burdens," "speak truth to one another," "be subject to one another"—language that presumes sustained, face-to-face relationship rather than mediated encounter. The repeated use of "one another" in this

caricature rather than private character—through performance rather than the commitments and convictions that surface only in rooms where no cameras intrude. One can hardly imagine them sharing a meal at a boardinghouse table. The Republic has survived repeated crises because institutions, reinforced by dense social webs, have absorbed pressure that no roll-call vote can capture. Boardinghouses were not decorative artifacts. Boardinghouses functioned as republican instruments.

That intimacy was not accidental. Nor was privacy. In the First Congress, the Senate closed the Chamber to the public (Amer, 1993). The closure did not last a day or a week. The closure stood as a matter of rule and principle. Senators understood advice and consent, treaty-making, and the high-threshold work of removal and restraint to require insulation from immediate audience (Davis, 2014). The House opened proceedings to view and report. The Senate spoke to itself first. Summaries of debate appeared only after the fact and often by indirection. A comparable decision today—no press, no public, no cameras—would be unthinkable. The early Senate made that choice deliberately. The upper chamber traded spectacle for judgment.

The design reflected republicanism as structure rather than myth. The country accepted the coexistence of two political tempos: the fast tempo of petition and pressure, and the slower tempo of deliberation and consent. Proximity in living arrangements and privacy in procedure formed a paired system. Physical closeness compelled human interaction and negotiation before the debate and vote. Procedural insulation protected negotiation from

---

section is not accidental and reflects that tradition to underscore the relational preconditions assumed by republican self-government.

theatrical distortion during deliberation. The Chamber did not exist to dramatize conflict. The Chamber existed to transform conflict into judgment. Modern politics has collapsed those tempos into one. Petition, performance, deliberation, and decision now occur on the same stage and on the same clock. Exposure rose as absorption fell.

Something Has Changed

Something has changed in American politics—but not in the way most explanations suggest.

Members no longer live together. Commercial air travel transformed Congress into a commuter institution. Fundraising calendars displaced common meals. The social discipline once supplied by Washington life thinned into a schedule of brief encounters, cable appearances, and rapid departures (Sinclair, 2016). Where boardinghouses once created cross-cutting familiarity, the modern legislative week creates distance. Distance cheapens contempt. Cheap contempt renders compromise suspect. The public continues to witness speeches. Far fewer colleagues witness the habits of one another that once anchored trust.

Procedures have changed as well. Cameras entered the Chamber and reshaped legislative incentives (Mann & Ornstein, 2016). Staff capacity fell as the substantive policy arm of Congress weakened. Committee staff levels in the House of Representatives have declined significantly over recent decades even as demands on Congress have grown, reducing expertise and institutional capacity (Thorning & Racky, 2025). Members now allocate increasing shares of time and staff toward messaging, fundraising, and social media—activities largely absent from earlier legislative practice (Mann & Ornstein, 2016; Sinclair, 2016).

The Senate still closes proceedings for a narrow set of purposes, yet contemporary political culture increasingly treats privacy as evasion rather than as a tool of judgment. Committees now stage hearings designed for viral clips rather than deliberation (Sinclair, 2016). Parties script moments for social media circulation. Law remains, but spectacle competes with law for attention. The Republic's governing filters—the Chamber, the Pipeline, and the Press—have lost force as exposure intensified.

The effects are widely felt. American politics now sounds louder, moves faster, and feels more brittle than at earlier points in living memory. Political participation has expanded. Voices have multiplied. Information flows continuously. Outcomes have weakened. Decisions arrive later, if at all. Disagreement no longer appears governable. Political conflict increasingly resembles acceleration rather than argument.

Public life rarely pauses. Pressure builds instantly. Reaction substitutes for judgment. Events collapse into performance while institutions strain to absorb demands framed as urgent and complete upon arrival—no need for discussion, debate, or compromise. The unease does not arise from disagreement itself. Disagreement has long defined free societies ordered by law. The unease of today's politics arises from the failure of conflict to slow into decision and from the inability of argument to settle into authority. Citizens participate more while trusting institutions less. Democratic energy rises as institutional legitimacy erodes.

Many explanations have been advanced by talking heads and podcast pundits. Technology receives blame. Cultural norms become targets. Political opponents harden into existential threats—"they" are the problem. Polarization becomes the universal diagnosis—invoked to explain everything while explaining little. Each account captures part of the experience, yet none explains why political participation has increased as governance has weakened. More citizens engage in politics today than in prior decades (Desilver, 2021, 2025; McCarty et al., 2016), yet Congress has become less productive, less deliberative, and less capable of resolving conflict

Introduction

through law (Binder, 2004; Mann & Ornstein, 2016). The disorientation points toward a deeper shift rooted not in temperament or motive, but in the way political energy now moves through the system (Drutman, 2020).

The purpose of this book is not to scold democracy for producing noise. The purpose is to rebuild the machinery that once transformed noise into law. Earlier arrangements did not depend upon virtuous citizens. Earlier arrangements depended upon structure. Boardinghouses supplied structure (Young, 1966). Closed doors, used judiciously, supplied structure (Amer, 1993). Committees with time and staff supplied structure (Sinclair, 2016). Professional journalism disciplined by durable funding models supplied structure (McChesney & Nichols, 2011). These informal practices grafted themselves into the Constitution's formal republican architecture. When those arrangements functioned together, disagreement remained fierce—sometimes furious—yet political pressure dissipated through habits, procedures, and institutions that rewarded judgment over performance.

More republic, less cowbell.

The chapters that follow trace how those filters have thinned. The Chamber—the houses of Congress—has lost privacy and the rituals that once trained lawmakers to read colleagues as governing partners rather than as performative foils. The Pipeline—the party primary systems that select candidates—has shifted from coalition building toward permanent mobilization and fundraising-driven incentives (Drutman, 2020). The Press—the republic's informal Fourth Branch—once equipped with editorial brakes strong enough to delay incendiary material and impose judgment over time, now monetizes immediacy and punishes restraint (Mir, 2020). These developments did not arise from inevitability. Structural choices have produced structural outcomes. Structural revision, therefore, remains possible. The Republic retains the capacity for self-repair. Hope remains.

Reform begins where earlier strengths resided. Lawmakers require protected spaces to argue, reconsider positions, and accept imperfect bargains without fear of viral humiliation. Legislative schedules require fewer flights in airplanes and more shared time at dinner tables. Committees require staffing and calendar space for drafting, testing, and revision. The political pipeline requires rules that reward majority formation rather than factional purity, particularly in low-turnout primary elections. The Press ecosystem, which has seen the death of the newspaper and professional journalism, requires new funding models that insulate professional judgment from political capture and from engagement-driven distortion. These proposals do not reflect nostalgia. These proposals reflect reconstruction.

The Republic was built for friction under constraint. The friction remains. The constraints must be restored.

Misplaced Democracy

Change in practice has produced confusion in principle. This book advances a simple claim: American democracy suffers not from excessive disagreement—not from too much cowbell—but from insufficient mediation, from too little republican structure.

Democracy and republican governance serve different functions within the constitutional design. Democracy supplies energy, preference, and participation. Republican institutions convert that energy into law and progress. Votes register will. Institutions impose delay, structure, and coalition before authority hardens. The Constitution treats democracy as a powerful input rather than as a governing mechanism, relying upon distance, time, and structure as instruments of self-government.

Introduction

That distinction eroded gradually across the last half-century. Democratic tools migrated into institutional spaces designed for republican mediation. Participation expanded as filtration thinned. Party nominations moved from smoke-filled rooms to mass primaries. Transparency exposed deliberation prematurely, as congressional committee bargaining gave way to live-streamed hearings and floor speeches crafted for immediate replay. Speed displaced settlement, with reaction cycles measured in hours rather than sessions. Pressure reached governing institutions before judgment could form, arriving through fundraising emails, social media storms, and cable news countdowns.

This book's argument does not oppose democratic participation. Democracy remains essential to republican legitimacy. The argument concerns placement. When democratic immediacy governs institutions designed to slow decision and broaden perspective, pressure overwhelms process. Elections cease to function as endpoints and become permanent conditions. Campaigning replaces governing, as members spend more time signaling positions than assembling coalitions. Compromise signals weakness under constant scrutiny. Delay appears illegitimate in an environment that rewards instant response.

The resulting frustration among American citizens reflects misalignment rather than civic decay. Citizens grow angry not because institutions resist democracy, but because institutions no longer transform democratic energy into durable authority. That misalignment proves difficult to perceive as today's events unfold. The difficulty has encouraged repeated calls for more democracy in spaces where stronger republican structure would better serve governance. Participation increases while outcomes weaken. Engagement rises as legitimacy erodes. These responses follow predictably from institutional design: unfiltered pressure accelerates toward decision without mediation. The system feels unresponsive not because citizens demand too much, but because contemporary institutions absorb too little. We the People are not the problem. The Republic's structures determine whether popular energy hardens to enable progress or devolves into tyranny.

Many of the reforms—in the name of democracy—that reshaped American politics over the last half-century pursued honorable aims across parties, legislatures, and the information environment. Reformers sought broader participation, greater transparency, and stronger accountability in response to real abuses in parties, legislatures, and media institutions. Closed processes excluded voices. Entrenched power resisted challenge. Backroom deals bred corruption and cynicism. Calls for openness carried democratic legitimacy.

The problem did not lie in motive. The problem lay in a misunderstanding of human nature and the demands of republican form.

Political institutions respond less to aspiration than to incentives and constraints rooted in human behavior. Altering rules alters behavior, often predictably. When reforms change how authority is gained, displayed, or rewarded, institutions adapt accordingly, regardless of intention. Across multiple domains, reforms have shared a common direction. Distance has shortened. Delay has thinned. Mediation has weakened. The space between democratic pressure and institutional decision has narrowed steadily. What now appears as polarization reflects a downstream effect of that narrowing rather than an independent cause.

For the Chamber, procedural changes centralized authority while exposing deliberation to constant visibility. For the Pipeline, party primary election reforms expanded participation while removing internal party filters that once required coalition before nomination. For the Press, media reforms and technological shifts lowered barriers to entry while weakening editorial discipline. Each change increased access. Each change reduced absorption. The combined effects have compounded across institutions. Legislators have learned to signal rather than negotiate. Candidates have

Introduction

learned to mobilize populist intensity rather than assemble governing majorities. Journalists have learned to prioritize speed over verification. Attention has increased even as governing capacity has declined. The Chamber, the Pipeline, and the Press have thus suffered the unseen toll of too much cowbell.

No conspiracy—despite exhortations from extremist fringes—was required. Institutional behavior followed design. Reformers frequently treated political friction among citizens and within Congress as failure. Such friction should not be feared. Delay came to appear undemocratic, even when delay served to overcome disagreement. Mediation resembled exclusion. Privacy suggested secrecy. Compromise became a four-letter word. Politics narrowed toward zero-sum outcomes. One side wins, and the other side must lose. Yet friction performs the essential work of governing in republican systems. Delay allows reconsideration. Mediation broadens perspective. Privacy protects bargaining space. Removing those features accelerates political pressure without producing judgment.

Today, the political disorder—the polarization, the anger, the turmoil, the uncertainty—that has followed reflects democratic correction without republican grounding. Democratic energy has flowed more freely, but the structures that once shaped that energy into law have weakened. The Republic has not failed from too much democracy. The Republic strains when democratic force bypasses republican form.

The Madisonian Insight

The tension between democratic force and republican form shaped the Constitution from the start. James Madison confronted that tension as a problem of design. Much of contemporary politics has drifted from the wisdom of Madison, the Founder best known as the Father of the Constitution. Madison approached self-government as a problem of design rather than aspiration. Madison did not begin with confidence in civic virtue. Madison began with acceptance of human limits. Ambition, rivalry, and faction appeared not as pathologies to be cured, but as permanent features of political life. The central question was never whether citizens would disagree. The question concerned whether disagreement could be structured to endure. These Madisonian lessons form the foundation of this book.

Madison treated politics as a system under stress. Large populations generate competing interests. Competing interests generate conflict. Conflict intensifies as proximity shortens and majorities form quickly. The constitutional response did not seek harmony. The response imposed structure. Distance mattered. Representation mattered. Time mattered. Power fractured across branches, chambers, and terms. Authority filtered. No single decision point allowed democratic energy to surge unchecked. Madison had studied the Ancients and their democracies. He understood the need for filtering democracy, characterized by energy, populism, and demagoguery, through republican forms.

Restraint within this framework does not signify elitism—governance reserved for a select few rather than the more common many. Madison distrusted concentrations of power, whether lodged in a narrow elite or in an unchecked majority. Restraint functions as engineering. Systems designed for endurance assume failure modes in advance. Republican government operates under the same logic. When institutions impose delay, compel coalition, and reward patience, behavior bends toward stability. When those constraints dissolve, behavior accelerates toward spectacle. Madison designed a system to survive disagreement without surrendering authority. Madison's insight provides the structural logic of this book. That distinction anchors the argument that follows.

Introduction

What This Book Is—and Is Not

This book is not a partisan indictment, a chronicle of outrage, a call for unity, or a project of moral renewal. Institutional erosion has accumulated across decades, particularly since the 1970s, through reforms supported by well-intentioned actors across ideological camps. Conservatives have advanced transparency. Progressives have expanded participation. Reformers on each side have sought accountability in response to real abuses. Closed processes excluded voices. Entrenched power resisted challenge. Backroom dealings bred corruption and cynicism. The resulting changes reflected democratic legitimacy rather than malice. Readers seeking vindication of grievance or affirmation of virtue will not find that work here. This book assigns responsibility to structure rather than motive.

This book is not an argument against democracy, nor a declaration of American collapse. Participation remains essential to self-government. Protest, persuasion, organization, and competition animate republican life. The concern addressed here involves the placement of democratic pressure within governing institutions, not the amount of participation. Democratic energy supplies legitimacy. Republican structure supplies durability. When democratic mechanisms operate inside institutions designed to slow decision-making, political pressure overwhelms deliberative process. Decline narratives flatter despair. Savior narratives flatter ambition. History supports neither indulgence. The American Republic has survived deeper divisions, sharper violence, and greater institutional strain than the present moment. Survival has followed structure, not sentiment.

The argument advanced here offers a structural diagnosis and a case for maintenance—reform, not revolution. Outcomes follow design. Behavior responds to constraints. Institutions shape incentives long before citizens recognize the consequences. When governing structures function properly, disagreement produces progress rather than rupture. Governance requires deliberation rather than rupture. When governing structures weaken, participation accelerates without settlement. Anger rises. Trust erodes. Legitimacy thins. Polarization widens. Repair begins not with moral correction, but with institutional restoration.

That restoration centers on three institutions that once stabilized American self-government by absorbing democratic pressure before pressure hardened into crisis. The Chamber concerns Congress as a deliberative body rather than a permanent stage. Committees, procedure, and privacy once forced repeated confrontation among interests before public decision. The Pipeline governs how ambition reaches authority through coalition rather than intensity. Parties once aggregated factions into governing majorities before elections rather than sorting citizens into permanent camps afterward. The Press sustains the shared informational foundation required for a divided people to remain a single polity. The Press, protected by the First Amendment and often described as the Republic's informal Fourth Branch, once operated under professional norms that slowed publication, verified claims, and filtered outrage before amplification.

Each institution has weakened over time. Yet each remains repairable today. Together, these institutions formed an architecture that converted conflict into judgment. The chapters that follow examine how that architecture functioned, how reform and neglect reduced absorption capacity, and how restoration remains possible without suppressing democratic participation. The goal is not nostalgia. The goal is governability.

Self-government demands habits modern politics rarely rewards. Speed flatters urgency. Performance gratifies immediately. Moral clarity feels decisive. Political leadership confined to binary narratives—victory or defeat, purity or betrayal—compresses republican government into majority tyranny, long feared by the

Introduction

Founders. Republican government survives through slower virtues. Judgment forms through repetition. Legitimacy emerges through process. Authority endures only when citizens tolerate outcomes that disappoint immediate desire. Institutions designed to slow decision-making now appear frustrating by design. That frustration reflects function rather than failure. Slowness protects deliberation. Friction forces accommodation. Restraint preserves legitimacy. Choosing patience over performance—accepting complexity, accepting ambiguity, accepting the gray shades—does not weaken democracy. Rather, choosing patience sustains the Republic.

In Limine*

Fear not. American self-government does not stand at the edge of collapse. The Republic has endured secession, mass violence, industrial unrest, global war, and internal terror. Survival has never depended upon civic harmony nor moral unanimity. Survival has depended upon institutions strong enough to absorb pressure without surrendering authority—a concept James Madison foresaw and encoded in the Constitution. Repair to that structure, when required, has proceeded through adjustment rather than rupture. Repair lacks romance. Repair is not sexy. Repair rarely survives a retweet. Yet repair—the continual renewal of the Republic—preserves self-government.

---

* This book employs a consistent set of Latin section titles to mark concluding thresholds. In Limine introduces the work by situating the reader at the boundary of the argument. In Sum concludes each chapter by distilling its governing claims. In Totum, reserved for the final chapter, gathers the argument as a whole. The usage reflects function rather than ornament.

The argument that follows does not ask citizens to withdraw, soften convictions, or quiet disagreement. The argument does not attempt to silence the cowbell. Democratic energy remains essential to republican legitimacy. Participation supplies force. Preference supplies direction. The work of governing begins afterward. Republican institutions exist to slow decisions, broaden perspective, and compel accommodation before authority hardens into law. When those institutions weaken, democratic pressure accelerates without settlement. The result feels like intensity without resolution—movement without destination.

This book begins from a simple premise: frustration is not evidence of democratic failure. Frustration often signals institutional function. Structures designed to slow decision-making will feel obstructive in moments of urgency. Processes built to force coalition will disappoint those seeking immediate victory. Contemporary frustration with both political parties reflects a design feature rather than a design collapse. Republican government asks citizens to tolerate delay, loss, and compromise in exchange for durability. Citizens do not remain in the majority across repeated elections. Democratic friction regularly places individuals on the losing side. The concern addressed here lies not with frustration over which party wins or loses, but with the failure of republican mechanisms to translate democratic win–loss friction into legislative progress. The tradeoff has never been popular. Yet the tradeoff has remained necessary.

What has changed is not disagreement, ambition, or faction. What has changed is the capacity of institutions to mediate those forces before they harden into spectacle. Pressure now reaches governing bodies faster than judgment can form. Performance now substitutes for deliberation. Reaction now crowds out settlement. These conditions did not arise by accident, nor do they reflect moral decline. Design choices altered incentives. Institutions adapted accordingly.

Introduction

The chapters that follow examine three sites where mediation once occurred and where absorption capacity has thinned. The Chamber governs how Congress works before it governs the nation. The Pipeline channels how ambition becomes authority through coalition rather than intensity. The Press sustains a shared informational foundation without collapsing into tribal narration. Each institution once slowed politics enough for judgment to emerge. Each now struggles under continuous exposure, compressed time horizons, and incentives that reward immediacy over resolution.

The question posed here is not whether democracy should speak more loudly—more cowbell. The question concerns whether republican institutions still possess the strength to listen without breaking—more republic. Self-government depends upon that distinction. Without mediation, pressure accumulates. Without delay, authority dissolves. Without structure, participation exhausts itself without producing progress.

This book does not offer comfort. The analysis that follows asks readers to reconsider assumptions that modern politics treats as self-evident: that speed signals responsiveness, that visibility ensures accountability, that openness always improves judgment, and that compromise reflects weakness. This book counters these claims. Each assumption deserves scrutiny. Each carries consequences when embedded into institutional design.

The threshold now stands open. Crossing requires patience rather than outrage, structure rather than spontaneity, and judgment rather than performance. The work ahead does not promise catharsis. The work promises *governability*.

The chapters that follow begin where mediation failed—and where repair remains possible.

CHAPTER 1

The Founding Fear

A COLLEGE CAMPUS IS meant to be a sanctuary for books, ideas, and above all, speech—free speech, free like a wilderness fire. Such freedom was never designed for comfort or ease. Free speech carries consequence by design. Fire warms when contained, but fire can destroy when left to rage. The difference lies not in the flame, but in the structures that hold the heat.

College marks the season when minds learn to handle that fire. Campus walkways line themselves with bulletin boards advertising lectures, rallies, auditions, and blood drives—kindling for thought. Patches of lawn double as soapboxes for fire breathers. Students linger at tables stacked with pamphlets and petitions, debating politics or faith or music or mathematics. The campus becomes a free-speech commons, where disagreements are rehearsed with more intensity than consequence, where sparks catch and flare. For many, these years offer rare permission to test boundaries, to argue boldly, to see which ideas survive contact with resistance.

The Founding Fear

James Madison was never an idealist. Madison was a pragmatist—and a college student. At Princeton from 1771 to 1772, Madison devoured philosophy and theology, studied the lessons of ancient republics, and sparred with classmates over liberty and authority. Debate sharpened conviction, but debate alone did not persuade him. Ideas required channels, rules, and structure to endure beyond youthful exchange. Campus argument revealed both promise and peril. The same heat that sharpened young minds could, when left uncontained, reduce institutions to ash. As biographer Noah Feldman (2017) observes, "At Princeton, Madison learned from Witherspoon that liberty required the discipline of reason. He was no firebrand. The Enlightenment appealed to his sense that passion must be governed if freedom was to last."*

Another campus, two and a half centuries later, appeared no different at first. At the center of a courtyard, a white canopy stood—familiar and unremarkable. Credit card companies often used such tents on campuses too. Student clubs sold baked goods beneath them. Free-speech lectures gathered crowds around them. Yellow *Do Not Cross* tape and bright orange pylons funneled the morning crowd into a loose semicircle, a makeshift audience awaiting the speaker (Brook, 2025). A microphone squealed, then settled. Student volunteers passed out flyers. A few campus police

---

* John Witherspoon (1723–1794) was a Scottish Presbyterian minister and Enlightenment thinker who served as president of the College of New Jersey (now Princeton) from 1768 to 1794. A signatory of the Declaration of Independence, Witherspoon brought Scottish Common Sense philosophy to American political education, emphasizing moral discipline, rational judgment, and the restraint of passion as prerequisites for liberty. Under his tutelage, James Madison absorbed the conviction that republican freedom depended not on enthusiasm or virtue alone, but on institutions capable of channeling human ambition through reasoned constraint.

officers leaned against nearby walls, watchful but relaxed. Rooftops loomed overhead, largely ignored. The scene carried the quiet confidence of a place accustomed to openness.

By noon, the plaza filled. Students and visitors pressed toward the canopy, smartphones raised to capture the exchange. Warm air hung heavy with expectation. Beneath the tent, the guest speaker worked the crowd with practiced ease. Hats—red ones—flew into the audience as the speaker tossed gifts from the stage. Hecklers met humor. Applause rolled across the courtyard, echoing off brick facades. The exchange felt familiar—loud, confident, unfiltered. Words struck sparks. Few considered how quickly fire can leap beyond restraint.

Only later did the details settle. The campus was Utah Valley University in Orem, Utah. The event, branded *The American Comeback Tour*, carried a familiar challenge—*Prove Me Wrong*. Roughly three thousand students and visitors had gathered in the plaza. Security remained minimal, with six campus police officers on site (Brook, 2025). At 12:23 p.m., a fatal shot rang out from a rooftop near the Losee Center (Goldin, 2025). The hats tossed moments earlier were red MAGA caps. The speaker beneath the canopy was Charlie Kirk. A campus morning that began as an exercise in free expression ended in assassination.

In the hours that followed on September 10, 2025, the nation divided once again—less over what happened than over how to respond. Outrage met indifference. Principles bent beneath partisanship. Some folks saw confirmation of moral decay across the aisle. Other folks barely registered the loss. A shared civic language fractured into rival tongues. Madison warned that democracy's gravest danger would not arrive by conquest, but from within—from passions left ungoverned, sharpened by resentment, inflamed by sympathy. Madison called that fever the *violence of faction*:* the moment opinion hardens into identity and the crowd forgets the individual's humanity. In Orem, Madison's warning read less like theory and more like diagnosis

Finger Pointing

Within hours, leaders from both parties and abroad condemned the killing as an assault on democratic discourse. *Reuters* compiled statements from Donald Trump, Joe Biden, Barack Obama, J. D. Vance, and foreign officials like Israel's prime minister—an unusual chorus that agreed on one point: political violence is intolerable (Reuters, 2025). Utah's governor, Spencer Cox, visibly shaken after viewing the viral video that captured the moment of the shooting and the crowd's stunned reaction, urged Americans simply to "stop shooting each other," a plea as narrow and urgent as a cease-fire (Vargas, 2025). The footage, replayed across television networks and social feeds, collapsed time and distance. Horror became performance, empathy divided by allegiance.

Online, however, a darker current surfaced. Some posts—a small minority—cheered or mocked Kirk's death. A handful of academics and staff amplified those digital comments, blurring the line between free expression and cruelty. Universities and employers responded with disciplinary measures that came faster than

---

* In *Federalist No. 10*, Madison warns that the "instability, injustice, and confusion introduced into the public councils, have, in truth, been the mortal diseases under which popular governments have everywhere perished" from what he called "the violence of faction." He opened his essay with this caution: "Among the numerous advantages promised by a well-constructed Union, none deserves to be more accurately developed than its tendency to break and control the violence of faction."

reflection. *Associated Press* reporting confirmed suspensions and terminations across multiple institutions for employees who posted or shared remarks celebrating or mocking the shooting (Bussewitz & Grantham-Phillips, 2025). The Chronicle of Higher Education and other outlets tracked firings, suspensions, and investigations of faculty and staff on multiple campuses for "callous" or celebratory remarks. In Texas alone, the state education agency opened probes in 124 school districts after hundreds of complaints about educators' social-media posts. Some cases were later reversed under legal scrutiny, but the signal was unmistakable: officials and employers were willing to police the boundary between free expression and applause for violence (Davis et al., 2025). The boundaries meant to contain liberty's flame can, if drawn in haste, suffocate the fire itself.

In the 48 hours before authorities named a suspect, false claims flooded social media feeds about the shooter's identity, party registration, and motives. Posts circulated alleging partisan revenge, foreign interference, and even staged conspiracy. Each new thread drew its own chorus of believers and debunkers. Screenshots became proof; outrage became evidence. The *Associated Press* ran back-to-back "Fact Focus" pieces debunking viral narratives and clarifying basic records such as voter status and party affiliation, underscoring how quickly a vacuum of verified information becomes a plebiscite of rumor (Goldin, 2025).

On campus, official statements spoke softly. They mourned the dead, tended to the shaken, and promised to review safety procedures without assigning blame. Utah Valley University's message to its community—"this tragedy has shaken us to our core"—was emblematic of institutions that must comfort first and explain later (Utah Valley University, 2025). The *Associated Press* follow-ups observed the dissonance between the school's image of security and the fragility that the day had exposed (Brown et al., 2025).

The Founding Fear

Together, those reactions sketched a country pulling in different directions at once. The nation's polarization lay bare. A broad public condemnation. A visible fringe celebration was punished in workplaces and schools—a torrent of disinformation that briefly set the narrative, an institutional silence that tended to grief while still assessing the facts. This pattern is familiar in American moments of political passion—the many speaking at once, the loudest and angriest amplified, the mediating institutions scrambling to catch up.

The question that remains is not whether the nation stands divided, but whether the Republic retains the resilience to turn volume into deliberation, heat into light, and passion into law. The Founders would not have been surprised by the noise. The constitutional generation anticipated conflict, faction, and fury as the price of liberty. Democracy, as Madison understood self-government, would argue loudly and often. What the Founders rejected was not contention, but collapse. Political murder was never a feature of the design; political murder marked a failure of restraint.[*] Yet the Founders also refused the easier path of silence. Free speech carried real risk, and republican government accepted that danger rather than extinguish liberty itself. The constitutional experiment sought neither calm nor purity, but structure—to channel tumult

---

[*] Madison's concern with political violence drew heavily from classical history, particularly the collapse of the Roman Republic (Beard, 2015). The assassination of Julius Caesar in 44 BCE—carried out by republican elites as an act of purported tyrannicide—failed to restore constitutional order and instead accelerated civil war and imperial rule. For James Madison, such episodes illustrated that political murder arises from institutional failure and hastens collapse rather than preserving liberty. Madison understood the risks inherent in unrestrained political expression, yet Madison and the other Founders rejected suppression as a remedy and instead designed institutions to absorb passion without allowing violence to govern outcomes.

without erasing disagreement, to contain fire without smothering flame. The Constitution stands as a firebreak against ourselves. The challenge, now as then, is whether that structure still holds.

Talk of Divorce

After Orem, the register shifted. "National divorce." "Disunion." "Secession." Phrases long confined to the political fringe—echoes of an unresolved American past—returned to public debate with new urgency. The crack of a rifle in Utah reverberated beyond the plaza, carrying forward not only accusation and grief, but renewed talk of ending the national marriage itself. In the days that followed, outcry, rumor, and recrimination rose faster than reflection, and some voices began to ask whether the Union could still endure. The question of civil war, once unspeakable, edged back into conversation.

Calls for a "national divorce" surfaced most prominently on the right. Representative Marjorie Taylor Greene, a frequent purveyor of rhetorical escalation, revived the phrase in the immediate aftermath of the shooting. Writing on X in 2025, Greene declared, "There is nothing left to talk about with the left. They hate us. They assassinated our nice guy who actually talked to them peacefully, debating ideas…I want a peaceful national divorce" (Ferguson, 2025). The statement framed separation not as tragedy, but as self-defense. Greene's language did not emerge in isolation.

Polling data suggests the idea has gained disturbing traction. A 2023 Axios survey found that roughly one in five Americans now entertains the possibility of secession or national divorce—and not just on the political right (Mbuqe, 2025; Talev, 2023). Even seasoned observers have expressed alarm at the normalization of such language. Political scientist Ryan Griffiths warns that appeals to irreconcilable difference ignore both the violent history of secession and the practical reality of American interdependence—political, geographic, and social (Richards, 2025). Separation, as history teaches, is neither clean nor peaceful. The nation has traveled that road before.

Scholars of civil conflict view this rhetoric as a warning sign rather than a forecast. Barbara F. Walter, who studies the origins of internal conflict worldwide, places the United States in what she terms a "danger zone"—a period in which democratic norms weaken without yet giving way to authoritarian control (Walter, 2023). Such conditions foster insurgent thinking rather than unity. In *How Civil Wars Start*, Walter identifies factionalized democracy as the most reliable predictor of modern civil conflict: societies where rival groups claim exclusive ownership of national identity. In such environments, political opponents cease to be adversaries and instead become illegitimate occupants of shared space. The noise following Kirk's assassination echoed that dynamic.

Most analysts nonetheless caution against alarmism. The Center for Strategic and International Studies concludes that the risk of organized civil war in the United States remains negligible (Jensen & Young, 2025). The structural precursors to rebellion—territorial control, rival armed forces, sustained leadership—remain absent. Walter, to be fair, also reaches a similar conclusion. Despite visible strain, American institutions continue to function. The greater danger lies not in sudden rupture, but in gradual erosion. Sporadic violence, rhetorical escalation, and declining trust corrode legitimacy over time rather than shatter the Union overnight.

Yet language matters. Word choice matters. When public figures speak casually of "divorce," "dissolution," or "the end of the Union," those phrases do more than capture frustration. Such language widens the horizon of acceptable thought and lowers the threshold of permissible action. As communication theorist George Lakoff observes, political language frames how citizens understand responsibility and blame (Lakoff, 2014). Political strategists James Carville and Paul Begala make the same point more bluntly:

language supplies the oxygen of politics (Carville & Begala, 2006). When leaders rehearse the vocabulary of disunion, those leaders legitimize the passions and factions that republican government exists to restrain.

The danger, then, is not that Americans will wake tomorrow divided into warring states. The danger lies in habituation—in treating separation as a reasonable answer to disagreement. Madison warned that republics fail not only through force, but through the slow abandonment of shared language and shared obligation. A people that speaks of divorce soon forgets the discipline of marriage. And a Union imagined as temporary will eventually behave that way.

The Founders' Warning

The Founders listened for the sound of politics slipping its restraints—the moment when argument hardens into identity and words cease to persuade and begin to license harm. The danger was not disagreement, but acceleration: passion outrunning judgment, rhetoric transforming grievance into justification. George Washington heard that danger in the rise of faction. Alexander Hamilton saw the demagogue waiting to seize the moment. John Adams feared majorities drunk on their own virtue. Thomas Jefferson doubted whether a republic, once set in motion, could hold its form indefinitely. Each approached the same problem from a different angle. Together, they described a common fear: that speed, not speech, would undo self-government. Each understood that when political speech abandons restraint, self-government enters its most fragile hour.

Washington was the first to sound the alarm. He feared political parties above other threats to the new Republic. In his *Farewell Address*, he warned that faction would lead to the "alternate domination of one faction over another, sharpened by the spirit of revenge, natural to party dissension, which in different ages and countries has perpetrated the most horrid enormities, is itself a frightful despotism" (Washington, 1931). The seed of tyranny, he believed, sprouted not from kings but from unrestrained popular will—what he called the "baneful effects of the spirit of party" (Washington, 1931). When the nation speaks without restraint and the loudest voices prevail, self-government begins to consume itself. As historian Thomas Ricks observes in *First Principles*, Washington's political philosophy was rooted in the classical ideal of self-command—the conviction that one must govern one's own passions before claiming the right to govern a nation (Ricks, 2020). His fear of faction was therefore not only structural but moral. Washington held a conviction that the survival of the Republic depended as much on the virtue of our citizens as on the design of our Constitution.

Hamilton, by contrast, located the danger less in the crowd itself than in those who would learn to command the crowd. As Washington's protégé, Hamilton shared his mentor's suspicion of unrestrained passion, but Hamilton focused on the figure who could weaponize that passion for personal gain. In *Federalist No. 71*, he warned of "the arts of men, who flatter [the People's] prejudices to betray their interests" (Hamilton et al., 2015). In the polished idiom of the eighteenth century, Hamilton was naming what we now call a demagogue.* At the Constitutional Convention, he cautioned that

---

* A demagogue, as legal scholar Eric Posner defines it, is "a charismatic leader who would gain and hold on to power by manipulating the public rather than by advancing the public good" (Posner, 2024). Patricia Roberts-Miller describes demagoguery not as a style of charisma but as a "discourse that promises stability, certainty, and escape from the responsibilities of rhetoric," a rhetoric that thrives by dividing citizens into the righteous and the damned Roberts-Miller (2019). Historian Ivan T. Berend reminds us,

"the people are turbulent and changing; they seldom judge or determine right" (Yates, 1821). Hamilton feared that the emotional volatility of democracy could be harnessed by the ambitious, turning liberty into theater. As biographer Ron Chernow observes, "Hamilton's besetting fear was that American democracy would be spoiled by demagogues who would mouth populist shibboleths* to conceal their despotism" (Chernow, 2016). That fear animates the modern spectacle, where tragedy mutates into performance within minutes. The rapid viral spread of the Kirk shooting—the instant mutation from tragedy into performance—feels as though Hamilton's ghost is scratching at our doors. The podium, once a stage for reason, has become a theater of spectacle, where persuasion yields to applause and the Republic's temperature rises with each cheer. Hamilton's insights remains perniciously relevant, even if American institutions have thus far proven resilient enough to outlast individual demagogues.

John Adams carried the warning further inward. Adams, ever the realist, believed that tyranny could arise not from kings but from

---

however, "to give an exact definition is not very easy." He goes on to offer the term "leader of the mob" (Berend, 2020).

* When I first read Chernow's sentence, I had to pause and look up the word shibboleth. The confession is perhaps proof that Ron Chernow's vocabulary is richer than my own. A *shibboleth* is a phrase or custom used by a particular group that serves as a test of belonging—or as a convenient slogan. The word originates from the Hebrew term used in the Old Testament (Judges 12:5–6), when the pronunciation of shibboleth was used to distinguish friend from foe. In modern use, it often describes empty or overused expressions that mark ideological tribes. For example, "Defend the Constitution!" or "Power to the People!" can function as populist *shibboleths*—rallying cries that conceal more than they clarify.

crowds. "Remember Democracy* never lasts long," Adams warned (Adams, 1814). "It soon wastes, exhausts, and murders itself. There never was a Democracy Yet, that did not commit suicide." For Adams, the danger lay not only in the mob but in the majority itself—the silent suffocation of minority voices by collective passion. Long before Alexis de Tocqueville coined the phrase *tyranny of the majority* (Mansfield & Winthrop, 2000), Adams had already diagnosed the condition: the tendency of popular rule to silence dissent and exalt passion over principle. He feared that equality, untethered from virtue, would decay into envy, and liberty—without restraint—would degenerate into disorder. As Dennis Rasmussen observes, Adams was perhaps the first American thinker to recognize that democracy's collapse could come not through conquest but through the slow erosion of character (Rasmussen, 2021). The modern environment—where social-media algorithms reward outrage over reason—is the very incubator for his concern. When tribal feeling becomes the law, the voice of conscience is drowned in applause.

Political psychologist Shawn Rosenberg hears the same warning in the present moment. In *Democracy Devouring Itself*, he argues that modern democracies place demanding cognitive burdens on

---

* Adam's capitalization of the word democracy unsettles me. As an engineer, I prefer consistent rules to arbitrary whims, and the capitalization habits of eighteenth- and early nineteenth-century writers—particularly the Founders—remain an ongoing source of irritation to my modern sensibilities, disciplined by years of standardized education. Fortunately, Dan Russell, an author and lecturer, has explored this strange orthographic behavior in a blog post devoted to the Founders' erratic use of capitals (Russell, 2025). Russell's research suggests that no firm capitalization conventions existed when they composed the nation's formative documents. Instead, capitalization served as a typographic tool for emphasis—a way to heighten drama or weight certain ideas.

citizens, including the need to tolerate ambiguity, engage opposing arguments, and weigh long-term consequences. Rosenberg concludes that many citizens retreat from those demands toward simpler, tribal frames that promise clarity and belonging (Rosenberg, 2019). His analysis echoes Adams's fear that democracy can collapse from within, not through conquest but through the steady erosion of patience, deliberation, and restraint. The Founders sensed this fragility without modern vocabulary. Rosenberg names the mechanism Adams described only in moral terms. Democratic self-government imposes a burden on citizens that demagoguery eagerly lifts and snatches.

Thomas Jefferson completes the arc. Jefferson, though a believer in the People's capacity for self-government, never placed blind faith in the permanence of democratic institutions. Even after serving as the nation's third president, he seemed uncertain that the Republic would outlast the passions that sustained our Union. In retirement at Monticello, Jefferson grew preoccupied with his legacy,* drafting his autobiography, preserving correspondence, and instructing that his gravestone bear only three achievements: "Author of the Declaration of American Independence, of the Statute of Virginia for Religious Freedom, & Father of the University of

---

* Jefferson's anxiety about posterity paralleled his doubts about the Republic's endurance. In one of his final letters to his lifelong friend and confidant James Madison, he implored, "take care of me when dead" (Jefferson, 1826b). The plea reveals not vanity but vulnerability—a recognition that the judgment of history, like that of democracy, could be fickle. In his last years, Jefferson worked tirelessly to shape his papers, organize his correspondence, and define how future generations would interpret his life and thought. His request to Madison was, in a sense, an appeal for republican stewardship beyond the grave—a hope that reason might prevail over rumor, and that legacy, like liberty, required tending.

Virginia" (Padover, 1952). His omission of the presidency is a telling insight to his long view through posterity's lens. Jefferson wished to be remembered for ideas, not office, for what he had built, not what might one day fall. "Because by these," he explained, "as testimonials that I have lived, I wish most to be remembered" (Jefferson, 1826a). His confidence in the Union's permanence remained cautious rather than assured.

His doubts predated his old age. During his years in Paris, he witnessed the early tremors of the French Revolution—an uprising that began in liberty and descended into blood. That experience left him wary of a government ruled by unchecked passion. Writing to Madison in 1789, Jefferson warned that "no society can make a perpetual constitution, or even a perpetual law. The earth belongs always to the living generation." He later continued, "Every constitution then, & every law, naturally expires at the end of 19 years. If it be enforced longer, it is an act of force, & not of right" (Jefferson, 1789). As Rasmussen observes, Jefferson held on to his faith in human progress longer than most of the Founders, yet even he came to doubt whether liberty could endure amid rising division and ambition (Rasmussen, 2021). He never ceased to believe that freedom was a flame worth tending, yet Jefferson understood—perhaps too late—that even light meant to enlighten can consume the house meant to shelter it.

In the aftermath of Charlie Kirk's death, the Union is not being asked to hold a line—we are being asked to contain a furnace. The noise we hear is not merely anger but a democratic wildfire without direction. Each outburst, each viral outrage, each rhetorical call for division adds pressure to the vessel that holds us together. The rhetoric of rupture, the spectral calls for separation, the recursive cycles of rumor and revenge—these patterns are ancient ones, familiar to the men who first imagined this Union. They feared the same combustion: passion overwhelming reason, noise replacing deliberation, citizens forgetting that disagreement is not disunion. The flames that consume free speech, civic trust, or simple grace burn from the same spark—the belief that persuasion has failed and force has become the only language left.

The question is not whether the nation stands divided, but whether the Republic retains the resilience to turn clamor into deliberation, heat into light, and passion into law. The Founders expected democracy to be noisy. The constitutional experiment never sought silence, but structure—the channeling of disagreement rather than the suppression of conflict. The Constitution was designed as a firebreak against ourselves, to prevent political flame from spreading beyond reason's reach. The challenge, now as then, concerns whether that structure still holds.

James Madison confronted the same dangers with greater confidence than his peers—Washington, Hamilton, Adams, or Jefferson. Madison outlived most of the Founding generation and witnessed more of the Republic's early turbulence than other architects of the Constitution, including the Nullification Crisis (1832–33).* Yet, he "largely kept the faith" (Rasmussen, 2021). Unlike Washington's moral caution, Hamilton's anxiety, Adams's pessimism, or Jefferson's doubt, Madison believed republican structure could endure human imperfection. Madison identified democracy's greatest danger as speed—the ease with which feeling could

---

* Madison witnessed the Nullification Crisis of 1832–33, when South Carolina claimed authority to void federal tariffs and threatened secession (Ketcham, 1990). Though retired from public office, Madison rejected nullification as incompatible with constitutional government, warning that allowing individual states to judge federal law would fracture the Union into competing sovereignties. Later historians have viewed the crisis as a constitutional precursor to the Civil War, not because war was inevitable in the 1830s, but because the episode exposed unresolved tensions over sovereignty, secession, and the permanence of the Union.

harden into law. The remedy lay in time and representation: a deliberate slowing of impulse through layered institutions, extended deliberation, and filtered consent. Madison trusted design to succeed where virtue alone could not. Yet the distance Madison built to cool passion has narrowed. The Republic, once an architecture of restraint, increasingly amplifies the noise that architecture was meant to absorb. Where citizens once argued through words, citizens now react through images. A single photograph or video clip can summon a crowd faster than a speech from the Senate floor.

That fear—the shared fear that passion could outrun structure—sets the stage for what follows.

Washington's Fear

We should not pass too quickly beyond Washington's anxiety. Washington's fear of parties was not a personal quirk; it was a historical judgment. English politics had taught him that factions rarely governed as loyal oppositions. Whigs and Tories treated power as spoil and defeat as humiliation. Parliamentary rivalry trained ambition to dominate rather than compromise. As Chernow documents, Washington associated party spirit with instability, corruption, and civic decay (Chernow, 2011).

That fear shaped Washington's Farewell Address. Parties, he warned, would foster cycles of domination and revenge, corroding legitimacy rather than contesting ideas. For Washington, faction trained citizens to substitute loyalty for judgment and victory for legitimacy. B. Scott Christmas captures this concern in Washington's Nightmare, arguing that Washington feared parties because parties accelerate conflict and convert rhetoric into permission for harm (Christmas, 2017).

Washington's fear also reflected a structural insight rather than a moral one. He did not assume factions would behave badly because their members were uniquely corrupt. He assumed factions would behave predictably once victory became the only recognized measure of legitimacy. When power rotates through narrow majorities, restraint becomes irrational. Compromise looks like weakness. Loss feels existential. Washington understood that repeated cycles of partisan domination would train citizens to expect punishment rather than persuasion, eroding the habits required for republican self-government.

This anxiety distinguished Washington from later critics of parties who focused on tone or civility. His concern ran deeper. Parties did not merely sharpen disagreement; they altered the incentives that governed political behavior. Once organized factions controlled access to office, reputation, and patronage, loyalty displaced judgment as the primary civic virtue. Leaders rose not by integrating interests but by mobilizing resentment. Institutions designed to refine public opinion instead amplified factional intensity.

Washington's experience commanding a revolutionary army reinforced this lesson. Coalition management—not ideological purity—had sustained the war effort (Chernow, 2011). Victory required constant negotiation among states, officers, Congress, and civilian authorities, each with competing priorities and grievances. That fragile equilibrium depended on personal trust and shared sacrifice rather than formal party alignment. Washington feared that partisan organization would harden those divisions, converting temporary disagreements into permanent identities and making future cooperation increasingly rare.

The tragedy of Washington's fear lies not in its accuracy, but in its incompleteness. He correctly identified the danger of unmediated factionalism but underestimated the inevitability of organized political rivalry in a mass republic. Parties emerged anyway, not because Washington was wrong about human nature, but because the Constitution did not supply sufficient lawful mechanisms to channel ambition at scale. His warning stands less as a rejection of parties than as a cautionary signal: when factions arise without structures designed to discipline them, fear becomes prophecy.

Tammany Hall

Washington's fear was justified—but incomplete. In the century that followed, American democracy collided with urban scale and mass immigration, and the formal Republic often refused to build the connective tissue that made citizenship usable in daily life. New York City became a republic in miniature—vast, diverse, volatile, and only lightly governed by institutions that operated at human scale.

Into that vacuum stepped Tammany Hall.

History remembers Tammany primarily for corruption, and that memory is earned. Patronage substituted for law. Loyalty displaced merit. Public funds leaked into private hands. Boss rule accumulated power beyond democratic warrant, most notoriously under William "Boss" Tweed (Golway, 2014).[*]

---

[*] William M. Tweed—better known as Boss Tweed—did not believe that mass voting itself posed the greatest threat to democratic control. Tweed understood that real power flowed upstream, long before ballots were cast. Control over nominations, party slates, and organizational access mattered more than turnout on Election Day. The sentiment is captured in a line widely attributed to Tweed: "I do not care who does the electing, just so as I can do the nominating."

Although the precise wording cannot be traced to a verbatim speech or document authored by Tweed, historians agree that the quotation accurately reflects Tweed's operating philosophy. As Terry Golway notes, Tammany Hall's power rested not in suppressing elections, but in managing candidate selection, party loyalty, and patronage networks that endured across election cycles. Tweed's insight was not democratic, but it was structurally astute. See Golway (2014).

Yet corruption alone does not explain Tammany's durability, or why similar machines emerged across industrial cities once universal suffrage, urban poverty, and immigrant density outgrew civic capacity. Scholars and contemporary observers have long noted that machines survived because machines delivered services, access, and problem-solving that municipal government did not reliably supply in the period before the modern welfare state (Reid & Kurth, 1992).

Ward politics operated at human scale. Captains and precinct workers knew blocks, families, churches, and workplaces. Machine organizations connected newcomers to jobs, legal help, and emergency assistance, while also guiding voters through naturalization and the practical mechanics of politics (Golway, 2014). In that sense, Tammany functioned as an informal layer of representation beneath the ballot box—an intermediary that translated diffuse needs into actionable demands and absorbed raw democratic energy before that energy overwhelmed City Hall.

That buffering function mattered. The late nineteenth century already saw riots, strikes, and ethnic conflict. Machines did not remove instability, but machines redistributed pressure downward, into negotiable spaces where favors, explanations, and face-to-face mediation could still operate (Reid & Kurth, 1992).

The danger lay not in mediation, but in how mediation occurred.

Tammany's authority remained informal, unaccountable, and unconstrained by constitutional design. Power accumulated without transparency. Loyalty replaced legitimacy. Corruption became systemic because lawful institutions did not perform the same connective work, and reform movements often treated the machine as a moral stain to erase rather than a civic function to replace (Golway, 2014). Civil service reforms and progressive reforms reduced patronage and professionalized administration, but the human-scale intermediary often vanished with the machine.

The Republic congratulated itself on moral victory while ignoring a structural loss.

The lesson is not that corruption deserves tolerance. The lesson is that mass democracy does not operate directly at scale. When formal institutions refuse to mediate between citizens and power, informal actors fill the void—party bosses, media entrepreneurs, activist networks, and now algorithmic platforms. Tammany stands as a warning not because Tammany existed, but because Tammany existed outside constitutional legitimacy, performing a necessary function poorly because the Republic declined to perform that function at all.

That failure did not end with the Progressive Era. The failure merely changed shape.

Tammany Hall emerged not because Americans abandoned republican restraint, but because republican structure failed to descend far enough to meet democracy where it lived. When formal institutions refused to organize mass participation at human scale, organization arose anyway—improvised, imperfect, and ultimately corrupt—setting the stage for the parties the Founders never designed but soon discovered they could not avoid.

Never Designed

The Founders did not design a party system. The Constitution never mentions parties. Early hopes rested on disinterested statesmen governing through shared civic purpose. That expectation collapsed almost immediately in the early republic. Disagreement organized itself. Coalitions formed. Ambition demanded structure.

Jefferson and Hamilton pivoted. Neither abandoned Washington's warnings. Both recognized that unorganized politics would not remain neutral. Power would flow somewhere. Better to channel rivalry into visible coalitions than to allow faction to operate informally and unchecked. The first national parties emerged not from theory, but from necessity.

This evolution revealed a truth the Founders underestimated: parties do not merely divide. Parties aggregate interests before elections and impose accountability after. That insight anchors the argument of Responsible Parties by Frances Rosenbluth and Ian Shapiro (2018). Strong parties, Rosenbluth and Shapiro argue, stabilize democracy by forcing coalition-building in advance rather than bargaining after victory. Weak parties invite personality politics, grievance performance, and unfiltered faction. Parties function as what the authors call the "core organs of democratic politics," resolving a paradox Washington never accepted and Madison only partially confronted.* Durable parties develop incentives to think beyond a single election cycle or charismatic figure—investing in policy coherence, candidate vetting, reputational capital, and governing capacity that outlasts one issue or personality.

Andrew Jackson institutionalized that lesson. Jackson did not invent political parties, but Jackson transformed loose alliances into disciplined national organizations. Party competition expanded participation while binding ambition to structure. The system remained

---

* Madison acknowledged the inevitability of faction in *Federalist No. 10* and argued for institutional design to control its effects rather than suppress its causes. Madison did not, however, anticipate the stabilizing role that disciplined political parties would later play in aggregating interests and enforcing accountability across elections. Over time, Madison came to accept political parties as a necessary—if dangerous—feature of republican government and worked with Thomas Jefferson to organize the Republican Party of the 1790s (often called the Democratic-Republican Party), which later fragmented and gave rise to the Jacksonian Democratic Party (Feldman, 2017). That lineage connects Madison's reluctant accommodation of parties to one of the world's longest-enduring political organizations—today's Democratic Party (Christmas, 2017).

noisy, imperfect, and often harsh—but durable. During the Jacksonian era (roughly 1828–1854), Jackson and his allies converted the remnants of the Democratic-Republican coalition, which Jefferson and Madison had pioneered, into the first mass national party. Local party committees, national conventions, coordinated newspapers, and patronage networks replaced the informal caucuses and personal followings of the early Republic (Wilentz, 2006).

Washington's nightmare never vanished. Parties can inflame passion and harden identity. History revealed the greater danger: ambition without structure. When parties weaken, faction does not disappear. Faction escapes containment. What Washington feared has returned in altered form—not parties too strong, but parties too weak to channel the noise.

A Hat and a Mob

What happens when that structure fails?

A crowd gathered on the steps of the Lincoln Memorial, one of the nation's most sacred civic spaces. The date was January 2019. A high school student from Kentucky, wearing a red "Make America Great Again" cap, stood face-to-face with a Native American elder beating a drum. The video from that moment lasted less than a minute. Yet within hours, the clip flooded the digital bloodstream—stripped of context, framed as confrontation. Social media amplified the singular moment across a multitude of screens. The boy's stillness was read as insolence, his half-smile as malice, his red hat as confession. Cable news filled the silence with moral certainty. "Honest question. Have you ever seen a more punchable face than this kid's?" declared one television commentator, his voice rising above the din (Gerstmann, 2025). The story metastasized by morning. The student's school, Covington Catholic High, received threats and closed for safety. The boy's family hired security. His name was Nick Sandmann.

Only later did longer footage emerge with more context—showing three groups shouting past each other: the Covington students waiting for their bus after the March for Life, a group of street preachers taunting them, and the Native elder, Nathan Phillips, approaching in an apparent attempt to defuse tension (Soave, 2019). The students did not surround the elder; he had approached them. The elder did not accuse the boy of mockery; he had seen confusion. The moment became raw material for demagoguery—a projection screen for a divided nation eager to see fears confirmed. Psychologists call this *motivated reasoning*—the tendency to interpret events in ways that preserve identity and moral certainty, even when evidence points elsewhere (Kunda, 1990; Westen, 2008). Each side saw what it needed to see, and the image became proof of its own invention. The scene was never simple. But the judgment had already been rendered.

Sandmann was condemned online not for what he said or did, but for what he wore. The red MAGA cap carried the weight of a movement and the baggage—in some eyes—of a president. The cap became shorthand for the perceived ills of America among those eager for an emblem of outrage. The cap was no longer a hat but a banner. In that moment, the symbol ceased to represent a boy and came to represent an entire tribe—white, rural, conservative, Christian. Judgment followed instantly because the symbol was already loaded. Those in opposing tribes did not need to ask what the boy believed. The digital image supplied conviction on its own terms. He was guilty by association, condemned by the symbol he wore. The digital crowd saw not a student waiting for a bus but a caricature of America's divide—one side clinging to power, the other clinging to grievance. Symbols have always been the language of mobs. Symbols allow passion to bypass comprehension.

As Sandmann later wrote, "I am being called every name in the book, including a racist, and I will not stand for this mob-like character assassination of my family's name" (Sandmann, 2019). He maintained that he had stood silently, hands behind his back, hoping calm might follow (Bowden & Nelson, 2020). That restraint became another provocation, silence another offense. In the public digital square, stillness reads as smirk, nuance as cowardice. Once labeled, no exit appears. The punishment is not prison but permanence—the unerasable association between face and accusation. As Edward Snowden titled his memoir, the internet keeps a *Permanent Record* (2019). Legal scholar Daniel Solove warned of the same condition in *The Future of Reputation* (2007): a society where rumor, once spoken, becomes data—searchable, shareable, and eternal. Each viral moment is stamped into collective memory, stripped of context, and archived for eternity. For a time, Sandmann's image joined the pantheon of viral morality tales—useful for fundraising, op-eds, and political sermons. Then the fabrication disappeared, replaced by another outrage, another public execution in the feed.

Sandmann sued several major media organizations for defamation. CNN quietly settled (Farhi, 2020). Others fought on until the courts, parsing motive and meaning, concluded that opinion—however mistaken—remains protected speech. Yet by then, the verdict of the crowd had long since hardened into folklore. Our democracy's culture of immediate judgment had triumphed over a republic's system of measured justice. What had once been a deliberative process—a slow calibration of truth and fairness—had become a reflex of accusation and retreat. The digital mob moves faster than evidence and forgets more slowly than history.

This vignette captures what Madison feared when passion escapes the bounds of structure. A single image, torn from context, summoned a national mob. A small faction swelled into a majority within minutes, flashing across the Union like lightning. The Founders assumed distance would restrain contagion—miles of geography and days of deliberation to cool blood before law or policy could form. Today, distance collapses to zero and time to seconds. The passions Madison sought to filter through representation now travel unmediated and unrepentant through digital fiber. A century ago, a rumor in a small town might ruin a man by sundown but fade by harvest. Today, the same rumor circles the globe before supper. What once ended in whispers over a fence now continues in hashtags and headlines. Madison warned that the fires of faction must be confined to local hearths; the internet has torn down those hearths. The mob no longer requires a town square. A digital signal suffices. Passion alone cools with time. Certainty does not. Once convinced of moral infallibility, citizens no longer deliberate—they crusade.

Battles Over Belief

Nowhere is this more visible than in our modern crusades of moral certainty, amplified by our digital connectivity that does not blink nor forget. In a school gym somewhere in America, a curriculum meeting turns into a crusade. One parent quotes Scripture; another cites science; each believes the other threatens the children. The scene is not new. A century ago, in Dayton, Tennessee, a young teacher named John Scopes was put on trial for teaching evolution. The trial—formally known as the Scopes Trial, and remembered in popular culture as the Scopes Monkey Trial—pitted Clarence Darrow against William Jennings Bryan and turned a small-town courtroom into a national referendum on faith and modernity (Larson, 2008). My daughter and I visited that courtroom one summer afternoon.* The wooden benches still creak; the ghosts still argue. The trial ended, but the quarrel has not.

---

* As a family, we live in Knoxville, and Dayton is only a short afternoon's drive along the back roads toward Chattanooga. Rather than taking the interstate, we wandered the slower route through Athens—one of two

In 1974, the evolution fight again reignited in Kanawha County, West Virginia, when new multicultural textbooks provoked protests so fierce that buses were bombed and schools shuttered. As Carol Mason notes, the conflict was less about the books themselves than about belonging—parents defending the moral language of their faith and community against a culture they no longer recognized (Mason, 2009). Three decades later, in Dover, Pennsylvania, a local board ordered teachers to read a statement reminding students that evolution was "not a fact," inviting intelligent design into the science classroom and a wider public debate about the boundary between faith and evidence (Kitzmiller, 2005; Lebo, 2008). Even now, in Rocklin, California, a school-board president calls for "Christ-centered parents" to serve on curriculum committees, blending theology with civics in a district once known for quiet suburban order (Hong & Murugan, 2025). These disputes are less about who is right than about who is heard. Each side believes they are defending truth—one through revelation, the other through reason—but both reveal a deeper anxiety about who speaks for the next generation. Democracy is messy.

Each dispute begins with a book but ends with a boundary—who belongs, whose truth prevails, whose children will inherit the

---

Tennessee towns flanking I-75 that have played their part in civic rebellion. In Athens, in 1946, returning World War II veterans seized the county jail to end a corrupt political machine—a brief, remarkable episode sometimes called "the last battle of the Second World War" (DeRose, 2020a, 2020b). My daughter was on spring break from her senior year of high school while my wife had to work, so the two of us made a father-daughter history day. She likes to remind me that a vacation with me is less like travel and more like class. We also detoured by the Watts Bar Nuclear Plant—sadly, closed to visitors—and then continued to Dayton, where we toured the courthouse of the Scopes Trial.

culture. As Lilliana Mason observes, Americans no longer disagree over policy but identity (Mason, 2018). These battles over books have become less about curriculum than about community—where faith, region, and heritage draw the battle lines more sharply than policy ever could. Partisanship has fused with tribe—race, religion, region—until political difference feels not like disagreement but moral defection: right against wrong, loyalty against betrayal. Neighbors retreat into opposing sanctuaries, each watching a different version of the same country through the lens of their preferred outlet—CNN, Fox News, or the endless scroll of social media that confirms their suspicions. The quarrel is no longer about education but about who we imagine ourselves to be as a people.

The Founders understood that unfiltered democracy carries the seeds of its own destruction. Madison warned that passion, once unrestrained by time and representation, would become "the mortal diseases under which popular governments have everywhere perished" (Hamilton et al., 2015). When the crowd's conviction hardens into moral certainty, debate gives way to denunciation. The mob no longer gathers in the town square; the crowd gathers in the digital feed. The quarrels once confined to classrooms and courthouses now flash across the nation in seconds, where reputation replaces reason and outrage becomes the coin of citizenship.

The Cult of Science

"Moral certainty" is not the exclusive province of faith.[*] Science, too, can become a creed when its advocates mistake evidence for ethics.

---

[*] For additional reading and insights, see Popper (2005), Kuhn and Hacking (1970), Hutchinson (2011), Polanyi (2012), or Jasanoff (2007).

The scientific method, by its nature, offers probability, not proof—confidence, not certainty. Yet in modern debate, appeals to "settled science" often carry the same absolutism once reserved for scripture. To wield science as moral authority is to abandon its first virtue: humility before the unknown.

Faith once wore robes—priests, fathers, bishops. Now faith wears a lab coat—scientists, professors, doctors. Separation of church and state remains a cornerstone of the American creed; yet some might wish the "faith" of science to observe a similar boundary. During the COVID-19 pandemic, the nation sought refuge in science but found instead another kind of creed. The slogan "follow the science" echoed from White House briefings, CDC podiums, and media headlines, promising certainty where none could stand. I can almost hear the chorus divide. From the left: "Here we go—another cynic mistaking doubt for denial." From the right: "At last, someone daring to say Saint Fauci might have been mortal after all." Although these replies are imagined in my mind's ear, the polarization the lines evoke is real. Studies during COVID found that liberals and conservatives treated the same public health evidence through sharply different prisms of trust and skepticism (Kerr et al., 2021). As the *New York Times* cautioned in "Follow the Science? If Only It Were So Easy," the phrase masked less a commanding truth than a public wish to make science a mandate rather than a method (Leonhardt, 2022). Yet science, rightly understood, is not a catechism but a discipline of organized doubt. The biologist's oath is not *I believe*, but *I test*. Science progresses by falsification, not by the confirmation of existing theories (Popper, 2005).

When Anthony Fauci declared, "I represent science" (Bice, 2021), he spoke with the authority of expertise. But many heard something older—the voice of infallibility. Early in the pandemic, Americans were told that masks were unnecessary, then that masks were essential, then that the vaccinated could remove them, then that folks should wear them again. As guidance shifted from no masks to masks to masks again,* what began as prudence became confusion, and confusion became distrust (Ramjee et al., 2023). Each turn was presented as *the science*, not as a shifting balance of science-based probabilities. The public absorbed guidance as decree, not as data under revision. Science was received as a noun—fixed, settled, complete—rather than as a verb: an ongoing act of testing what might be wrong. When those probabilities changed, certainty shattered. The scientific process had not failed, but the public's expectation of certainty had (Bundgaard et al., 2021; Jefferson et al., 2023). A hypothesis revised looked like hypocrisy revealed. The method built to question itself collided with a culture that mistakes change for weakness. Our culture's faith in science is misplaced.

A similar confusion surrounded the economic science of COVID. While epidemiologists focused—rightly—on transmission and mortality, economists raised parallel warnings about the costs of prolonged shutdowns: lost livelihoods, educational disruption, delayed medical care, psychological strain, and widening inequality (Cutler & Summers, 2020; Goolsbee & Syverson, 2021). These arguments were not denials of viral risk, but attempts to weigh competing

---

* In February 2020, the Centers for Disease Control (CDC) advised that healthy individuals did not need to wear masks, citing supply shortages and limited evidence of community spread. By April 3, 2020, new data on asymptomatic transmission prompted the CDC to recommend universal masking. In May 2021, vaccinated individuals were told they could remove masks indoors, only to be advised again in July 2021 to resume masking amid a mutation surge. The rapid reversals—driven by evolving evidence but communicated as definitive—became partisan flashpoints: critics on the right saw inconsistency and overreach, while voices on the left hardened the changing guidance into an article of faith, treating dissent less as skepticism than as heresy (Ramjee et al., 2023). The reality, however, is that science is simply provisional.

The Founding Fear

harms. Yet economic analysis was often dismissed as moral evasion, as though counting costs were equivalent to denying lives. One science—epidemiology—was elevated to command; the other—economics—was treated as suspect. The error was not choosing health over wealth. The error was refusing to acknowledge that tradeoffs existed at all. Weighing such tradeoffs belongs to politics and democratic governance, not to science alone.

As an engineer, I have seen this misunderstanding of science firsthand—the collision between scientific uncertainty and moral certainty. People want direct answers; scientists offer conditional ones—answers in probability, not decree. In a comical popular movie scene, the same frustration plays out between Han Solo and C-3PO in *The Empire Strikes Back*. Solo embodies human decisiveness; C-3PO embodies the qualifying logic of science. As the *Millennium Falcon* hurtles through an asteroid field, C-3PO warns, "Sir, the possibility of successfully navigating an asteroid field is approximately 3,720 to 1!" Han cuts him off: "Never tell me the odds!" The line endures because the boldness captures something deeply human—our instinct to reject uncertainty, to hear caution as cowardice. Scientists, like C-3PO, speak in probabilities. Politicians, like Han, prefer bravado. One measures truth; the other commands belief. When those languages collide, probability sounds like doubt, and doubt sounds like weakness. In the modern age, democracy struggles with the conditional, contingent, and provisional nature of science, and both sides, the political left and right alike, remain blind to that misunderstanding.[*]

---

[*] For empirical evidence of symmetric misunderstanding of science across ideological lines, see (Altenmüller et al., 2024; Marino et al., 2024; Milkoreit & Smith, 2025; Rekker, 2021). Together, these studies show that individuals across the ideological spectrum interpret or dismiss scientific

Science and democracy share the same peril. Both depend on humility—the willingness to doubt one's own conclusions. Science demands humility before nature; democracy demands humility before one another. When either forgets that discipline of self-questioning, evidence becomes ideology and politics becomes faith. Both assume that truth is provisional and must survive argument. Yet in recent years, the appeal to "science" has hardened into something closer to faith. Citizens and politicians alike invoke science as a moral certainty, not an empirical method.

The phrase "the science says" has become a modern indulgence—an absolution that attempts to spare the speaker from debate. If science says, then the conclusion that follows must not be questioned. When politics demands obedience in the name of science, the boundary between method and mandate collapses. What was meant to guide policy begins to rule that very policy. The Founders feared a union of church and state because dogma, once enthroned, silences dissent (Madison, 1785). The same caution now applies to what might be called the *Church of Science*—a growing impulse to treat scientific consensus as moral decree, and disagreement as sin (Lessl, 2007; Stenmark, 2017). "Science says" is starting to sound like "God says" through the filter of the Founders. The noise of democracy grows louder when citizens mistake expertise for authority and skepticism for heresy. We are relearning, in the age of algorithms and pandemics, that truth cannot be compelled by religion or by a religion masquerading as science.

---

evidence through partisan identity, reinforcing rather than resolving misunderstanding. These findings are, surprisingly, independent of education level and economic background.

The Founding Fear

Abortion, perhaps more so than COVID, exposes our modern confusion over the role of science in our democracy. Biology can describe life's continuity—from fertilization to birth—but science cannot pronounce where life begins in the moral sense. That question crosses from microscope to metaphysics. Yet politicians, both on the left and the right, invoke "the science" as if biology carried the force of revelation. As with COVID, one domain of science—biology—tends to dominate the conversation, while other relevant disciplines such as economics, psychology, ethics, and social consequence take a backseat (Gould, 2011).

Pro-life advocates often cite embryology textbooks such as Moore et al. (2008) to claim that "life begins at fertilization." Scientifically, that statement is accurate as a description of biological development, but philosophically incomplete. The laboratory can identify when an organism begins, but not when a person does. That line—between cell and soul—is one science can describe but should not cross. Science is not equipped to answer moral questions. Biologically, however, the embryo is not the mother's body but a genetically distinct organism that directs its own continuous development (Noden, 2003). Recognizing that individuality is a matter of description, not prescription—explains *how* life begins, not *what it means*.

Pro-choice advocates, in turn, appeal to neuroscience and neonatology, arguing that moral consideration attaches not at conception but with the emergence of cortical function or independent viability (Steinbock, 2011). Studies of fetal brain development show that organized cortical activity necessary for consciousness does not appear until well into the third trimester (Derbyshire & Bockmann, 2020), and obstetric data mark viability around twenty-four weeks, varying by technology and circumstance (Horbar et al., 2002). These findings are genuine contributions of science, yet they too are used rhetorically—as if biology could resolve a moral debate by decree. Each side selects the evidence that fits their belief—and that belief is just that *belief*. The laboratory becomes another pulpit in the nation's argument.

We must insist: science should never decide when human life begins or ends (Warren, 1973). That judgment belongs to morality. Science can tell us *how* cells divide, how organs form, or how brain signals evolve—but not *why* personhood matters. As Stephen Jay Gould argued in his doctrine of *non-overlapping magisteria*, science and moral truth lie in separate domains (Gould, 2011). And critics of scientism have argued that scientific methods can yield empirical data, but cannot bridge the gap from "is" to "ought" (Earp, 2016). Over the last hundred years, science has brought us through the industrial revolution and the information age, lightening humanity's burden—but we must resist the temptation to turn science into religion and subjugate democracy to scientific claims alone. We may debate whether our morality comes from God, gods, reason, or some cosmological source—but we ought never abdicate moral responsibility to scientists. Science is a process, not another king or priest.

The Founders, men of the Enlightenment, trusted reason but not perfection. They revered science as a tool of discovery, not as a source of moral law. They sought a republic governed by deliberation, not decree—a system that balanced evidence with ethics, experiment with experience. The Founders could not have foreseen an age when science itself might harden into a creed, or when practitioners might be treated as a priesthood of truth. Yet the caution endures. A free people must welcome knowledge without surrendering conscience. Citizens who question morality dictated by a god, the God, many gods, or scientists acting as gods are not heretics to be crucified. Such citizens perform the essential labor of republican self-government: testing authority, resisting certainty, and insisting that power—no matter its source—remain accountable to human judgment in the realm of Caesar, where no earthly authority is beyond question.

Scientific certainty, like moral certainty, breeds noise when authority crosses beyond proper bounds. The friction arises not between truth and falsehood, but between disciplines that speak different languages—evidence and ethics, data and duty. Democracy requires both, but confusion between the two corrodes judgment. Science tests; politics decides. When either claims authority beyond proper limits, public trust collapses.

Noise emerges when humility disappears. The clamor over masks, vaccines, and fetal heartbeats turns less on data than identity, less on uncertainty than discomfort with ambiguity. The Founders designed a republic to slow passion long enough for reason to arrive. The scientific method serves a similar purpose. Each structure contains human overconfidence. Each depends on time, transparency, and the courage to say, "we may be wrong."

Science, at its best, invites revision and change. A democratic republic, at its best, endures revision and change without demanding submission.

Cameras in the Chamber

The delegates who framed the Constitution met behind closed doors in the Pennsylvania State House, later known as Independence Hall. They agreed to maintain secrecy so that discussion would remain frank and positions could evolve without fear of public fixation. Under the watchful authority of George Washington, who presided as both symbol and sentinel, the Chamber held fast to this vow (Chernow, 2011). Windows were shut, guards were posted, and no delegate was permitted to leak debate beyond those walls. James Madison's notes, kept surreptitiously and published only after his death, would become the record the public was never meant to see (Ketcham, 1990). The rule was clear: nothing said inside the hall could be repeated outside (Farrand, 1911). The secrecy was deliberate. The delegates feared that half-formed ideas, once heard by the public, would harden into dogma before they could be refined. The intent was to create an environment that fostered deliberation and compromise. Former Chief Justice Warren Burger once wrote of the Founders assembled in 1787, "A delegate who spoke positively to a point on Monday would find it easy to modify his position on Friday" (Burger, 1995). The Republic began in silence so that reason could still be heard above the noise of democracy.

Two centuries later, Congress opened its doors to the live camera—the television camera. When C-SPAN* began broadcasting in 1979, the nation could, for the first time, observe our legislative branch in continuous session (C-SPAN, 2025; Frantzich, 1996). In the post-Watergate world, we hailed this new-found transparency as a democratic triumph, a visible confirmation that public institutions belonged to the public. Yet visibility is never neutral; exposure alters behavior. Aim a camera at a family dinner and the quietest relative becomes a performer. Congress is no different. Attention transforms character faster than authority does. The constant gaze of the camera has transformed deliberation into performance and subtly rewired the incentives of speech.† Members no longer

---

* C-SPAN—the Cable-Satellite Public Affairs Network—was founded in 1979 by former journalist Brian Lamb as a nonprofit cooperative of cable television companies. The network's first live broadcast aired on March 19, 1979, carrying floor proceedings of the U.S. House of Representatives. The network's creation marked a pivotal moment in the visual transparency of Congress and forever changed the rhythm of legislative performance (Frantzich, 1996).

† As an anecdotal reminder of the camera's influence in legal settings, the O.J. Simpson trial remains instructive. Influential skeptics include Nancy Marder, whose *The Conundrum of Cameras in the Courtroom* (2012) surveys state experiments and argues that cameras can alter a lawyer's strategy, a witness's demeanor, and a courtroom's pacing. Marder contends that participants act more cautiously—or more theatrically—under visible

address their colleagues across the aisle but appeal to the unseen audience beyond the lens. The camera has become a new constituent, and attention has become the new currency of representation.

No one grasped this opportunity more quickly than a young congressman from Georgia named Newt Gingrich (Coppins, 2018). In the 1980s, House rules allowed the C-SPAN cameras to show only the person speaking, never the empty seats. Gingrich began addressing the Chamber late at night, delivering fierce monologues against Democratic leaders who were long gone home. On television, the small screen looked as though he were confronting a full house. The image was convincing enough that Speaker Tip O'Neill eventually ordered the cameras to pan across the vacant floor—provoking an uproar and making Gingrich a national figure. The episode marked a turning point in American politics: the discovery that the camera could legislate as powerfully as Congress itself. From John F. Kennedy's calm poise against Richard Nixon's shadowed fatigue,* to George W. Bush's "Mission Accomplished" tableau

---

scrutiny. Kyu Ho Youm revisits those same concerns in the digital age, warning that cameras may exacerbate bias and transform trials into media events rather than factfinding proceedings (Youm, 2012). R.J. Fuoco, in *The Prejudicial Effects of Cameras in the Courtroom*, also emphasizes how performance pressures can distort testimony (Fuoco, 1981). To be clear, these scholars do not claim that a camera altered a specific verdict, such as O.J.'s trial, but each insists that the risks are real and consequential. If the courtroom—where truth is sworn and evidence weighed—can bend beneath the lens, why would politics, the most performative of professions, be immune to its pull?

* The first televised presidential debate, held on September 26, 1960, marked a watershed in American political communication. According to post-debate surveys, radio listeners judged Richard Nixon the winner, favoring his detailed policy answers, while television viewers overwhelmingly thought John F. Kennedy had prevailed—drawn to his calm demeanor, direct gaze, and camera-ready composure (Druckman, 2003; Kraus, 1977).

aboard the *Abraham Lincoln*, to Donald Trump's Bible-in-hand photo outside St. John's Church after Lafayette Square was cleared, each moment has revealed the same new media order—appearance governs faster than fact. The image no longer accompanies power; the image *is* power.

This round-the-clock medium of instant broadcast and global reach—unthinkable to the Founders—has overtaken Congress. A smartphone screen now sits in each citizen's hand, ready to record, replay, and react. The modern committee room has become a stage built for replay. Lights. Camera. Action. Each exchange is framed for an audience far beyond the hearing room. Cameras capture not only the testimony but the angle, the pause, the raised eyebrow—each gesture preserved, captioned, and sent into the digital world, where virality is the real verdict. Members now arrive with rehearsed cross-examinations designed for live streaming. The object is no longer persuasion or governance, but the crafting of a line sharp enough to pierce the noise. A gotcha moment. A sound bite. A viral clip. A meme. Each one is designed not to persuade the mind but to claim the moment.

Like Gingrich before them, representatives such as Alexandria Ocasio-Cortez, the progressive star from New York, and Jim Jordan, the Republican firebrand from Ohio, intuitively understand this medium's power in the modern committee room. Ocasio-Cortez has crafted multiple viral moments from her seat. One of the first, known as the *"Lightning Round,"* on campaign-finance loopholes in 2019, unfolded like courtroom theater—rapid-fire questions, rising

---

The event revealed that visual impressions could outweigh argument, inaugurating an era when image began to rival—or even eclipse—substance in presidential politics.

tension, a final line delivered for both the record and the replay (Wyatt, 2019). "It's already super legal, as we have seen, for me to be a pretty bad guy," she said. "So it's even easier for the president to be one" (C-SPAN, 2019b). Weeks later, in the hearing with Michael Cohen, she blurred the line between governance and performance, interrogating with a precision that played equally to the record and the replay (C-SPAN, 2019c).

That same year, she cornered Facebook's Mark Zuckerberg with a hypothetical—could she pay to run ads falsely claiming that Republicans had backed the Green New Deal?—forcing him to stammer on live television (Paul, 2019). "So you will not take down lies?" she asked (C-SPAN, 2019a). Each exchange blended substance with stagecraft, designed as much for the camera as for the Chamber. Ocasio-Cortez and others have learned to fire questions in rapid succession with little expectation of a genuine response, knowing the cameras reward the impact more than the answer. The resulting clips have raced through social-media feeds—cut, captioned, and remixed—celebrated or condemned according to taste. Supporters have praised her precision; opponents see choreography. Both reactions have revealed the same reality: the committee room has become a studio, and politics has become the art of going viral.

On the other side of the aisle, Representative Jim Jordan wields the same medium with opposite force. His hearings move like press conferences turned combat—rapid-fire exchanges, voices colliding, the tone pitched halfway between cross-examination and confrontation. In a 2024 Justice Department oversight hearing (C-SPAN, 2024a), he drove a clash so sharp that Attorney General Merrick Garland answered on camera, "We will not be intimidated," a line replayed across feeds before the gavel fell (Rabinowitz, 2024). A year earlier, during FBI oversight, Jordan's barrage of questions about "weaponization" produced tight close-ups, clipped retorts, and the kind of cutaway shots that travel fast once detached from context (C-SPAN, 2023). In another widely shared moment, Jordan came to the defense of former CBS reporter Catherine Herridge, condemning her firing and the network's seizure of her notes (C-SPAN, 2024b). Jordan asked Herridge if she had written critical stories about the Biden family. She replied, "I reported out the facts of the story. I called balls and strikes." "You sure did," Jordan said. "You reported the facts and then CBS fired you!" (Steigrad, 2024). The exchange, delivered as an act of protection, played online as confrontation—an image of righteous anger tailored for replay. To admirers, he was fearless; to critics, theatrical. Each faction circulated the same footage as proof of the other's decay. The substance drained out in the digital echo; what remained was the image—raised voice, leaning frame, frozen glare—looped until the performance became the point.

Jefferson, Hamilton, Adams, and Madison spoke to history through the flurry of their pen. Ocasio-Cortez, Jordan, and their generation speak only to the moment through the lashings of their tongue. Both scenes—AOC's precision and Jordan's aggression—mirror the same shift that began with Gingrich's midnight monologues. Visibility has become the currency of influence. The committee table now functions like a broadcast booth. The exchanges are less about policy than about owning the frame—creating a viral moment. The feedback is instantaneous. As soon as a clip appears online, the public replies directly through the scroll—thousands of comments addressed to the member by name, equal parts praise and derision. In that swarm of responses, deliberation bends toward performance. Members no longer wait weeks to gauge public sentiment; they can read the comment trail in real time on their phones. Yet for all their prominence, neither Ocasio-Cortez nor Jordan ranks high where one would hope that ranking matters most—in legislative effectiveness. The Center for Effective Lawmaking places AOC 230th of 240 House Democrats and Jordan near the bottom of his caucus 202nd of 205 House Republicans with one of the lowest scores in the 116th Congress. As *USA Today* noted, their

The Founding Fear

power lies not in passing bills but in shaping narratives—punching far above their legislative weight in the theater of attention (Bedford, 2023; 2025; Elbeshbishi, 2021).

The theatrical use of committee hearings by figures like Ocasio-Cortez and Jordan has spilled beyond the hearing room, finding parallel in the Chambers of Congress itself, where decorum has become part of the performance. A striking example came early in the Barack Obama presidency when Congressman Joe Wilson shouted "You lie!" from the House gallery as Obama declared that illegal immigrants would not be insured under the proposed health-care reform—an eruption that prompted a House reprimand and foreshadowed the collapse of floor protocol (Hulse, 2009). A comparable moment of high drama occurred again when President Obama, in his 2010 State of the Union, turned his critique on the Supreme Court with justices sitting just rows before him. "With all due deference to the separation of powers," scolded Obama, "last week the Supreme Court reversed a century of law that I believe will open the floodgates for special interests" (Liptak, 2010).[*] Justice

---

[*] The Supreme Court, often described as the least dangerous branch (Hamilton, Federalist No. 78), possesses neither sword nor purse. The Court depends on the Executive for enforcement and on Congress for funding and jurisdiction. Presidents from Jefferson to Jackson to Lincoln have—for good or for bad—resisted or ignored the Court's rulings. Such tension is built into our Constitutional design. Yet Obama's rebuke in 2010 was striking for its setting and style. Delivered face-to-face, with the Justices seated silently before him and cameras broadcasting nationwide, the moment resembled a man taunting lions from behind the zoo bars—safe in the knowledge that the cage would hold. The bravado, however cathartic, seemed hardly becoming of a Nobel Peace laureate.

Samuel Alito was captured mouthing, "Not true," at the rebuke (Memmott, 2010).*

More recently, during a joint session address by Donald Trump, a group of House Democrats—beginning with Democrat Al Green, a 20-year Representative from Texas, and backed by colleagues holding protest signs and turning their backs—staged a public interruption and were subsequently censured by the House (Erikson, 2025). These episodes reveal how the norms of legislative decorum are being subsumed by spectacle. Cameras in the Chamber, partisan and theatrical gestures, and direct audience engagement have transformed what were once serious deliberations into staged contests of performance and grievance.

The Founders built a republic that required distance—geographical, temporal, and emotional—between the governed and their representatives. That distance gave reason space to cool passion before law took form. The modern Republic has erased that buffer. Each statement now encounters a digital echo before the final word settles. Cameras no longer observe power from the margins; cameras now participate in the act of governing. The Republic once spoke through elected representatives. Today, the Republic speaks through the lens—and the lens never blinks.

---

* Some commentators have argued that Alito was factually correct in his objection, noting the ruling did not overturn the Tillman Act of 1907 but rather struck down parts of the 2002 Bipartisan Campaign Reform Act (Memmott, 2010; Taranto, 2024). Yet, years of empirical analysis have shown that Obama's warning did prove prescient. Outside-spending by corporations and special-interest groups has surged, and the concerns he raised about the erosion of democratic equality and the rise of big-money influence in elections now appear widely validated (Waldman, 2022).

The Founding Fear

Coronations, Not Conventions

I was eleven years old the summer Ronald Reagan accepted the Republican nomination for President in Detroit, Michigan. I was old enough to follow the faces on television, but too young to understand fully what those faces signified. I remember sitting cross-legged in our wood-paneled den beside my father—he was still alive then, though he would pass away that fall—watching the blue glow of the television wash the room in soft light. The crowd inside Joe Louis Arena rippled with campaign signs and sequined hats, the band punctuating applause lines with practiced precision. Somewhere in the background, a reporter's voice searched for tension on the convention floor—Sam Donaldson, perhaps, or someone like him—microphone raised as if a skirmish might break out among the delegates.

None did.

The roll call unfolded like a script already memorized. Even to a child, the outcome felt foreordained. Reagan won the party's nomination.

That same summer, I also helped my uncle, Lon V. Boyd—or *Uncle MoMo*,* as my brother and I called him—campaign for a local political office. MoMo was well known in our town, and that early introduction to campaigning made for a remarkable season for an energetic boy. My mother had T-shirts printed for my brother and me that read *Vote for My Uncle* in crushed-velvet white block letters—classic 1980s attire. We went door to door handing out push

---

* My uncle served as an officer in the U.S. Navy's Underwater Demolition Teams, the precursor to today's SEALs. His shipmates called him *MoMo*—a teasing nod to his height and to a tall totem pole character from a 1950s movie whose name and title have both been lost to time.

cards and matchbooks*— remember, this was the 1980s—and rode in parades, waving from pickup trucks during town festivals.

Politics, at that scale, felt tangible. I remember spirited conversations on front porches, neighbors who disagreed without retreating, hands that shook across difference. Campaigning involved persuasion, uncertainty, and risk. Watching the national convention later that summer felt different. The parade rolled past, but the floats had already been judged.

I would later learn that the absence of drama was not a failure of the convention—it was the point. By 1980, Reagan had swept forty-two states in the primaries; the delegate count was never in doubt (Busch, 2005). Four years earlier, the Republican Party had fought itself to exhaustion in Kansas City, where Reagan nearly unseated President Gerald Ford on the convention floor (Ceaser, 2017; Polsby, 1983). That bruising contest would prove the last genuinely contested Republican convention of the twentieth century.

In Detroit, television anchors spoke instead of unity and momentum. Observers noted that conventions had shifted from arenas of persuasion to staged affirmations. In Dan Rather's words, "The people who run the conventions have given the networks every reason to pass up the full coverage of the past by squeezing out any real news" (Morris & Francia, 2005). What had once been deliberative had become ceremonial. Conventions no longer

---

* A blog post by Alison Turtledove (2018) offers both written insight and photographic evidence of traditional campaign matchbooks. As she explains, "In the days when nearly everybody was a smoker, printing up a book of matches with your logo and phone number was a smart way to market your business"—or your campaign. My Uncle MoMo had thousands of these matchbooks printed, and I still come across them from time to time when I clean out an old memorabilia trunk in storage. Good memories.

selected nominees; they ratified decisions made elsewhere. They had become coronations.

The contrast with earlier party history is stark. In 1880, Republicans required thirty-six ballots to settle on James Garfield, a compromise forged through fatigue and negotiation. In 1920, party leaders emerged from a smoke-filled room having chosen Warren Harding after ten ballots and countless bargains (Fabry, 2016). Even as late as 1976, reporters crowded the Kansas City floor as Reagan's and Ford's camps counted and recounted delegates, unsure which way the tide would turn (Little, 2020). As Zachary Karabell later observed, that convention was "the last major party convention in which the outcome was not a foregone conclusion" (Karabell, 1998).

What followed only confirmed the transformation. By the mid-1990s, journalists were walking away. Karabell recounts that ABC's Ted Koppel stormed out of the 1996 Republican convention, declaring that the event offered no controversy and therefore no news. Nearly every minute had been choreographed; nearly every word had been scripted. The reform movements of the late 1960s and early 1970s—intended to democratize candidate selection—had drained conventions of suspense. Delegates no longer decided. Delegates confirmed. The drama that remained was theatrical rather than political.

I did not grasp this shift at the time. I only sensed that something had changed. The energy I experienced in my uncle's local campaign—the door-knocking, the debate, the uncertainty—had been replaced, at the national level, by a pageant of certainty. That summer's convention became a template. Today's gatherings are scripted down to the second, roll calls arranged for prime time, dissent carefully seated beyond the camera's reach. Conflict no longer unfolds on the floor. Conflict is front-loaded into primaries that reward intensity over persuasion and visibility over coalition-building.

The result is a democracy that amplifies division while choreographing unity. The microphones still search for conflict, but the microphones no longer decide anything.

This transformation of candidate selection marks a pivotal moment in the Republic's drift away from republicanism—too much noise, too much unfiltered democracy. The fight moved earlier, louder, and closer to the public stage, while the institutional mechanisms designed to absorb conflict quietly receded. We will return to the rise of political primaries and their unintended consequences in later chapters. For now, we observe that when politics becomes full audition and no deliberation, spectacle fills the space once occupied by judgment—and the noise grows louder just as governance grows thinner. The modern party primary is a solution that solved no problem.

The modern party primary did little to repair genuine defects in American democracy. The reforms addressed perceived rather than structural flaws, amplifying participation without strengthening governance.

When 30,000 Became 760,000

Somewhere between Charlotte and Greensboro, a congressional district once traced a path so thin that drivers joked one could lose the seat with a sneeze. Reporters called the district the *I-85 snake*— North Carolina's 12th, a ribbon of asphalt politics running the length of the highway (Kokai, 2016). Longtime Representative Mel Watt, a Yale-trained attorney from Charlotte, represented the district for two decades. Locals joked that he could campaign its length without ever leaving the car or touching the steering wheel.

A generation later, similarly contorted districts have multiplied across the country. Illinois's 4th District—the "earmuffs"—links two Latino neighborhoods in Chicago with a narrow strip of expressway that nearly disappears on a printed map (Outlook Staff, 2012;

Scales, 2020). Maryland's 3rd District, drawn in 2011, resembled a "broken-winged pterodactyl," a sprawl of disconnected suburbs later struck down as an extreme partisan gerrymander (Creitz, 2025).

Together, these districts read like a Rorschach test for democracy—each outline revealing what a partisan mind most wants to preserve. Figure 1 illustrates the point: a snake, an earmuff, and a pterodactyl—districts engineered for outcomes rather than neighborhoods.

Yet, gerrymandering itself is hardly new. Elbridge Gerry's salamander first slithered across Massachusetts in 1812, when party leaders twisted the Essex South District into a serpentine shape to secure advantage for roughly 30,000 constituents (*The Birth of the Gerrymander*, 2008).* What began as a crude manipulation of proximity has matured into a science of precision. Modern mapmakers employ geographic information systems and voter databases—tools once reserved for military planning—to tune districts down to the household level (Altman & McDonald, 2010; Suzuki, 2015). Each address becomes a coordinate. Each voter, a data point.

---

* The word *gerrymander* is a portmanteau, combining the name of Massachusetts Governor Elbridge Gerry with *salamander*. The term originated in 1812 after a newspaper cartoon depicted one of Gerry's party-drawn districts as a salamander-shaped creature, and it has since come to describe the deliberate manipulation of electoral boundaries to favor a political party or group.

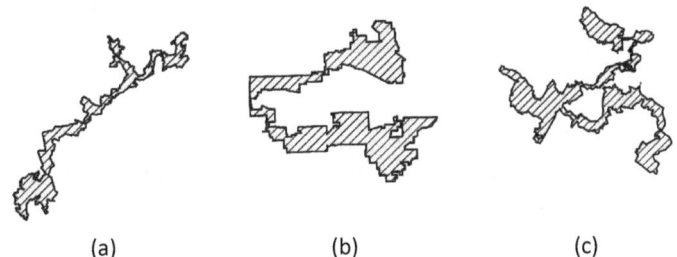

(a) (b) (c)

Figure 1. Three emblematic gerrymanders from the 113th Congress. North Carolina's 12th (the "I-85 snake"), Illinois's 4th (the "earmuffs"), and Maryland's 3rd (the "pterodactyl"). Maps rendered from U.S. Census congressional district boundaries (TIGER/Line 2013 for the 113th).

James Madison imagined representation as proximity—one representative for every 40,000 souls, a ratio small enough to sustain trust yet large enough to preserve distance (Ketcham, 1990; Suzuki, 2015). George Washington intervened during the Constitutional Convention to lower the proposed ratio from 40,000 to 30,000, believing political intimacy should remain within reach of a handshake (Chernow, 2011). The delegates assumed representation would remain a relationship—letters answered, reputations earned, accountability felt.

Two centuries later, that intimacy has dissolved into arithmetic. Each member of Congress now represents roughly 760,000 people. The growth, shown in Fig. 2, follows a clear path: steady expansion through the nineteenth century, followed by a sharp break after 1929, when Congress permanently fixed the House at 435 members. The cap resolved a decade-long stalemate after the 1920 Census, when rural lawmakers resisted reapportionment that would have shifted power to industrial cities. The compromise ended the dispute but severed representation from population. What began as a procedural solution hardened into a structural constraint.

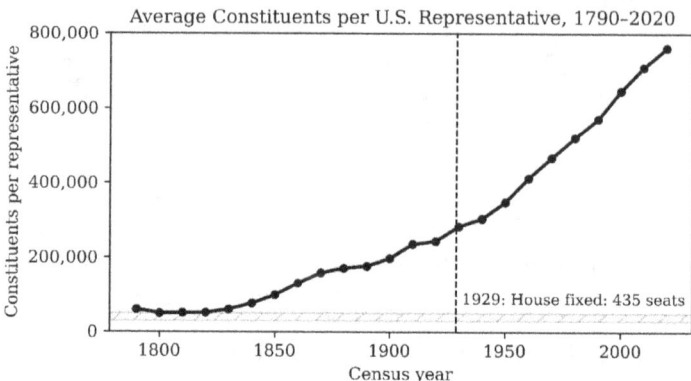

Figure 2. Growth of Constituents per U.S. Representative, 1790–2020. The line traces the historical increase in the average number of constituents represented by each member of the House of Representatives from the first census to the present. The shaded band between 30,000 and 50,000 marks the cognitive and constitutional range envisioned by the Founders—a scale within which trust and reciprocity remain humanly manageable. The sharp rise after 1929 reflects the permanent cap of 435 seats, driving today's ratio to roughly 760,000 constituents per representative.

As the nation tripled in size, representation stood still. Modern cognitive science helps explain why that scale feels alien. Robin Dunbar's research on social cognition suggests that human beings maintain stable trust networks at limited sizes, with meaningful recognition fading as numbers grow (Dunbar, 2010; Dunbar, 1992). These findings do not prescribe institutional design, but they confirm a basic truth the Founders understood through experience: political trust weakens as relational distance grows. Beyond a certain scale, familiarity gives way to abstraction. Citizens become categories rather than neighbors.

Madison did not oppose scale. *Federalist No. 10* famously argued for enlarging the sphere to dilute faction, and Rosenbluth and Shapiro extend that logic by showing how large districts force parties to aggregate interests before elections rather than bargain afterward. In that sense, size strengthens governance. The difficulty emerges elsewhere. A district large enough to stabilize coalitions may also become too large to sustain connection. The modern expansion of congressional districts has therefore exposed a paradox at the heart of representation: scale disciplines factions, while proximity sustains trust.

The modern House satisfies the logic of aggregation while violating the logic of intimacy. Representation once measured relationships. Today, representation measures reach. The distance meant to cool passion has dulled connection instead. The House of the People increasingly resembles an auditorium—loud, crowded, impersonal—where voices blend into static and passion amplifies without restraint. Madison warned that the fires of faction must be confined to local hearths. In a nation where one representative speaks for three-quarters of a million, the hearth has gone cold, even as the noise grows louder. The digital age has exposed this scale–intimacy paradox with a clarity unimaginable to the Founders. Resolving that paradox—recovering structure without surrendering scale—forms a central theme of more republic—not less—developed in the chapters ahead.

Congress on Borrowed Time

Congress is not functioning properly. The twelve appropriations bills that once marked a working legislature rarely pass before the start of the fiscal year. In their place comes a procession of continuing resolutions—temporary lifelines extended to avoid shutdowns, colloquially known as CRs (Congressional Research Service, 2024; Davidson et al., 2019). Each missed deadline now threatens not only federal paychecks but the coordination of a $30 trillion economy, the largest in the world (U.S. Bureau of Economic Analysis, 2025). For better or for worse, nearly one in every three dollars in the American economy flows through federal contracts, programs, and salaries—through channels Congress alone is constitutionally authorized to fund (Saturno, 2023). The absurdity is structural. The world's largest marketplace depends on a legislature that cannot pass a budget. What James Madison described as the "power of the purse" has become a hostage to faction (Mann & Ornstein, 2006), and the noise of democracy now echoes in the silence of appropriations.

For much of the Republic's history, this paralysis would have been unthinkable. Before the 1970s, Congress generally completed annual appropriations near the start of the fiscal year, and short-term funding measures remained rare exceptions rather than routine practice (Congressional Research Service, 2024). The modern budget process emerged in 1974, when Congress—reeling from Vietnam, Watergate, and years of presidential impoundment—attempted to reclaim authority through the Congressional Budget and Impoundment Control Act (Mann & Ornstein, 2006). The Act created the Congressional Budget Office, established budget committees in each chamber, and shifted the fiscal year from July 1 to October 1 (Saturno, 2023). The ambition was restorative. Congress sought to impose order, reclaim initiative, and discipline executive overreach. Yet the framework multiplied deadlines and diffused responsibility. Missed deadlines required temporary fixes. Temporary fixes became routine. The statute designed to restore control instead institutionalized avoidance.

The deeper surrender, however, preceded 1974. Congress had already yielded first-mover advantage on the budget half a century earlier. The Budget and Accounting Act of 1921 required the President to submit an annual, comprehensive federal budget to Congress and created what later became the Office of Management and Budget (Schick, 2008; White, 2003). The reform promised coordination and efficiency after World War I. The cost was initiative. From that moment forward, the Executive Branch proposed an integrated fiscal agenda, while the House—constitutionally charged with originating revenue—reacted. Over time, reaction hardened into dependency. Congress retained formal authority over appropriations but ceded narrative control, agenda setting, and timing to the Executive. Power followed first move. By the late twentieth century, the President's budget had become the baseline from which Congress amended, delayed, or failed.

Other democracies resolved this tension differently. In Westminster parliamentary systems, as in the United Kingdom, budgets are treated as matters of confidence. A government that cannot secure passage of a budget falls, triggering elections (Dicey & Wade, 1982; McLean & McMillan, 2005). Deadlines matter because survival depends on them. The American system deliberately rejected such fusion of powers. Madison designed separation to slow decision and force compromise, not to guarantee efficiency. Yet the comparison is instructive. In Westminster systems, failure produces consequence. In the American system, failure produces continuation. When Congress cannot decide, the government proceeds on autopilot—little to no consequence. The tincan gets kicked down the road.

Continuing resolutions have therefore become instruments of congressional survival. Since the 1970s, Congress has seldom completed a fiscal year without resorting to at least one CR (Bahal, 2025). Over the past twenty-eight years, lawmakers have enacted more than one hundred interim continuing resolutions and several full-year substitutes, ranging in duration from weeks to months. Figure 3 presents the record, with bars showing the number of continuing resolutions and a curve marking days of government shutdown—periods when Congress failed to enact even temporary funding.

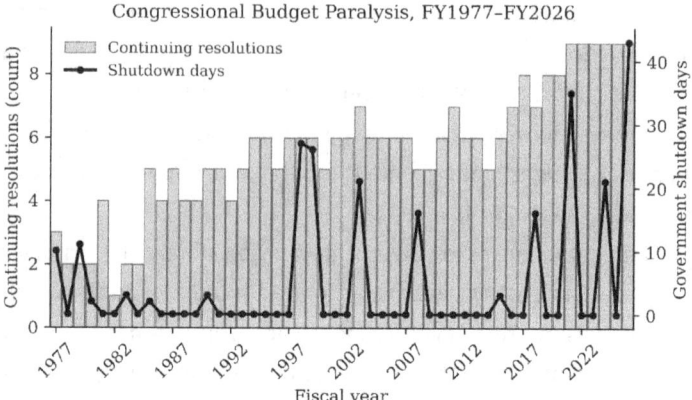

Figure 3. Congressional Budget Paralysis, FY 1977–2026. Number of continuing resolutions enacted per fiscal year (bars) and total days of federal government shutdowns (line) following implementation of the Congressional Budget and Impoundment Control Act of 1974. Continuing resolutions and shutdown days are allocated by fiscal year; partial and full shutdowns are counted uniformly. Sources: Congressional Research Service; Office of Management and Budget.

From 1998 through 2026, Congress has averaged roughly five CRs per fiscal year. In the twenty-first century, federal agencies have operated under temporary funding for approximately one-third of each year. The measure meant to buy time for deliberation has displaced deliberation itself. Each missed deadline weakens Congress's standing. The longer the government operates on borrowed time, the more the Executive Branch governs by necessity. Improvisation hardens into habit.

Political scientists Thomas Mann and Norman Ornstein warned of this collapse nearly two decades ago in The Broken Branch (2006). They described a Congress that had ceased to legislate in the Madisonian sense—not balancing ambition with ambition, but collapsing into tribal performance. What once functioned as the deliberative core of government increasingly operates as a partisan stage, reactive to presidential cues and public outrage. The abdication is not a single event but a pattern. Each crisis Congress avoids—by continuing resolution, by executive order, or by judicial deferral—deepens the rut. The branch erodes not by force but by disuse.

The consequences extend beyond budgets. Figure 4 reveals a parallel inversion in lawmaking itself. While the number of public laws enacted annually has fallen to a fraction of mid-century levels, the Federal Register—the daily ledger of executive rulemaking—has expanded to nearly ninety thousand pages per year (Office of the Federal Register, 2025). In the 1950s, Congress routinely enacted more than seven hundred statutes annually. In recent years, that figure has fallen below two hundred.* Fewer laws are not inherently a failure. The danger lies in the asymmetry. Clyde Wayne Crews calculates that in 2024 federal agencies issued nineteen rules for every law enacted by Congress (Crews, 2025). Scholars such as Philip Wallach identify this inversion as the defining feature of modern governance: a Republic legislating by notice and comment rather than by vote (Wallach, 2023). Madison's "predominant" branch has become the quietest.

---

* The decline in public laws should not be read as an argument for producing more laws. For a free country, the United States already has an abundance of laws—too many, in the view of many jurists (Hayek, 2011). The point here is relational. As congressional activity has diminished, executive rulemaking has expanded to fill the vacuum (Wallach, 2023).

The Founding Fear

Figure 4. The New Lawmakers: Executive Rulemaking and Acts of Congress, 1940–2024. Annual public laws enacted by Congress in selected benchmark years (bars) compared with total pages published annually in the *Federal Register* (line), a commonly used proxy for administrative rulemaking activity. The figure illustrates the long-term divergence between declining legislative output and the growth of executive and administrative governance. Sources: Office of the Federal Register. *Federal Register Statistics*, various years. U.S. Congress. *Statutes at Large*; Congressional Research Service legislative summaries.

The same pattern appears in matters of war. The War Powers Resolution of 1973—passed one year before the Budget Act—sought to reclaim congressional authority after decades of executive expansion (Ely, 1993; Fisher, 2013). Like the budget reforms, the statute announced limits without enforcing them. Military action proceeded under open-ended authorizations. The 2001 Authorization for Use of Military Force passed with a single dissenting vote and has remained operative for more than two decades, spanning multiple administrations, theaters, and conflicts without renewed congressional approval, yet still authorizing executive military action (Fisher, 2013). Congress wrote the rules, then declined to revisit them. Fiscal deadlines slipped as steadily as war authorizations blurred. Legislators governed by deferral.

What Congress has yielded, the other branches have absorbed. Executive power expands through orders and rules. Judicial power expands through interpretation. Abortion, marriage, campaign finance, and affirmative action have been settled less by statute than by decree—through litigation rather than legislation (Sunstein, 2019; Teles, 2008).* Legislators respond as spectators, praising or condemning outcomes without attempting translation into law. Constitutional interpretation has become the default mode of national policymaking not because judges seize authority, but because representatives decline to exercise their authority (Mann & Ornstein, 2006). Judicial supremacy, like executive unilateralism, thrives on legislative retreat. When elected branches refuse to deliberate, judges become lawmakers by vacancy rather than usurpation.

---

* Conservatives, in particular, did not merely inherit judicial ascendancy; conservative leaders actively cultivated judicial power. Beginning in the 1970s, after repeated defeats in the elected branches, conservative legal strategists deliberately redirected political energy toward the courts. As Steven Teles demonstrates, this effort coalesced through the Federalist Society, a network of public-interest law firms, and a disciplined philanthropic infrastructure designed to shape legal education and advance judges committed to textualism and originalism (Teles, 2008). Julian Zelizer traces the same arc in *The Atlantic*, showing how this long campaign—from the Nixon appointments through the Reagan Justice Department to the Trump confirmations—transformed the federal judiciary into the Right's most reliable instrument of governance (Zelizer, 2018). The result was not a coup but a gradual transfer of authority, achieved through persistence rather than seizure. That strategy itself is not the problem. The deeper failure lies elsewhere. Congress has surrendered so much legislative authority to the courts that judicial victories now substitute for lawmaking. Under those conditions, disciplined legal movements appear not merely effective but inevitable. What looks like judicial overreach is more accurately legislative retreat.

Gridlock, therefore, does not describe a Congress at rest. Gridlock marks motion displaced to the other branches. Authority flows downhill to whoever still moves—the President by pen, the Court by judgment. Congress governs by outrage and resolution, democratic energy consumed by performance rather than persuasion. The abdication began with the purse, extended through war, and settled into judgment. Each surrender shifted power from deliberation to decree. The People's branch, designed to lead, has become the echo chamber of the Republic's disorder. What once filtered democratic passion now amplifies into noise so constant that progress yields to paralysis. The imbalance is institutional and cultural alike, born of a nation that confuses immediacy with action and volume with governance. As this chapter turns toward conclusion, the question remains whether the structure still holds—whether a Republic designed to channel conflict can still contain a democracy that no longer pauses to deliberate.

In Sum

In the old *Saturday Night Live* sketch, Christopher Walken keeps interrupting a recording session to demand "More cowbell!"—each take louder and more absurd than the last.* The music never improves, only the volume. The scene endures because the captures something familiar—the moment when confidence drowns out coordination. Modern democracy often sounds the same. Each faction

---

* The pop-cultural persistence of the "cowbell" has been taken quite seriously. At the University of Maryland a doctoral candidate published *The Cowbell in Music and Culture* (McGovern 2023), tracing the instrument's evolution from livestock signal to orchestral implement to a symbol of humor, derision, and sub-culture.

More Republic, Less Cowbell

wants to be heard above the others; few stop to ask whether the song still holds together.

Each generation must decide whether liberty warrants the discipline necessary to sustain a free government. Liberty without responsibility cannot endure. The Founders feared pure democracy for that reason—not from distrust of the People, but from recognition that the People possess power strong enough to undo the Republic when unrestrained by responsibility and structure. Madison's design never sought to quiet the crowd but to contain the democratic fire—turning passion into policy, heat into light, speech into law. That alchemy required distance, delay, and protected deliberative space—features of republican government now dismissed as defects rather than safeguards. The genius of the Republic lay in constitutional structure, not in a Kumbaya chorus with more cowbell.

That 250-year structure, carefully crafted by the delegates in Philadelphia and tested by storms—including a civil war, *the Civil War*—now strains beneath the new noise of a hyper-connected electronic world. The distance within Madison's extended sphere, once a buffer that cooled emotion, has collapsed under the Pressure of mass instantaneous reaction. The camera, the feed, and the algorithm have erased the pauses that once protected responsible judgment from the reckless crowd. Factions now move at the speed of digital signals, and social-media 'certainty' arrives long before evidence.* Congress, meant to serve as the ballast of the ship, drifts

---

* The phenomenon of social-media 'certainty' arriving ahead of evidence can be understood through the lens of motivated reasoning. As Kunda (1990) demonstrated, cognitive processes shift when the goal is affirmation rather than accuracy. In digital environments, the rapid circulation of social posts and the reinforcement of identity-aligned content allow

with the current of outrage. Only a legislature can legitimately translate plural disagreement into binding law without coercion, yet Congress increasingly performs that role for the camera rather than exercising their power through deliberation. The Executive—well suited to exploit this velocity—governs by decree, the Court by interpretation, and the People's branch by performance. The Republic still speaks, yet the language has changed—from deliberation to display.

The danger is not necessarily that democracy has grown too loud, but that the noise no longer passes through reason's filters. Free speech, once a furnace of thought, now burns without boundaries. Moral certainty parades as virtue; scientific certainty masquerades as law. Each one forgets the humility that both democracy and science demand—the courage to admit we may be wrong. Noise is what remains when humility is lost. The present crisis is not one of corruption, but of abdication—a steady withdrawal from responsibility that leaves authority to migrate elsewhere. Yet democracy's fire still warms. The same heat that threatens to consume can still forge. We should not give up on our democratic republic just yet. America has stumbled through louder seasons than this one and has emerged, scorched but unbroken, each time rebuilding the channels that keep passion and reason in uneasy balance. This time—this hour, this moment—should be no different. The task before us is the same one Madison left unfinished: to rebuild those channels in a world where distance and delay have vanished. We can rebuild the American Republic.

'misplaced certainty'—a subjective conviction untethered from evidence—to take root and resist correction (Olcaysoy Okten et al., 2023).

More Republic, Less Cowbell

The Republic was never promised permanence. The structure the Founders built has endured wars, depressions, and reinventions, yet each era has added weight to the frame. Today's noise began when the slow disciplines of republican government yielded, piece by piece, to the temptations of speed. Each reform born of openness—a tilt toward more democracy, more cowbell—each shortcut toward efficiency, each gesture of purity has carried a hidden cost—another loosened joint in the architecture Madison designed to restrain us from ourselves. The time has come to remember what the Founders knew: a nation cannot be saved by a louder democracy, only by a steadier republic—*more Republic, less cowbell.*

CHAPTER 2

The Long Unraveling

ON A WINTER EVENING in 1976, a handful of reporters in Des Moines gathered around a black-and-white television and watched a political universe tilt. Snow clung to the edges of car tires outside the caucus halls, and most Americans had never heard the name Jimmy Carter. Inside one cramped headquarters, volunteers passed Styrofoam cups of weak coffee, waiting for numbers few believed would matter. Then the networks declared Carter the winner in Iowa, and something subtle but seismic shifted within American politics. A system designed to filter ambition through deliberation yielded to a process that rewarded momentum, visibility, and performance. The startled smiles in that room marked more than a candidate's breakthrough. Those expressions marked the opening of a new political era—a republic beginning to shed restraint.

The Long Unraveling did not arrive through a single decision or a single figure. The process emerged through reforms pursued in good faith, through technologies that expanded access, and through a civic culture that confused exposure with wisdom. Over time, those forces strained the constitutional architecture that once moderated democratic passion, deepening polarization and inviting demagoguery to fill the resulting void.

This chapter traces how a nation once governed by the cool logic of a constitutional republic drifted toward the heat of democratic immediacy. The habits, institutions, and rhythms that once tempered public life gradually thinned, grew louder, and became more fragile. The unraveling unfolded incrementally rather than abruptly, but the consequences proved substantial. Understanding that descent remains essential for understanding how a republic rebuilds and calms the clang of too much cowbell. The story begins where the new system first revealed its leverage point: a cold caucus night in Iowa, when a little-known candidate discovered that sequencing could substitute for stature.

The Iowa Shock

The night Jimmy Carter won Iowa, even members of his own staff seemed startled. The date was January 19, 1976—a cold Monday in Des Moines. I was six years old, yet memory preserves fragments of that campaign season. Carter did not inspire affection at the time. The Southern peanut farmer from Georgia carried a smile full of teeth and an otherwise unreadable face. The fuller account comes not from childhood recollection, but from later reading and reflection.

Snow dusted the parking lots outside the caucus halls, where turnout was light and expectations lower still. Inside a cramped campaign office, a small group of volunteers watched county returns flicker across a television screen. When the networks declared Carter the winner—technically first among candidates receiving pledged support—he smiled, shook a few hands, and said quietly, "Well, maybe we did something tonight" (Witcover, 1977).

They had. By dawn, newspapers ran triumphant headlines announcing Carter's Iowa surge—*Carter Wins Iowa!* For many readers that morning, a single question followed: *Jimmy who?* Even seasoned political reporters appeared caught off guard. Few news organizations had bothered to send correspondents to Iowa, treating the caucuses as a quaint Midwestern ritual rather than a consequential political event. Party rules had changed after 1968, and the meaning of early contests had changed with them. Most observers missed the shift. Jimmy Carter did not.

When Carter's name topped the wire copy, editors scrambled to locate file photographs and background notes. By breakfast, the small team in Des Moines fielded calls from national networks eager to book interviews with a candidate most Americans had never seen.

Carter's campaign violated nearly every expectation of modern presidential politics. No national organization stood behind the effort. Financial resources remained thin. Party leaders withheld endorsement. Headquarters in Atlanta operated on a shoestring, staffed by volunteers who answered phones, licked envelopes, and slept on office floors. While better-known rivals focused on fundraising and television appearances, Carter spent more than a year quietly visiting county after county across Iowa—attending potluck dinners, staying in spare bedrooms, and learning voters' names firsthand (Witcover, 1977).

The Press initially treated the effort as a novelty. Reporters joked about the "peanut brigade" from Georgia, charming but doomed (Witcover, 1977). he state party chair later recalled that many professionals did not even realize Carter was running. Once the returns came in, that casual dismissal vanished. An unknown candidate had finished ahead of "uncommitted," demonstrating that momentum could substitute for money and that visibility could generate viability (Shafer & Claggett, 1995).

The Iowa result did not merely elevate a candidate. The Iowa result revealed a transformation already underway. Early contests now shaped national perception, press attention amplified minor advantages, and democratic immediacy began to overwhelm deliberative restraint. The Carter victory marked an early step away from republican filtration and toward a politics driven by volume, momentum, and performance—an early clang of too much cowbell. The only remaining question was whether the system could convert that kind of momentum into national power.

Jimmy Who?

That question became the story. Iowa did not deliver many delegates toward securing the 1976 Democratic nomination at the New York City convention, but Iowa delivered something more valuable—momentum. That momentum carried Jimmy Carter from obscurity to the White House. Reporters, eager for redemption after Watergate, searched for an outsider who appeared decent, uncorrupted, and recognizably human. Many found that figure in the peanut farmer from Plains, Georgia (Witcover, 1977). Within days, press accounts described Carter as "the man to watch" in the nomination race. Within a month, donors phoned campaign headquarters faster than volunteers could answer. Within a year, Carter stood on the inaugural platform, hand raised, pledging never to lie to the American people (Carter, 2003).

Carter's ascent appeared improbable but followed a discernible logic. The Iowa victory emerged from a political system rewired after 1968—a system Carter understood better than many party leaders who constructed the reforms in the name of democratic renewal (Shafer & Claggett, 1995). Momentum required a mechanism. Iowa became decisive only because party rules had already been rewritten to treat early contests as legitimate measures of authority. That transformation began eight years earlier, when the

Democratic National Convention in Chicago, intended to display party unity, instead revealed institutional collapse. Mayor Richard J. Daley's police confronted antiwar protesters with clubs as tear gas drifted across streets illuminated by television lights.* Inside the convention hall, delegates shouted over one another while cameras lingered on faces contorted by anger. Outside, chants of "The whole world is watching" echoed into millions of living rooms (White, 1969). In the age of television, the 1968 convention became a national spectacle of disorder.

Inside the International Amphitheatre on Chicago's South Side, delegates nominated Vice President Hubert H. Humphrey—despite Humphrey's absence from every primary contest. Party leaders still governed nominations in the traditional manner. Governors, county bosses, and union heads assembled blocs of delegates and exchanged support through negotiation rather than voter appeal (Witcover, 1977).† Before 1968, presidential nominations rarely depended on popular voting. Urban political machines in cities such as New York, Chicago, and Philadelphia delivered loyal delegations as political currency. Negotiations unfolded in hotel suites. Promises

---

* The confrontation outside the Conrad Hilton Hotel on August 28, 1968—later known as *the Battle of Michigan Avenue*—became one of the most widely televised episodes of civil unrest in American political history. Officers from the Chicago Police Department charged demonstrators and bystanders with clubs and tear gas as network cameras broadcast the scene live. A subsequent federal investigation concluded that the violence constituted a "police riot" (History.com, 2018; Little, 1996).

† The archetype of this older order was Tammany Hall. Comparable party machines operated elsewhere, most notably in Chicago under Richard J. Daley and in Jersey City under Frank Hague. These organizations exemplified a nomination system rooted in hierarchy, loyalty, and negotiated authority rather than popular enthusiasm. See Jenkinson (2022) and Golway (2014).

of patronage and cabinet appointments lubricated agreement. The system rewarded loyalty over ideology and hierarchy over enthusiasm.

To a public exhausted by war and shaken by the assassination of Robert Kennedy, closed-door politics appeared indistinguishable from betrayal—despite the same process having elevated Lincoln, Roosevelt, Eisenhower, and Kennedy. Television reframed perception. Through that lens, the old party system no longer looked legitimate.

When Humphrey lost the general election to Richard Nixon, reckoning followed. The Democratic Party established the McGovern–Fraser Commission, chaired by Senator George McGovern and Representative Donald M. Fraser, and charged the group with reforming presidential nominations. The commission sought openness: written rules, transparent procedures, and inclusive participation. Delegate selection would become more democratic, more accountable, and more visible (Shafer, 1983). Less republic. More democracy.

As constitutional scholar Richard H. Pildes later observed, reformers never intended to eliminate the institutional party or create a fully populist, primary-dominated system. Committee member Austin Ranney later reflected, "We accomplished the opposite of what we intended" (Pildes, 2016). Reformers hoped to broaden representation within the caucus structure rather than dismantle party authority. The rules produced by the commission proved complex and burdensome. Many state parties abandoned caucuses altogether in favor of simpler, state-run primaries. Within two election cycles, the United States had "stumbled—and I do mean stumbled—into a system that eliminated any meaningful role for party figures" (Pildes, 2016).

The result amounted to a quiet revolution. New requirements mandated written procedures, proportional representation for women and minorities, and a decisive shift away from smoke-filled rooms toward primaries and caucuses (Shafer & Claggett, 1995).* On the surface, the reforms appeared sensible. Greater democratic participation sounded virtuous. More democracy rarely draws objection. More cowbell.

The nomination system that emerged by 1972 bore little resemblance to the constitutional design envisioned by the Founders. The new primary–caucus regime rewarded energy over seniority and visibility over experience—a structural invitation to demagoguery (Berend, 2020). Candidates appealed directly to voters rather than to party leaders responsible for governing coalitions. Reformers believed democratic legitimacy had been strengthened. Republican stability had been weakened. Political authority no longer flowed downward through institutions but surged upward from mass participation (Aldrich, 1995; Pildes, 2016).

Pildes notes that the pre-1968 nomination process resembled a constitutional separation of powers. Popular primaries functioned as a lower chamber expressing public sentiment, while party leaders served as an upper chamber filtering passion through

---

* A *primary* is a state-administered election in which registered voters cast secret ballots—commonly referred to as *Australian ballots*—for their preferred presidential candidate. A caucus, by contrast, is a party-run gathering in which participants meet at a designated time and location, openly deliberate, and register support through public methods such as physical grouping, standing, or voice votes. Although both mechanisms were introduced to broaden participation in presidential nominations, caucuses consistently attract fewer and more ideologically committed participants, magnifying the influence of highly engaged party activists. As political scientist Sean J. Wright argues in *Time to End Presidential Caucuses* (2016), caucuses are less representative, more burdensome to attend, and systematically favor motivated minorities. That imbalance has repeatedly shaped early-state momentum by rewarding organizational intensity over broad appeal—a dynamic first revealed at scale during Jimmy Carter's Iowa breakthrough in 1976.

experience. The system balanced these forces, much as Madison and Hamilton designed the House and Senate to restrain one another. Presidential nominations once combined popular impulse with institutional judgment. When that internal equilibrium collapsed after 1968, presidential selection drifted toward immediacy, amplification, and spectacle—and away from republican restraint. Jimmy Carter became the first modern candidate to treat those redesigned incentives as a set of instructions rather than a set of traditions.

The Carter Method

Jimmy Carter studied the post-1968 shift with the patience of an engineer. Carter and his team recognized that under the new rules, early victories in primaries and caucuses mattered more than national name recognition. Carter wagered that success in Iowa or New Hampshire could dominate headlines for weeks, converting obscurity into inevitability (Witcover, 1977). While most rivals chased endorsements and money, Carter chased delegates. The campaign focused on small states that voted early, with Carter shaking hands in diners, visiting church basements, and staying overnight with local families to stretch limited resources. While better-known Democrats concentrated on large states and elite donors, Carter appeared everywhere else. As Carter later recalled, "Our basic plan was to start early and work harder than anyone else" (Carter, 1995).

His Iowa strategy followed a simple rule: arrive early, remain visible, and win something—anything—that could be framed as success. Finishing ahead of better-known candidates triggered a rush of press attention. Television, rather than delegate math, produced the breakthrough (Witcover, 1977). Each interview multiplied exposure. Each headline attracted donations for the next contest. Carter grasped the emerging feedback loop before political science supplied a name for the phenomenon (Shafer & Claggett, 1995).

Trained as an engineer,* Carter became the first presidential candidate to treat the modern primary system as a design problem. Carter mapped incentives, modeled feedback effects, and exploited the mechanics with precision—the moment, as one historian later observed, when the primary system found its first engineer (Pildes, 2016). The campaign assembled a machine built not from gears and levers, but from momentum and perception. Rising visibility produced assumptions of viability, and assumed viability produced votes.

In that sense, Carter's triumph was structural rather than merely personal. The campaign demonstrated a new political logic: sequential victories could substitute for national consensus. Small, early wins created momentum disproportionate to underlying support. Observers later described Carter's success as superior strategy, but that description obscures the deeper cost. A republic depends on the slow aggregation of broad agreement. A system that allows momentum to outrun consensus rewards sequencing over synthesis. Carter did not persuade a national majority at the outset; Carter assembled inevitability step by step, converting narrow victories into presumed legitimacy.

The distinction matters. Strategy alone does not weaken a republic. A system that elevates momentum above deliberation does.

---

* Jimmy Carter graduated from the U.S. Naval Academy at Annapolis in 1946 with a Bachelor of Science degree, ranking 59th in a class of 820. Trained as a naval engineer, he later completed graduate-level studies in nuclear reactor technology and physics at Union College while serving under Admiral Hyman G. Rickover in the Navy's nascent nuclear submarine program. See Carter (1995) and Brinkley and Lewis (1999).

The reformed nomination process privileged candidates capable of dominating early attention rather than candidates capable of assembling durable governing coalitions. Carter succeeded because the rules allowed momentum to masquerade as mandate.

When Carter walked down Pennsylvania Avenue in 1977 rather than riding in a limousine, the gesture symbolized humility and moral repair after Nixon (Dumbrell, 1995). Yet the path that carried Carter to the presidency revealed a deeper transformation. The McGovern–Fraser reforms democratized nominations while dismantling the mediating structures that once filtered passion through deliberation. Party leaders surrendered control in favor of openness. Hierarchy yielded to spontaneity. Procedural reform quietly redefined political authority (Shafer & Claggett, 1995).

Carter's campaign proved—first and decisively—that a presidential candidate could bypass traditional authority by mastering primary sequencing, crafting a personal narrative, and feeding that narrative into a media environment increasingly attuned to political theater. Carter's success redefined the meaning of a presidential campaign. Campaigning became the governing model. Subsequent elections followed the same pattern: momentum first, message second, meaning last.

Republicans soon adopted the same machinery, partly because Democratic-controlled state legislatures designed primary laws that governed both parties, and partly because televised Democratic contests framed primaries as the legitimate measure of public will (Aldrich, 1995; Pildes, 2016). By 1980, both parties operated within the same populist architecture.

In the name of transparency, party leaders created a new form of opacity. Public performance replaced internal debate. Carter's decency was genuine, but the system rewarded spectacle alongside substance. The Founders' fear of faction evolved into a subtler danger—the faction of personality. Later campaigns echoed the same dynamic. Reagan's Revolution, Obama's Hope, and Trump's Drain the Swamp each drew power from direct emotional connection unmediated by party hierarchy (Aldrich, 1995).

After the trauma of the 1968 convention, Democrats sought to prevent another crisis of legitimacy. In pursuing that goal, party leaders altered the means by which legitimacy itself was earned. A democratic republic became more democratized—perhaps excessively so. Transparency hardened into permanence. Campaigns ceased to end. Politics ceased to rest. Republican restraint yielded to passions once confined by institutional design (Shafer & Claggett, 1995). The election of Jimmy Carter marked the emergence of a system that rewarded celebrity over statesmanship.

The reforms that enabled Carter emerged from Nixon's collapse. The hunger for honesty after Watergate produced a culture of surveillance disguised as transparency. Presidents thereafter governed before a permanent tribunal of cameras, committees, and prosecutors. Modern politics does not progress cleanly from Nixon to Carter. Modern politics loops backward, each figure defined by the consequences left in the other's wake.

Carter's breakthrough revealed more than a new path to the White House. The breakthrough revealed a transfer of authority inside the parties themselves. When nominations moved outward, party leadership could no longer manage ambition through structure. Ambition learned to manage structure through campaigns.

That shift raises a deeper question. If parties once mediated ambition, what performed that mediating function before national campaigns, mass media, and primaries assumed control? American politics did not always operate without intermediaries. Earlier systems relied on human-scale brokers who absorbed pressure, translated demands, and negotiated conflict long before passion reached national institutions. Those brokers were imperfect. Many were corrupt. Yet those brokers performed a function that modern reform would later remove without replacement.

The Machine and the Missing Middle

The destruction of political machines in the early twentieth century is often told as a story of democratic progress. Corruption receded. Civil service replaced patronage. Elections grew cleaner. Government professionalized. Each reform addressed genuine abuses and delivered tangible improvements.

Reform, however, imposed an unacknowledged cost.

Political machines such as Tammany Hall did more than traffic in favors or manipulate ballots. Machines performed mediation. Ward captains translated the demands of immigrant neighborhoods into negotiable claims. Local brokers absorbed anger before anger reached city hall. Patronage, however unsavory, anchored politics in human-scale relationships that allowed conflict to be managed rather than merely expressed (Banfield & Wilson, 1963; Gamm, 1999).

When Progressive reformers dismantled the machines, reformers eliminated corruption—but reformers also erased the last widely functioning layer of informal political intermediation in American public life. That loss coincided with a structural change moving in the same direction. As the population grew while the size of the House remained fixed, the ratio of citizens to representatives expanded dramatically. Fewer members served more people, and representation stretched thinner with each census. Human-scale brokerage became harder to sustain. The disappearance of ward-level mediation combined with expanding district size to sever the daily, personal links that once absorbed pressure and translated grievance before conflict reached national institutions.

No constitutional substitute followed.

Progressive reform assumed that purified procedures could replace personal intermediaries. Voters would interact directly with institutions. Law would speak clearly for itself. Administration would operate neutrally. Politics would elevate reason over relationship (Hofstadter, 1955). The vision reflected optimism about rational governance, professional expertise, and civic virtue. That optimism proved incomplete.

As electorates expanded and government responsibilities multiplied, citizens confronted institutions too large, too distant, and too abstract for direct engagement. Local knowledge thinned. Informal translation vanished. Representation flattened. The political system grew cleaner—and colder. Access shifted from neighbors to forms, from relationships to rules, from conversation to compliance.

Mediation did not disappear. Mediation merely changed character.

Party organizations lost authority while campaigns gained independence. Local brokers vanished while national figures rose. Mass media replaced ward captains as translators of public demand. Later, digital platforms replaced editors. Each step increased distance between citizens and decision-makers while preserving the appearance of direct democracy. Where machines once negotiated upward, modern politics amplifies outward.

This shift altered the nature of faction itself. Factions no longer passed through layered human filters before reaching governing institutions. Emotional intensity traveled faster than deliberation. Mobilization outpaced negotiation. Political identity hardened without the softening effect of local compromise and reciprocal obligation.

James Madison anticipated this danger. *Federalist No. 10* did not propose eliminating factions. Madison proposed managing faction through structure—by extending the sphere, multiplying interests, and interposing representative layers between impulse and authority. The constitutional design depended not on purity, but on filtration.

Political machines violated Madison's design by operating outside constitutional bounds. Progressive reform violated Madison's design by eliminating filtration altogether. Both errors shared a common root.

The Republic resisted the idea that representation must occur at multiple scales. Either power flowed upward without structure, or intermediaries emerged without legitimacy. No durable middle ground developed. Reform addressed corruption but neglected function. Purification removed pathology but also removed capacity.

Modern polarization reflects this unresolved tension. Citizens experience politics either as distant abstraction or as raw tribal struggle. Trust erodes because no visible layer exists to absorb pressure, resolve disputes, and translate interests before conflict reaches national institutions. National politics now bears emotional weight once distributed across neighborhoods, parishes, unions, and wards.

The lesson of the machine era is not nostalgic. The lesson is structural.

Mass democracy requires mediation. When lawful mediation disappears, informal mediation returns. When informal mediation dominates, corruption follows. Stability demands a third option: mediation that is constitutional, accountable, and deliberately designed.

The American system once stumbled into that function by accident. The future demands performing that function on purpose. To understand what such mediation once looked like—and how it was lost—it is necessary to examine how party authority operated before its modern reconfiguration.

The Axis of Party Power

Before 1968, the American presidency operated *within* a party rather than *above* it. The president was a visible leader, often the most prominent figure associated with the party, but not its organizational head. Party authority resided elsewhere—distributed across state organizations, congressional leadership, and national committees that predated, outlasted, and often constrained any single administration (Aldrich, 1995; Rauch, 1994). Parties governed continuity. Presidents governed episodes.

This distinction mattered. Presidential elections did not trigger wholesale reorganization of party authority. Victory elevated a candidate to office, not to ownership. The party's structure—fundraising channels, nomination processes, committee systems, and internal discipline—remained largely intact regardless of who occupied the White House. A president needed the party's cooperation to govern, but the party did not become an extension of the president's personal campaign.

That balance no longer holds.

After 1968, the presidency increasingly became the *de facto* center of party leadership. Fundraising, messaging, candidate recruitment, and agenda-setting gravitated toward the presidential nominee and, once elected, toward the president. This shift did not occur because presidents formally seized control of party institutions. The shift occurred because the institutions that once mediated ambition lost their gatekeeping role.

Each presidential contender in the primary system now had to construct a separate organization—a mini-party within the party—to survive a long, media-driven nomination process. These campaign bureaucracies made little sense to dismantle once the general election began. Over time, this inertia hollowed out the standing party structure. Rather than spanning presidential cycles, party infrastructure increasingly had to be rebuilt around each nominee.

The decisive change came from the reorganization of nominations. When party-controlled selection gave way to voter-centered primaries following the reforms recommended by the McGovern–Fraser Commission, the locus of political legitimacy moved decisively outward (Ceaser, 2017). Candidates no longer rose through party structures. Candidates built parallel organizations designed to win primaries, dominate media attention, and mobilize voters directly. These organizations operated beside the party, not within it. Once successful, they displaced the party as the primary vehicle of authority.

The modern presidential campaign is therefore not a party instrument but a self-contained enterprise. The campaign recruits staff, raises funds, builds data operations, and crafts messaging independently of existing party infrastructure. The candidate owes tactical loyalty to the campaign team that delivered the nomination, not to party leaders who maintained the organization across cycles. The party, in turn, becomes a vessel rather than a driver—expected to align, amplify, and defend, but no longer empowered to discipline or direct.

This transformation produces a three-entity dynamic that did not exist in the same form prior to the 1968 reforms.

First, the candidate and campaign apparatus operate as an autonomous force. Primary success depends on mobilization and media dominance rather than coalition maintenance. Incentives reward intensity, visibility, and speed. Loyalty flows upward toward the candidate rather than outward toward the party (Skowronek, 1997). The candidate therefore owes little to the party after securing the nomination.

Second, party leadership and party loyalists remain responsible for institutional continuity. They manage local organizations, ballot access, fundraising compliance, and down-ballot coordination. They preserve brand and structure over time. Yet these actors exercise diminishing influence over candidate behavior, messaging, or coalition strategy. Authority persists without control, as party apparatchiks are often disconnected from the candidate.

Third, party voters engage episodically. Participation centers on primary contests and general elections, with little interaction between cycles. Voters select nominees but do not govern organizations. Most party voters are not active party members or part of party leadership. They wear the party jersey but are not party loyalists. The act of choice replaces the work of maintenance. Accountability narrows to election day (Rosenbluth & Shapiro, 2018).

The resulting system weakens each component, particularly relative to its more cohesive form prior to 1968. Candidates command attention but lack durable constraint. Party institutions endure but struggle to enforce coherence, as candidates feel little loyalty to a system that played little role in securing the nomination. Voters possess formal power without sustained engagement. What once functioned as a layered structure now operates as a loose alignment of interests held together by electoral necessity rather than organizational discipline.

Two recent presidential contests illustrate this realignment with unusual clarity.

On the Republican side, Donald Trump secured the 2016 nomination over the open resistance of party leadership. Contemporary coverage consistently described Republican officials as "alarmed," "scrambling," and ultimately "falling in line" after the primary electorate had spoken (Nguyen, 2016). The party neither selected nor shaped the nominee in advance. The party merely ratified the outcome after the fact. Once in office, conflict between Trump and party stalwarts persisted, underscoring the absence of effective organizational discipline within the modern party structure (Haberman, 2022).

A similar, if less confrontational, pattern appeared within the Democratic Party in 2008. Barack Obama defeated Hillary Clinton, the candidate most closely aligned with party leadership and institutional continuity. Early endorsements, donor networks, and organizational support favored Clinton. Yet Obama's campaign mobilized primary voters directly, bypassing much of the party's traditional infrastructure. Party leaders unified only after the nomination was decided by the electorate, not before (Balz & Johnson, 2010; Halperin & Heilemann, 2013).

In both cases, the party followed rather than led. Authority flowed from voters to candidates, then back to party institutions tasked with absorbing the result. These episodes were not aberrations. They were predictable consequences of a system in which nomination legitimacy precedes organizational accountability. More democracy, less republic.

The presidency did not absorb party leadership by design. Party leadership receded by attrition. As nomination authority migrated outward, organizational gravity shifted upward. The presidency became the visible center not because it was intended to govern the party, but because nothing else remained capable of doing so.

This repeated toggling of party infrastructure with each presidential cycle has contributed substantially to modern polarization. Primary candidates now vie not only for the presidency but, unknowingly, for control of the party itself. Party loyalists grow frustrated by abrupt ideological swings from one election to the next. Presidential nominees confront resistance from institutional leaders they did not rely upon to win. The average party voter stands confused, observing persistent infighting without clear lines of authority.

This structural realignment explains much of modern partisan instability. Parties appear simultaneously dominant and hollow—powerful in elections, fragile in governance. Presidents appear omnipotent in rhetoric and constrained in practice. The system amplifies voice while thinning authority.

Scandal as Politics

The unraveling did not stop with nomination reform; the same weakening of mediation soon reshaped accountability into a politics of exposure. The same post-Watergate impulse that weakened party mediation also transformed how accountability operated in American politics. In the years immediately following President

Richard Nixon's resignation, reformers sought to ensure that no future administration could escape scrutiny. That corrective instinct, however, produced consequences that reached far beyond Watergate itself.

Investigations conducted in 1975–1976 by the Church Committee—formally the *United States Senate Select Committee to Study Governmental Operations with Respect to Intelligence Activities*, chaired by Senator Frank Church of Idaho—revealed a pattern of executive abuse that predated Nixon. During the administrations of John F. Kennedy and Lyndon B. Johnson, federal agencies authorized warrantless wiretaps of civil-rights leaders, conducted domestic surveillance of antiwar organizations, and directed intelligence operations toward purely political targets (Church Committee, 1976; DeRosa, 2021; Epsley-Jone & Frenzel, 2025). The committee concluded that these practices posed a deeper constitutional danger than the Watergate break-in itself, even when the conduct could not be prosecuted under existing law. Executive overreach, the committee emphasized, was systemic rather than episodic.

The Kennedy administration, for example, authorized the FBI to wiretap the residence and offices of Martin Luther King Jr. beginning in late 1963 (Church Committee, 1976; Lacy, 2019). Although officials initially justified the surveillance on national-security grounds, the operation soon devolved into an effort to discredit a domestic political figure. Two years later, the Supreme Court's decision in *Katz v. United States* (1967) clarified that warrantless electronic surveillance violated the Fourth Amendment, rendering such practices plainly unconstitutional. The Church Committee later described the King wiretaps as flagrant violations of privacy and civil liberty (Church Committee, 1976). President Johnson ordered tighter constraints on future surveillance, yet the investigation revealed a continuity of executive excess that long preceded Nixon. Earlier presidents had already fused intelligence with politics. Nixon became the first to face exposure, and then compounded failure through concealment.

Nixon did not invent partisan misuse of government power. Nixon escalated the scale, secrecy, and recklessness of those practices at the precise moment when investigative journalism and television converged into a formidable force. The reporting surrounding the 1972 Watergate break-in and the subsequent televised Senate hearings transformed political accountability into national spectacle. The Press served a necessary watchdog function, but the pivot occurred when exposure itself became the objective. Attention shifted from deliberative governance toward prosecutorial triumph. The emerging pattern rewarded relentless accusation, encouraging journalists and political actors alike to pursue fragments of misconduct until repetition hardened suspicion into presumed guilt. The logic echoes a dark maxim attributed to Lavrentiy Beria, the longtime head of Stalin's secret police and one of the principal architects of Soviet terror: repeat an accusation often enough, and guilt eventually adheres.

Subsequent administrations operated within that new logic. Scandal multiplied. Whether the proliferation reflected declining presidential ethics or an increasingly adversarial media environment remains contested. What changed unmistakably was the incentive structure. President Ronald Reagan confronted the Iran–Contra affair (Draper, 1991). President Bill Clinton faced impeachment following revelations concerning Monica Lewinsky (Posner, 1999). President George W. Bush navigated investigations tied to the Dick Cheney energy task force (Dean, 2004) and the exposure of CIA officer Valerie Plame (Wilson, 2008). President Barack Obama endured delegitimization campaigns such as birtherism, which, though non-criminal, weaponized suspicion through the language of investigation (Corsi, 2011). Scholars describe this evolution as the rise of a "politics of scandal," where legal process and media visibility function as routine tools of partisan conflict rather than exceptional remedies (Markovits & Silverstein, 1988; Rottinghaus, 2015; Thompson, 2013).

The modern presidency has operated under permanent scrutiny since Nixon's fall. Presidential legitimacy now faces testing not only at the ballot box, but in hearings, subpoenas, and headlines. Exposure carries political force independent of adjudication. The boundary between oversight and weaponization has thinned, converting safeguards of republican accountability into instruments of partisan warfare.

This argument does not excuse Nixon's conduct, nor dismiss the necessity of accountability. Watergate warranted consequence. The danger lies in the procedural transformation Watergate catalyzed. The suffix "-gate" now attaches reflexively to controversy—Contragate, Whitewatergate, Travelgate, Nannygate, Troopergate, Deflategate, Spygate, Obamagate—turning disagreement into presumed criminality by linguistic habit alone (Rowland, 2022). Scandal has become political currency. A journalist seeking attention or a faction seeking advantage can elevate grievance into crisis by invoking investigation as performance and tagging with -gate escalates gravity. The constitutional tools of impeachment and oversight long existed; what changed after Watergate was the habit of converting political conflict into legal combat—the criminalization of politics.

That habit soon received statutory form. In 1978, Congress enacted the *Ethics in Government Act*, creating the office of independent counsel to ensure that presidents remained subject to the law. The intention was honorable: restore public confidence through impartial scrutiny. The outcome proved paradoxical. The statute normalized perpetual investigation, embedding inquiry as a standing feature of governance. Scholars observed that the law "institutionalized the permanent investigation of presidents" and transformed prosecution into "a weapon of political combat" (Posner, 1999; Teles, 2008). A safeguard against corruption evolved into an engine of distrust.

Every administration since has governed under that shadow. The Republic surrendered part of its deliberative culture to the courtroom. When success in legal proceedings rivaled success at the ballot box, persuasion yielded to prosecution. Convincing a small panel of jurists requires far less consensus than persuading a nation, subtly shifting power toward the Judicial Branch beyond the Founders' design. The cowbell of scandal rings loudly. Once politics learned to govern through investigation and spectacle, the same method inevitably reached nominations and confirmations.

The Bork Precedent

The logic of scandal did not remain confined to elections and executive oversight. That logic soon migrated into the judiciary. The nomination of Robert Bork to the Supreme Court in 1987 marked a decisive turning point in American confirmation politics. The hearings did not revolve around competence or character in any traditional sense. The hearings became a trial of belief. Cameras lined the walls. Congressional staff circulated talking points before the nominee completed answers. Bork possessed formidable intellect, but the scholar's manner invited confrontation rather than deflection. He answered with analytical precision rather than political caution, and the effect proved combustible. Words unsoftened by charm supplied opponents with material easily framed as menace. Within weeks, the verb *to bork* entered the national lexicon, meaning to destroy a nominee through organized caricature (Sabato, 1991). Judicial philosophy had become theater. Senate deliberation had become performance. The cowbell rang again.

The spectacle did not arise in isolation. For nearly two centuries, Senate confirmations rested on two informal but powerful norms: presidents enjoyed broad discretion in selecting qualified jurists, and senators refrained from demanding advance commitments on questions likely to reach the Court. Ideological litmus tests* violated judicial decorum and threatened the separation of powers (Epstein & Segal, 2005; Goldman, 2004; Slotnick, 1983). Even contentious nominations—Louis Brandeis in 1916, Hugo Black in 1937, or Earl Warren in 1953—were debated primarily on grounds of temperament or experience rather than ideology (Gibson & Caldeira, 2009). That restraint eroded after *Roe v. Wade*, when constitutional law absorbed moral language and judicial nominations acquired existential stakes (Greenhouse, 2024).

Bork's nomination shattered the remaining convention. His unapologetic originalism—expressed clearly and extensively across decades of scholarship—left little room for strategic ambiguity. Bork had written too much, and too plainly, for evasion to serve as shelter. Judicial philosophy became the battlefield. Senators no longer treated ideology as inappropriate to discuss; ideology became the central charge. The *Washington Post* later observed that the campaign against Bork "did not resemble an argument so much as a lynching" (White, 2012). Televised scrutiny collapsed the

---

* The term *litmus test*—borrowed from chemistry, where a strip of paper changes color to reveal acidity or alkalinity—entered American political vocabulary in the early 1970s and ramped up during the Carter–Reagan election (Turner, 1980). The earliest documented uses appeared in discussions of Supreme Court nominations following *Roe v. Wade* (1973), when activists on both sides of the abortion debate began demanding that nominees declare their moral and constitutional positions in advance. By the late 1980s the phrase had become common shorthand for ideological prerequisites in judicial selection. In the 1980s, Senator Daniel Patrick Moynihan went so far as to declare "ideological tests for the judiciary" a form of "corruption" (Schmidt, 2018). Yet, his declaration carried little weight for his fellow Democrat, Senator Ted Kennedy. See Epstein and Segal (2005) and Goldman (2004).

The Long Unraveling

distinction between jurisprudence and politics. A confirmation became a referendum on the Constitution itself (Teles, 2008).

The episode revealed a deeper shift in the Republic's understanding of virtue and power. The Founders envisioned the judiciary as the cool branch—insulated from popular passion and guided by reasoned restraint (Hamilton et al., 2015). Bork's hearings destroyed that insulation. Television, which had already reshaped elections, now reshaped confirmations (Zelizer, 2018). Senators addressed the camera rather than colleagues. Rhetoric displaced reasoning. Law yielded to moral theater. Confirmation became a cowbell campaign conducted within constitutional walls.

Ted Kennedy supplied the defining voice of that transformation. Within hours of President Reagan's announcement, Kennedy delivered a floor speech that established the template for modern confirmation warfare. "Robert Bork's America is a land in which women would be forced into back-alley abortions, blacks would sit at segregated lunch counters, rogue police could break down citizens' doors in midnight raids, school children could not be taught about evolution," Kennedy declared (C-SPAN, 1987).* The speech

---

* Ted Kennedy's venomous attack of Bork had context—the two had history. During the infamous "Saturday Night Massacre" of October 20, 1973, then Solicitor General Bork became Acting Attorney General after Elliot Richardson and William Ruckelshaus resigned rather than obey President Nixon's order to dismiss Watergate Special Prosecutor Archibald Cox. Bork carried out the dismissal, later contending that he acted to preserve continuity within the Justice Department and to prevent institutional collapse. The decision, though legally defensible, left a lasting political scar—one that Kennedy could not let go. Fourteen years later, Senator Kennedy invoked that event as emblematic of Bork's willingness to defer to executive power during the battle over his Supreme Court nomination. Kennedy's tone carried the gravity of vengeance—retribution delivered in the

preceded hearings, evidence, or testimony. The indictment awaited the defendant. Advocacy organizations, media allies, and interest groups mobilized around the frame Kennedy supplied, defining Bork before Bork could define himself (Binder & Maltzman, 2009; White, 2012). Senate procedure became a weapon of moral accusation—an echo of Joseph McCarthy's earlier abuses. McCarthy's enemy had been communism. Kennedy's enemy was conservatism. Both derived power from fear.*

The effects endured. Confirmation hearings shifted from examinations of intellect and integrity toward performances of moral condemnation. Kennedy's strategy succeeded—Bork was rejected 58–42—but the cost reached beyond a single nominee. Future candidates learned to speak in abstraction. Presidents learned to nominate thinner records. Senators learned that outrage could substitute for argument. The Senate's filtering function eroded. Democratic passions were no longer restrained; democratic passions were amplified.

The following decade did not reverse the pattern. The Clinton years expanded and normalized the method. Political operatives such as James Carville and Paul Begala openly described rapid counterattack and message control as civic hygiene rather than political

---

language of justice. See his biography in Bork (2013) and PBS *Frontline* interview in Bork (2019).

* McCarthyism refers to the anti-communist investigations led by Senator Joseph R. McCarthy during the early 1950s, when congressional hearings became instruments of accusation rather than inquiry. Although McCarthy claimed to expose subversives in government and the arts, his methods—public naming, guilt by association, and disregard for evidence—turned oversight into spectacle and fear into governance. The era's name has since become shorthand for the use of state power to punish political dissent. See Ellen Schrecker, *Many Are the Crimes: McCarthyism in America* (1998), the definitive history of the period.

warfare (Carville & Begala, 2006; Matalin & Carville, 1995). The approach perfected techniques earlier deployed against Bork—frame first, argue later. Republicans adopted similar methods. Karl Rove articulated the same logic from the opposite flank, converting permanent campaigning into governing strategy (Rove, 2010). Investigations migrated from questions of public conduct into exposures of private life, dissolving the boundary between law and politics (Posner, 1999). The *Ethics in Government Act* had already normalized perpetual investigation (Posner, 1999; Teles, 2008). Scandal became a governing instrument.

By the time the Brett Kavanaugh hearings unfolded in 2018, the transformation was complete. Jurisprudence yielded to accusation. Memory, identity, and belief eclipsed legal reasoning (Liptak, 2018; Toobin, 2018). An allegation rooted decades earlier became a national spectacle adjudicated in a partisan forum unsuited for determining guilt or innocence. The hearings revealed the end state of Kennedy's precedent: accusation replaced argument, performance replaced principle. The process neither resolved truth nor preserved legitimacy. A partisan committee cannot substitute for a courtroom, just as moral theater cannot substitute for deliberation. A republic that adjudicates character through spectacle confesses the loss of confidence in deliberation itself.

The consequences extend beyond individual nominations. When confirmations become moral referenda, the judiciary forfeits the quiet dignity upon which legitimacy depends. Each justice arrives framed as partisan conquest. Robes signify belief rather than impartial judgment. In that perception lies the true cost of being *borked*—the erosion of faith in neutrality itself (Gibson & Caldeira, 2009). The cowbells, once rung, do not fall silent. Their echo stains decisions that follow, wounding the Court's fragile authority. A justice becomes martyr to one side and villain to the other. Either outcome corrodes trust.

The art of confirmation has drifted from deliberation toward spectacle. That drift began with Kennedy. The Senate once prided itself on restraint as a mark of wisdom rather than weakness. Alexander Hamilton described the judiciary as possessing "neither force nor will, but merely judgment" (Hamilton et al., 2015). The distance from that ideal measures how far the Republic has strayed. Political assassination—once unthinkable within advice and consent—now anchors the performance. Oversight masquerades as outrage. Rhetoric displaces reason.

The Senate's transformation did not remain confined to confirmations. The performance incentives that remade judicial politics soon remade legislative politics, especially after partisan control of the House became a prize worth redesigning the institution to hold.

The New House

That summer, I had worked the campaign trail for Fred Thompson and Bill Frist, new faces in Tennessee politics who embodied the rising confidence of the Republican Party. When the return trip began that evening, darkness had settled over the road. The radio filled the cabin with static and results. Station by station, county by county, the numbers tilted red. By the time Cookeville came back into view, the outcome was unmistakable: Republicans had captured the House of Representatives for the first time in forty years. Alone on the highway, headlights cutting through fog, I felt the exhilaration of history turning—personal effort briefly aligned with national change.

November 8, 1994, entered political memory as the so-called Republican Revolution. Under Newt Gingrich's leadership, and anchored by the *Contract with America*, Republicans moved from minority to majority with gains of 54 seats (Gingrich, 1994; Kennedy, 2018). The Contract outlined a ten-point reform agenda, including a balanced-budget amendment, tax cuts, welfare reform, and term limits. For a moment, the political horizon appeared newly open. As the miles slipped past beneath my tires that night, the radio returns sounded like possibility.

What followed in Washington diverged sharply from that promise. The divergence was neither malicious nor fully anticipated. The revolution proved structural as much as electoral. Control of the House changed hands, but the institution itself soon changed character. Reforms enacted under Gingrich's leadership reshaped the internal machinery of Congress and, in doing so, altered the governing incentives of its members. Political scientists Thomas E. Mann and Norman J. Ornstein describe in *The Broken Branch* (2006) how revised rules and leadership practices converted the House from a forum of deliberation into an engine of party control. Seniority yielded to loyalty. Committees lost independence as authority concentrated in the Speaker's office. Legislative debate shifted from negotiation toward partisan display. The new order rewarded confrontation over collaboration and elevated message discipline above institutional stewardship. At the time, I welcomed the Republican victory without grasping the institutional cost—and few, including Gingrich himself, likely foresaw that cost. Only years later, through scholarship such as Mann and Ornstein's, did the consequences become clear.

Gingrich centralized authority within House leadership, weakened traditions of seniority and committee autonomy, and imposed rules that rewarded party loyalty over chamber independence. Committee chairs no longer rose through experience; leadership selected chairs for obedience and fundraising capacity (Heberlig & Larson, 2012). The congressional workweek shortened as fundraising and messaging displaced policy formation. The Speaker's office evolved into a command center for partisan strategy rather than a steward of deliberation for the People. Decision-making increasingly reflected party objectives rather than institutional responsibility (Simon, 2019).

The changes reached beyond formal rules. The connective tissue of governance frayed. Matt Grossmann, in *Artists of the Possible* (2014), describes how informal networks among senior members and committee chairs once formed the quiet architecture of policymaking. Trust accumulated through repetition—through private negotiation, reciprocal restraint, and the patient work of compromise, often shielded from cameras. The structural upheaval after 1994 fractured that architecture. Authority flowed upward to leadership. Committee autonomy yielded to command. Horizontal cooperation gave way to vertical obedience. The House no longer resembled a living ecosystem of legislators bargaining toward policy. The Chamber began to function as two rival machines engineered for partisan victory rather than institutional care.

As structure hardened, psychology followed. Lilliana Mason, in *Uncivil Agreement* (2018) documents how partisan identity deepened into social identity during this period. Lawmakers increasingly defined themselves by tribal allegiance rather than policy orientation. The opposing party came to resemble an enemy to be defeated rather than a competitor to be persuaded. Such passions had long existed among voters, yet Congress historically absorbed and moderated those divisions (Fiorina et al., 2004). That buffer weakened. Research now shows elite polarization advancing faster than mass polarization, driven by incentives that reward ideological rigidity (Leonard et al., 2021; Seimel, 2024). Congress increasingly amplified divisions rather than translating conflict into governance. Emotional polarization migrated upward into the governing class. Identity displaced policy. The cowbell echoed through the Chamber.

Procedural consequences followed. Laurel Harbridge-Yong's research in *Is Bipartisanship Dead?* (2015) shows that while bipartisan cosponsorship persisted, leadership control over the floor prevented most bipartisan legislation from reaching debate or vote. The public face of Congress—televised sessions, press conferences, hearings—projected conflict rather than cooperation. Legislation still passed, but deliberation gave way to performance.

Taken together, these dynamics reshaped not only House procedure but legislative self-conception. The victory of 1994, once celebrated as accountability restored, ushered in instability. Party control began to change hands with increasing frequency, a condition Frances Lee describes as the "age of insecure majorities" (2022). Each turnover reproduced the same governing style: centralized authority, permanent campaign posture, and public confrontation (Mann & Ornstein, 2006; Sinclair, 2014). Both parties adopted the model. Committee assignments became rewards for loyalty. Expertise lost value. Visibility displaced policy. The House that once embodied the deliberative heart of the Republic increasingly resembled a stage designed for applause rather than judgment.

Figure 5 illustrates this transformation. Long eras of stable party control before mid-century give way after 1994 to frequent shifts across the presidency, Senate, and House. The pattern reflects not renewed balance but heightened instability, as partisan incentives eclipsed institutional continuity.

I recall that drive back toward Cookeville in 1994, the exhilaration of possibility still sharp in memory. Over time, a different recognition emerged. The House, once a place of negotiation and institutional governance, increasingly resembled partisan theater. Members aligned not with committee deliberation but with leadership messaging. The Speaker ceased to function as first among equals and assumed the role of field commander. The Chamber marched to the cowbell's metronome, each strike signaling obedience rather than judgment. That rhythm has polarized Congress and, by extension, the People.

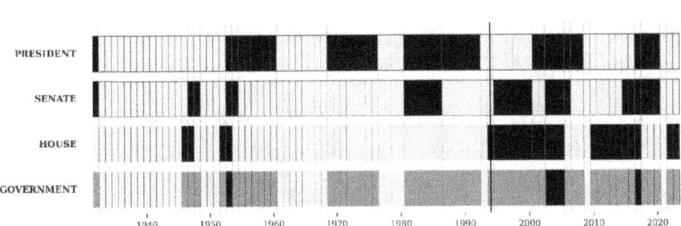

Figure 5. Party control of the presidency, Senate, House of Representatives, and unified versus divided government, 1932–2024. Each horizontal band shows party control in a given year: light gray denotes Democratic control, and dark gray denotes Republican control. The lowest band summarizes periods of unified and divided government—near white for unified Democratic control, near black for unified Republican control, and mid-gray for divided government. Vertical dashed lines mark years of party turnover. The timeline shows extended periods of single-party dominance before the mid-twentieth century, followed by increasingly frequent shifts after 1994 as partisan control across the branches grew more unstable.

The Old Order Ends

For nearly half a century before 1994, the House of Representatives operated under a quiet—though somewhat biased—equilibrium. Power was stable, procedure was predictable, and the Democratic majority functioned less as an ideological bloc than as a coalition held together by habit, seniority, and geography. From the 1950s through the early 1990s, as Fig. 5 shows, that equilibrium persisted through nine presidents, two wars, and waves of social upheaval. To outside observers, Congress appeared static. To insiders, the House felt like ballast—a system built for continuity rather than speed.

That pre-1994 House rested on four durable foundations. First, the Solid South supplied a dependable bloc of Democratic seats—conservatives known as Dixiecrats. Southern committee chairs, conservative on economics and segregationist on race, dominated the agenda through the seniority system and often shaped national legislation regardless of the president's party (Rohde, 1991). Second, *seniority* reinforced institutional memory. Advancement came through longevity, not loyalty. The rules rewarded patience and ensured that the Chamber's culture prized deliberation over discipline (Fenno, 1978). Third, *incumbency* offered protection from national tides. House elections were intensely local, built on district service and personal reputation (Mayhew, 2004). Fourth, members shared an institutional identity that transcended party—at least more often than not. Rivalries were sharp, yet a tacit respect for procedure—what Nelson Polsby (1968) once called "institutionalization"—anchored the Chamber.

Within that order, Democrats governed with remarkable consistency. Their caucus encompassed Southern conservatives, Northern liberals, and labor populists who quarreled over policy, region, and philosophy, yet shared a common faith in the institution itself. Cross-pressured coalitions forced compromise. Republicans, meanwhile, operated as a regional minority: disciplined but limited. Their power came less from numbers than from rhetorical opposition. The result was not harmony, but stability. Conflict often remained inside the majority rather than between majorities.

Over time, that internal pluralism began to collapse. Civil-rights legislation fractured the Democratic coalition, confirming President Lyndon Johnson's private prediction after signing the Civil Rights Act that "we have lost the South for a generation" (Caro, 2002; Goodwin, 1991). He was right. Conservative Southern Democrats gradually disappeared as their districts realigned under the Republican banner. Economic realignment then drew portions of the industrial Midwest toward the GOP*. Still, the House lagged behind the electorate. Localism, seniority, and casework insulated incumbents from presidential coattails. Political scientist David Mayhew (2004) described this era as one of "electoral independence," when legislators built careers by separating themselves from Washington's national battles. The House remained a deliberative buffer, absorbing social conflict through procedure rather than performance.

That insulation was reinforced by another structural feature of the pre-1968 order: the limited role of the president as party leader. Presidential elections did not reorganize congressional authority, redirect fundraising networks, or reset party hierarchy. Presidents governed administrations; parties governed Congress. Democratic control of the House endured not because Democratic presidents dominated the party, but because presidential power remained largely separate from legislative organization—dampening nationalized swings and preserving Congress as a semi-autonomous branch that did not reflexively bow to the Executive, even under unified party control.

As a Republican, I confess discomfort in admitting that the House's long Democratic era delivered stability. That order, however, did carry costs. The seniority system that preserved continuity also calcified power. Committee barons ruled through secrecy and

---

* GOP is an abbreviation for Grand Old Party, a nickname for the Republican Party that emerged in the late nineteenth century. The term originally emphasized the party's identity as the institutional heir to the Union, the Constitution, and the victory of the Civil War. While informal and never official, GOP became a durable shorthand that linked Republican partisanship to longevity, tradition, and national preservation rather than ideology alone.

procedural manipulation, deciding which bills lived or died behind closed doors. Party leaders, fortified by control of fundraising networks and floor scheduling, learned to protect their majority as much as govern the nation (Heberlig & Larson, 2012; Rohde, 1991; Sinclair, 1999). By the early 1990s, the House's calm concealed a quiet authoritarianism—less ideological than procedural. When Gingrich finally shattered that structure, the upheaval revealed not only partisan ambition but also the brittle regime that had settled beneath the veneer of institutional routine.

Comparing the two eras reveals how institutional design shapes political temperament. The pre-1994 House functioned as a legislature of accommodation—slow, opaque, and internally divided, yet capable of converting conflict into incremental policy. The primary dysfunctions were procedural rather than emotional. The post-1994 House evolved into a legislature of alignment—faster, transparent, and highly responsive, yet prone to gridlock whenever party control fractured. The new dysfunctions were psychological. Lilliana Mason (2018) shows that partisan identity during this era hardened into social identity; opponents came to resemble enemies. Elite polarization soon outpaced polarization within the public (McCarty et al., 2016). The Chamber no longer mediated the passions of democracy and instead began to magnify them.

Laurel Harbridge's (2015) research documents the procedural fallout. While bipartisan co-sponsorship remained common, leadership control of the floor agenda meant that few cross-party bills reached debate. The public face of the House—televised votes, press conferences, and hearings—displayed constant conflict even when quiet collaboration persisted out of view. Visibility became its own reward. The institution's incentives shifted from policy achievement toward partisan performance.

The difference, then, was not merely who held the gavel, but what the gavel meant. For forty years, the Democratic majority treated the House less as a partisan weapon than as a governing institution whose continuity sustained the Republic—often in ways that preserved power as much as principle. After 1994, the majority, whether Republican or Democratic, treated the House as a means to an external end: winning the next election. When reelection and message control replaced deliberation, the House entered a state of permanent campaign. A chamber once built to absorb political passion began instead to project it.

In that light, Gingrich's revolution was both accomplishment and caution. By modernizing Congress—making the House responsive, disciplined, and electorally agile—he weakened the virtues that had stabilized the structure: patience, trust, and institutional humility. The House that emerged from 1994 was not yet broken, but the House had been optimized for a different purpose. An institution designed for governance became an engine of polarization. The rules changed, and with them began the long unraveling of congressional deliberation—the slow replacement of self-government with perpetual campaign.

The comparison between the pre- and post-1994 eras reveals a larger pattern. Each reform, conceived as a correction of the last, provokes reactions that magnify the imbalance the reform sought to fix. Such transformations warn reformers. In a complex system, the effort to cure one distortion often creates another, and no rule can anticipate the full chain of incentives set in motion. The House did not fall to malice. The House fell to miscalculation—an earnest attempt to restore balance that instead accelerated the descent into partisanship.

The Permanent Campaign

The Constitution tethered the House of Representatives to the People through biennial elections—frequent but not too frequent elections. James Madison described the design as creating an "immediate dependence on, and an intimate sympathy with, the people," *Federalist No. 52* (Madison, 2016). He went on to add, "Frequent elections are unquestionably the only policy by which this dependence and sympathy can be effectually secured." The Founders built the system on a steady cycle of campaigning, governing, and earning renewed consent through elections. That cycle has now accelerated beyond recognition, transforming a mechanism for democratic renewal into a treadmill of constant performance. Representatives now campaign without ceasing, governed less by deliberation than by polling, and less by what is best for the country in the long term than by what is best in the near term for fundraising. The logic of campaigning has devoured the logic of governing.

Madison predicted this danger with unusual clarity. Madison's concern was never with elections themselves but with their tempo. In *Federalist No. 53*, he warned that "no man can be a competent legislator who does not add to an upright intention and a sound judgment." He went on to reveal that the development of such judgment "requires time." Madison explained that "a year is little enough." Madison accepted that some members, "by frequent reelections, [would] become members of long standing" and "thoroughly masters of the public business." That continuity, though not without danger, was essential to guard the House against manipulation by the more seasoned Senate or Executive. Experience, he implied, was not corruption but competence—the necessary counterweight to the volatility of popular politics. His defense of the two-year term thus balanced accountability with competence—frequent enough to preserve dependence on the People, yet long enough to cultivate judgment. A chamber that lived in perpetual electioneering, Madison implied, would produce dependence not on the People's reason but on their passions—a dangerous dependence.

Modern research confirms Madison's warning. Political scientists Mann and Ornstein note that "shortened time horizons and continuous campaigning leave little room for the slow, difficult work of deliberation" (Mann & Ornstein, 2006). Similarly, Professor of Law at Stetson University and a Fellow at the Brennan Center for Justice at NYU Ciara Torres-Spelliscy observes that perpetual fundraising "diminishes effective governance" by crowding out legislative preparation (Torres-Spelliscy, 2017). Legislators spend more time mingling with the wealthy and special interests than with their constituents and public interests. Former Representative Dan Glickman, a Democrat from Kansas, has confessed, "The sad truth is ... there simply isn't enough time in the day to stay competitive in campaign finance and do the actual job of policymaking" (Penniman & Potter, 2016). The pathology Madison feared—the substitution of constant election for deliberative reflection—has become the governing norm. The permanent campaign is not a modern invention so much as an unfortunate realization of the danger Madison foresaw when the imbalance exists. What Madison diagnosed in theory and scholars later measured in practice, political operatives soon formalized as strategy.

Political journalist Sidney Blumenthal gave this phenomenon its name in *The Permanent Campaign: Inside the World of Elite Political Operatives* (1982). Blumenthal documented how twentieth-century advances in mass media and professional consulting have replaced the party apparatus of the nineteenth century with a permanent infrastructure of pollsters, advertisers, and strategists. Campaigns no longer end on election night. Rather, the same personnel and methods remain active and chugging away until the next election—no time to govern. Governing has become a continuation of campaigning by other means. Blumenthal warned that the new structure "remakes government into an instrument designed to sustain an elected official's popularity" (Blumenthal, 1982). The boundaries between persuasion and policy have dissolved.

Although Blumenthal focused primarily on presidential politics, the same logic soon migrated into the House. The Founders' two-year election cycle, designed for accountability, has become an existential constraint. House members now weigh each decision, statement, and vote for electoral impact rather than for long-term judgment or institutional stewardship. Members of Congress govern under the shadow of their next campaign rather than the light of their last mandate. Gingrich's reorganization of the House in the 1990s intensified this dynamic, binding congressional advancement to party loyalty and fundraising performance. The result is a chamber in constant motion—its schedule and substance dictated less by deliberation than by the race for exposure and resources. Time pressure does not merely exhaust legislators; time redirects their attention.

Legal scholar Torres-Spelliscy, in her peer-reviewed law-review study (2017), gives empirical precision to Blumenthal's conceptual warning. She describes congressional fundraising as an "incredible 'time suck'," documenting how elected officials devote substantial portions of their week to donor calls, travel, and political maintenance rather than legislative or oversight work (Torres-Spelliscy, 2017). The burden is especially acute for members from competitive districts, who must raise millions of dollars each election cycle simply to remain viable. Torres-Spelliscy shows that the modern campaign-finance regime has transformed legislative time allocation such that campaign activity has expanded into the governing calendar, leaving little space for policy development or deliberation. The cowbells ring continuously, echoing through each phone call and donor event, drowning the quiet work of governance beneath the rhythm of perpetual solicitation. The price of entry has climbed steadily. Figure 6 shows that the average cost of winning a House seat has more than doubled since the 1980s—even after adjusting for inflation (Campaign Finance Institute & Brookings Institution, 2019).

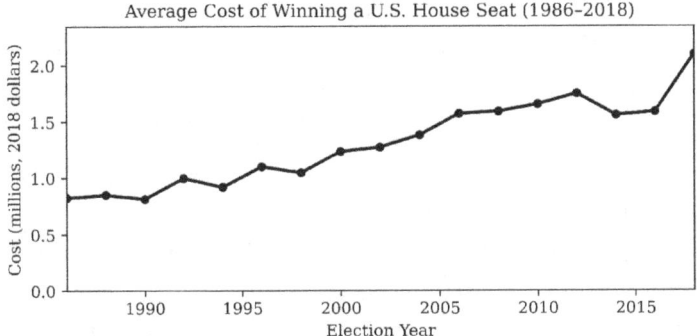

Figure 6. Average Cost of Winning a U.S. House Seat, 1986–2018 (2018 Dollars). Inflation-adjusted data from the Campaign Finance Institute and Brookings Institution show the steady rise in the financial burden of congressional campaigns. Values represent average spending by winning House candidates; independent expenditures are excluded (Campaign Finance Institute & Brookings Institution, 2019).

The Congressional Management Foundation's *Life in Congress* (2013) survey reveals the gap between perception and reality. The study, based on confidential questionnaires completed by House and Senate members and senior staff, examined how legislators allocate their time among policy work, constituent service, campaign activity, and administrative duties. Designed to capture members' own perceptions rather than direct observation, the findings illuminate how lawmakers portray the balance between governing and campaigning—a portrayal that contrasts sharply with independent analyses of their actual schedules. Members described spending roughly one-third of their time on legislative duties and less than one-fifth on campaign activity—figures that reflect aspiration more than practice. The difference resembles a patient trimming the truth on a medical form—reporting good habits, omitting the late-night meals, hoping the numbers still look respectable.

Independent investigations, including those by *Issue One*, depict a more demanding reality in which members, particularly those in competitive districts, devote twenty to thirty hours each week to fundraising and political maintenance (Issue One, 2017). Former members quoted in that study conceded the toll: "Constantly raising funds for the political parties interferes with the work of serving your constituents and your country. Hours spent fundraising—and worrying about fundraising—are time and energy diverted away from lawmakers' legislative responsibilities" (Issue One, 2017). Party leadership reinforces the pattern by tying committee influence and leadership advancement to fundraising performance. The official calendar may list votes and hearings, but the practical schedule revolves around call sheets and donor events. The House has drifted from a workshop of deliberation toward a political marketplace governed by financial quotas and perpetual campaigns

The marketplace soon reshapes representation itself. The fundraising treadmill privileges those with disposable income and organized interests capable of delivering campaign resources. Ordinary constituents gain attention only when their stories serve narrative or fundraising utility. The representative's dependence shifts from the median voter to the high-value donor, from civic equality to transactional access. That distortion is measurable, and a handful of elite contributors now dominate political giving. Between 2009 and 2020, just twelve major donors accounted for roughly one of every thirteen dollars spent in federal elections—a concentration of influence unprecedented in modern American politics (Issue One, 2017). Former Representative Cliff Stearns captured the consequence from inside Congress: "Committee leadership is decided by who can raise and give the most money—not the most competitive or competent or best speaker or most politically astute, but who is able to raise the mega bucks" (Stearns, 2016). The House remains close to the People geographically but drifts far from them in substance—another turn in the Long Unraveling of a republic designed for reflection, not solicitation.

When Congress Stopped Mingling

A wise friend once taught me how he discerns the strength of a church community. When I first moved to Dahlgren, Virginia, for my first job away from my hometown in Tennessee, I spent several Sundays searching for a congregation that felt alive. I told my friend about my visits, and he smiled. He offered the following wisdom, "Watch what happens after the service," he said. "That is how you will know." He explained what he called *the Mingle Factor*. A strong church, he said, has a long Mingle Factor—the longer people linger after the benediction, talking in the aisles, helping one another with strollers or schedules, the more they mingle, the stronger the fellowship. A short Mingle Factor means people flee as soon as the last hymn ends. They may worship together, but they do not *belong* together. That same distinction—between shared ritual and shared life—applies just as clearly to political institutions.

That simple measure—a count of how long people remain when their formal business ends—turns out to be a sound diagnostic for institutions far larger than a church. Congress once had a high Mingle Factor. Members lived in Washington with their families, attended the same schools, and gathered for dinners that crossed partisan lines. Lyndon Johnson's famous "Johnson treatment"—a hand on the shoulder, a shared drink, an argument turned negotiation—worked because Johnson knew his colleagues as people. He shared meals with them. He spent social time with them outside the Capitol Building. He knew them as persons as much as politicians. Washington was still a village disguised as a capital, and those small social ties sustained the Republic's capacity for compromise (Caro, 2002).

The Long Unraveling

That world has vanished—not through choice alone, but through structural change. The modern Congress measures its Mingle Factor in minutes rather than hours or days. Members now commute to Washington rather than reside there. The "Tuesday-to-Thursday Club" flies in for votes and leaves before the ink dries on the roll call (Mann & Ornstein, 2006). Their families remain back in their districts, not in the District. The dinner tables where colleagues once broke bread together now gather dust, and hallway conversations have become rare. Without repeated informal contact, familiarity tends to decay. When legislators no longer know one another as individuals, negotiation feels unnatural, and disagreement feels personal.

I must confess that I once believed the opposite. I used to think shorter weeks in Washington were healthy—that members who spent more time in their home districts would remember their roots, their people, and the smell of their own soil. Time at home would feel like an antidote to Washington's self-importance. I no longer find that case persuasive. Distance, I have learned, cuts both ways. A representative who spends too little time in the Capitol forgets not the People but the process—how the collective work of governing depends on proximity to fellow legislators. Too much time in Washington can indeed pull one away from constituents—just ask Al Gore Jr.*—but too little time there can just as easily pull one away from colleagues.

---

* Al Gore Jr.'s upbringing reflected the dual identity that shaped both his politics and his public perception. Though born and educated in Washington, D.C., Gore spent summers on his family's farm near Carthage, Tennessee, where he performed demanding physical labor. During later campaigns, he often invoked those farm experiences to emphasize his Tennessee roots. Some commentators and constituents viewed those stories

Social science confirms what experience slowly teaches. Social psychology reached this conclusion long before Congress did. In the early 1950s, researcher Muzafer Sherif conducted what became known as the Robbers Cave experiment. He divided a group of boys at a summer camp into two teams, separated them physically, and encouraged competition. Hostility emerged quickly—name-calling, sabotage, and even violence. Sherif then attempted to reduce the conflict by preaching cooperation and shared values. Those efforts failed. Only when the groups were brought together in close proximity to one another, face to face, repeatedly to solve practical problems—repairing a broken water line, pulling a stalled truck—did hostility subside (Perry, 2019; Sherif, 1988). Cooperation emerged not from moral instruction but from shared experience in close proximity. The lesson was blunt: human beings do not learn to cooperate at a distance.

A generation later, political scientist Robert Axelrod and evolutionary biologist William Hamilton demonstrated the same principle mathematically. Using the Iterated Prisoner's Dilemma, they showed that cooperation does not require altruism or trust in advance. It requires repetition. When individuals expect to encounter one another again—and can remember how the other behaved previously—cooperative strategies outperform selfish ones. The most successful approach, which Axelrod called *Tit for Tat*, began with cooperation, responded firmly to betrayal, and returned to cooperation once the opponent did (Axelrod & Hamilton, 1981). Trust, in

---

as contrived, but biographer Bill Turque and journalist Melinda Henneberger both found them substantially true, noting that Gore's life was "punctuated by two homes and two audiences"—Tennessee and Washington—each genuine, each incomplete (Henneberger, 2000; Turque, 2000). Gore's life proves both the rule and, ironically, the exception.

this model, is not a virtue; trust is an equilibrium produced by ongoing interaction.

Later research extended these insights into modern organizations. Studies of workplace collaboration consistently find that proximity and face-to-face interaction remain among the strongest predictors of cooperation and creativity, even in an age of digital communication (Kraut et al., 2002; Pentland, 2012). Physical presence lowers misunderstanding, humanizes disagreement, and makes reciprocity visible. Across disciplines and decades, the conclusion converges: good intentions alone do not sustain cooperation. Cooperation requires repeated contact within environments that allow memory, accountability, and repair.

The COVID-19 pandemic functioned as a large-scale natural experiment in remote interaction, offering additional insight into the role of proximity in collective decision-making. When work and governance shifted abruptly to virtual contact, in-person interaction retained a stronger influence on social bonding and mutual understanding than communication mediated by calls, texts, or video (Liang et al., 2024). At the same time, forced reliance on remote communication coincided with increased interaction among like-minded individuals and fewer spontaneous cross-cutting encounters—a pattern that reinforces echo chambers rather than bridges them (Lee et al., 2023). These findings confirm the structural pattern at issue here: proximity matters not merely for psychology, but for the social networks and cooperative habits that undergird collective governance.

The quality of interaction depends not only on frequency but on the environment that rewards or punishes behavior. Repetition alone does not produce trust; the context must favor cooperation over combat. The contrast between two well-known experiments illustrates the point. In Robert Axelrod and William Hamilton's model, cooperation flourished when players met repeatedly under rules that rewarded reciprocity and punished betrayal with proportional fairness (Axelrod & Hamilton, 1981). In Philip Zimbardo's *Stanford Prison Experiment*, by contrast, participants were placed in a hierarchy that rewarded aggression and submission rather than empathy or restraint. Within days, volunteers assigned to play guards adopted cruelty as a norm while those cast as prisoners withdrew or rebelled (Haney et al., 1973; Zimbardo, 1973). The experiment was halted after six days, undone by the hostility it produced.

Congress today operates under similarly perverse incentives—not because members lack interaction, but because the institutional environment rewards confrontation over reciprocity. Members interact constantly through hearings, media appearances, and social media exchanges, yet those interactions occur within a structure that penalizes conciliation and elevates conflict. The institution has recreated the dynamics of a prison yard more than a deliberative chamber. Until the environment once again rewards reciprocity, repeated interaction will deepen division rather than mend the bonds of trust.

The longer members stay away from one another, the less human their adversaries become—as the Stanford experiment sadly demonstrated. A Congress that governs by commuting and swooping into Washington for mere days is a Congress that forgets how to mingle. Will Rogers used to say that he had "never met a man he didn't like," a creed born of curiosity and constant contact. Rogers met people from many walks of life and found something decent in each of them because he met them face to face. The modern Congress no longer lives by that wisdom. Distance turns rivals into caricatures. When the Republic conducts business in transit, hope cannot hope discover the art of belonging.

Moral intuition alone cannot explain this change. The shift is structural as well as cultural. Air travel made commuting possible; fundraising made it mandatory. As the cost of campaigns rose, members spent weekends courting donors rather than colleagues (Issue One, 2017). The social infrastructure of Congress—shared apartments, bipartisan prayer breakfasts, evening receptions—has collapsed under the weight of partisan media and relentless travel. Mann and Ornstein describe Congress's transformation from a *community of legislators* into a *collection of political entrepreneurs*—a body of solo practitioners more focused on survival than on governing (Mann & Ornstein, 2006).

In the 1950s and 1960s, mingling softened partisanship. Southern Democrats and Midwestern Republicans played poker together and shared drinks after floor fights. Speaker Sam Rayburn hosted informal gatherings in his modest apartment, serving bourbon and chili to members from both parties. Those evenings produced trust that carried into committee rooms. Such trust did not arise from goodwill alone; it emerged from proximity enforced by institutional design. Robert Caro notes that Johnson could fight a senator by day and dine with him by night; the argument ended when the door closed (Caro, 2002).

That door rarely opens today. Many members now sleep in their offices, a habit that began as a show of frugality after the 1994 Republican Revolution but has since become a bipartisan necessity. Roughly one in five House members live this way—unrolling cots behind their desks, showering in the House gym, and turning workspaces into bedrooms (McCaskill, 2018; Sprunt, 2020). The practice began as a gesture of humility, a signal that representatives were not wasting taxpayer money on Washington apartments. Over time, it became a symptom of institutional decline: fewer families relocate to the capital, fewer friendships form across parties, and the building designed for deliberation doubles as a dormitory. The Capitol corridors, once alive with conversation, now resemble airports between flights.

Physical separation eventually produces psychological distance.

The decline is psychological as well as logistical. When members lose personal contact, they replace knowledge with caricature. The

More Republic, Less Cowbell

opponent becomes not a colleague but an abstraction—a villain of a fundraising email. Political scientist Ezra Klein has shown that when social circles contract to ideological likeness, partisan identity hardens and empathy weakens (Klein, 2020). As social networks become more homogeneous, differences no longer temper one another; they stack. Religion, geography, class, and party converge into a single tribal identity that resists compromise. In that condition, political disagreement feels personal, and persuasion feels futile. The same transformation that has fractured neighborhoods and congregations through Facebook and social media isolation now defines Congress itself. Members live among the like-minded, raise funds from the same audiences, and consume the same partisan media. The loss of mingling has turned representation into self-affirmation. A legislature without mingling becomes a legislature without mercy.

The friendship between Democrat Norm Mineta and Republican Alan Simpson illustrates what has been lost. The two first met as teenagers at a Boy Scout jamboree near a Japanese internment camp during World War II. Decades later, they served together in Congress and worked to pass the Civil Liberties Act of 1988 (Beck, 2019; Lim, 2018). Their friendship began in empathy and endured through policy. As Philip Wallach notes, relationships like theirs once sustained the everyday trust that made governance possible, but such bonds have become rare in today's Congress (Ganz, 2024). Their story was not an anomaly but the last of a vanishing species. Sam Rayburn and Joseph Martin, Lyndon Johnson and Everett Dirksen, Daniel Patrick Moynihan and Alan Simpson, Ted Kennedy and Orrin Hatch—each pair embodied the trust that proximity once nurtured. When those relationships disappeared, the Republic lost not only civility but also the human architecture of compromise (Caro, 2002; Hatch, 2009; Kennedy, 2009; Zelizer, 2006).

Robert Putnam's study of civic life, *Bowling Alone*, provides the larger frame (Putnam, 2000). Trust grows through repeated, low-stakes encounters. When people share meals, teams, and rituals, they develop what Putnam called social capital—a reservoir of goodwill that enables collective action. Congress once embodied that capital. Modern schedules have drained the social capital that once sustained the institution. A legislature designed for conversation now operates without conversation.

What feels like cultural loss is also empirically visible. Political scientists have even measured the Mingle Factor in other terms. James Fowler mapped legislative co-sponsorship networks and found that the density of cross-party ties predicts bipartisanship and legislative productivity (Fowler, 2006). Mason Porter and colleagues analyzed overlapping committee memberships and discovered that shared assignments once functioned as bridges between factions (Porter et al., 2005). When those overlaps narrowed, polarization deepened. The empirical record affirms what personal experience suggests that when people stop mingling, cooperation collapses.

A healthy republic requires more than procedural order. The Republic depends on a rhythm of fellowship. Rules alone cannot replace the human bond that turns opposition into partnership. The Founders understood this truth when they designed a legislature built for deliberation rather than haste. They assumed that conversation would fill the spaces between votes. Today, those spaces stand empty.

A church with a short Mingle Factor still conducts the service. The hymns are sung, the prayers recited, the sermon delivered. Yet once the benediction ends, the pews empty in silence. The congregation performs worship without fellowship. Congress has reached the same condition. The noise remains—the fundraising, the floor speeches, the partisan cowbells—but the fellowship has faded. A republic that no longer mingles no longer moderates. The Mingle Factor has fallen near zero, and the trust that once made disagreement safe has disappeared.

Self-Inflicted Contempt

Mark Twain once quipped, "Suppose you were an idiot. And suppose you were a member of Congress. But I repeat myself" (Paine, 1912). Twain's joke captured a sentiment older than himself—a wry skepticism toward the political class that has shaped the American mood. Bad-mouthing Congress is an American tradition. From the beginning, the public treated Congress as both a mirror and a target, mocking congressional quarrels while relying on the institution's endurance. Such ridicule, when restrained, served a democratic purpose. Laughter deflated arrogance. Ridicule restrained ambition. A republic that tolerates humor at the expense of its leaders remains healthy so long as humor does not curdle into hate.

For much of American history, mockery of Congress came from the outside looking in. Citizens jeered at corruption and folly, yet still expected the legislature to function. Lawmakers absorbed the blows and carried on with the rough dignity of a profession accustomed to scorn. Even during periods of chaos, Congress remained a stage where disagreement signaled vitality rather than decay. Public frustration formed part of the civic bargain—a release valve rather than a solvent—where voters could curse their representatives on Saturday and still trust those representatives to vote on Monday.

Recently, that civic bargain has begun to fracture. Candidates now win elections by scorning Washington with calls to "drain the swamp."* Political scientist Richard Fenno (1978) described the

---

* The phrase *drain the swamp*, now a staple of populist rhetoric, predates the modern era by more than a century. Progressive and socialist reformers first used the metaphor in the early twentieth century to describe structural reform rather than cosmetic change. In 1912, Socialist

paradox decades ago. Voters despise Congress yet admire their own representative. Such ambivalence once reflected a healthy skepticism toward power. In recent years, however, skepticism has hardened into contempt, and contempt has crept inward. Members of Congress no longer absorb public anger—they amplify public disgust. They are no longer merely its objects; they have become its authors. The transformation has produced a peculiar form of political masochism, performed not only on the campaign trail but also within the marble halls of the Capitol.

The change is measurable. As shown in Fig. 7, Congressional self-contempt has become not only audible but quantifiable. The figure traces the rise of what might be called institutional masochism—a steady shift in how members of Congress describe their own institution. Using the digitized *Congressional Record* prepared by (Gentzkow, 2018), I analyzed more than four million floor speeches delivered between 1961 and 2015.

Congressman Victor L. Berger of Wisconsin urged that reformers must "drain the swamp," a call to confront the systemic roots of political and economic corruption rather than the visible symptoms (Berger, 1912). The expression later migrated across the political spectrum—from socialist to capitalist imagery—when Ronald Reagan adopted the metaphor during the 1980s to describe clearing Washington of bureaucratic excess and inertia. "When you're up to your armpits in alligators," Reagan remarked with his characteristic humor, "it's sometimes hard to remember that your original intention was to drain the swamp" (Reagan, 1982). Donald Trump revived the slogan in 2016 as a populist battle cry against establishment politics, transforming a century-old metaphor of reform into a declaration of revolt against the governing order.

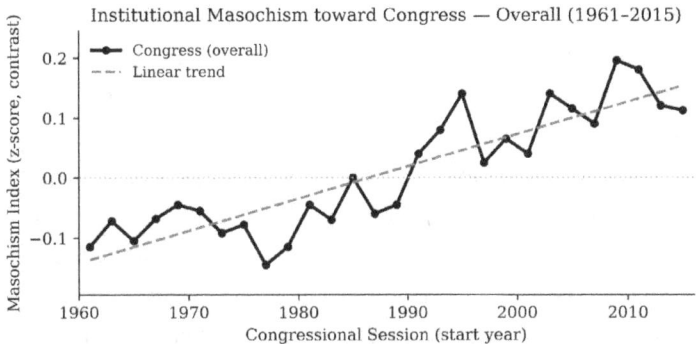

Figure 7. Congressional Self-Denigration, 1961–2015. The Masochism Index measures the degree to which members of Congress use self-critical language when referring to their own institution. The analysis draws on more than four million speeches from the *Congressional Record* (Gentzkow, 2018), comparing semantic proximity to dictionaries of esteem ("honorable," "deliberative," "responsible") and contempt ("broken," "corrupt," "dysfunctional"). Values above zero indicate increasingly self-denigrating rhetoric. Values below zero reflect greater institutional pride. The steady upward trend reveals a decades-long shift from mild self-respect to habitual self-contempt, with the steepest rise beginning after the partisan realignment of the 1994 House revolution.

Each speech was converted into a numerical representation using modern word-embedding techniques, which allow computers to measure the semantic distance between ideas. Two thematic dictionaries—one for institutional esteem ("honorable," "deliberative," "responsible") and another for institutional contempt ("broken," "corrupt," "dysfunctional")—served as reference poles. The difference between these associations yields what I call the *Masochism Index*, a z-scored measure of self-regard within congressional language over time.

A score above zero indicates that members of Congress are, on average, speaking about the institution in more self-critical or self-loathing terms than the historical norm. A score below zero suggests greater institutional pride or self-defense. The trend line rises steadily across five decades, from roughly −0.10 in the 1960s to +0.20 by the 2010s—a three-tenths standard deviation increase in rhetorical self-contempt. The shift coincides with major structural changes that include the advent of televised sessions, the collapse of bipartisan norms in the post-reform era, and the rise of permanent campaigning (Fenno, 1978; Mann & Ornstein, 2006). By the early twenty-first century, members of Congress had learned to echo the cynicism once reserved for their critics. The institution's self-regard, like its approval rating, had entered long-term decline.

Early legislators distrusted one another but not the institution that housed their rivalry. Their quarrels strengthened the constitutional order rather than eroding the framework of governance.

The distinction between argument and contempt is not unique to legislatures. Psychologist John Gottman, whose longitudinal studies of married couples span decades, reached a parallel conclusion about intimate institutions. Disagreement, even heated disagreement, does not predict divorce. Couples who argue can remain stable so long as mutual respect endures. Contempt, however—eye-rolling, mockery, sneering dismissal—proves far more corrosive. Gottman identifies contempt as the strongest behavioral predictor of marital dissolution because contempt signals not frustration with a position but disdain for the partner's worth (Gottman & Silver, 2015). Marriage can survive conflict; marriage rarely survives sustained contempt.

A legislature functions in a similar register. Debate may bruise egos, but contempt strikes at legitimacy. When members attack an argument, the institution absorbs the blow. When members attack the institution itself—branding Congress as "broken," "corrupt," or "useless"—they mimic the marital dynamic Gottman warned against. The quarrel shifts from policy to identity. The Chamber ceases to be a forum for disagreement and becomes the object of disdain.

The modern age has redirected that distrust inward. When members privately echo the public's contempt for Congress, skepticism hardens into corrosion. The greater danger now arises not from external critics but from disbelief seeded within the legislature itself. Earlier generations carried their arguments onto the floor, not against the Chamber that gave them voice. Clay, Webster, and Calhoun—giants of American history—clashed in open debate, yet still defended the dignity of the body that framed their contests (Remini, 2006).

The implications of this trend extend beyond language. Teams that habitually denigrate themselves rarely perform well. Jim Collins, in his study of high-performing organizations, observed that greatness begins not with strategy or structure but with getting the right people on the bus—leaders who believe in the mission and one another (Collins, 2001).* Successful teams may disagree fiercely, yet they preserve confidence in the institution that binds them. Congress, by contrast, increasingly resembles a bus whose passengers despise the vehicle itself. The more members mock the institution they inhabit, the less capable they become of steering that institution anywhere.

The analogy is imperfect. Government is not a bus nor a business, nor should it operate as one. A legislature is not designed for

---

* The analogy between Congress and a business has limits. Elections do not function like executive recruitment, and voters cannot simply "hire" the right people to get the institution on course. The electorate chooses representation through election conflict, not hiring consensus, and members enter office with opposing mandates by design. The relevant lesson from Collins lies not in selection but in culture: high-performing teams, whatever their purpose, avoid self-sabotage. Bad-mouthing colleagues—or the institution itself—within the walls of Congress serves no constructive end. Campaign rhetoric has a political purpose; congressional self-loathing does not.

profit or efficiency but for deliberation, balance, and restraint. Still, the civic principle that underlies Collins's insight remains true. Cohesion matters. A Congress that ceases to respect itself forfeits the moral authority required to command the public's respect. Disagreement across parties defines American democracy, but when contempt turns inward—when members of Congress learn to loathe *Congress*—the Republic's deliberative core begins to erode. The upward slope in Fig. 7, crossing the zero line, is therefore more than a linguistic curiosity. The trend marks a cultural failure of self-belief within the branch Madison called the "first of the first."

Today, many in Congress now treat the institution with little respect. The marble halls resemble a fraternity house more than the People's House—temporary quarters where ambition outpaces reflection. Brief stays and nights spent on office couches mark a culture of rivalry and performance rather than duty and deliberation. The building still bears the nation's seal, yet conduct within too often falls short of the dignity that seal demands—Congressman Wilson's "You lie!" outburst comes to mind.

The direction of distrust has reversed. Americans have long questioned Congress from the outside looking in, but only in recent decades has Congress begun to question itself from the inside looking out. The older pattern of rivalry—state against state, region against region, party against party—has given way to a new pattern of self-negation. Members now campaign as if Congress were an occupying power rather than a Constitutional trust. The tone once reserved for tyrants abroad or bureaucrats in the Executive Branch now targets the very legislature that represents the People. Contempt for Congress has become the *lingua franca* of Congressional politics.

Such inversion marks a fundamental break from the Founders' design. The Constitution welcomed external criticism as a sign of republican vigilance. The same framework never anticipated a legislature that would absorb that criticism, transform the angst into identity, and treat self-denigration as a badge of virtue. The Republic was built to endure dissent; the Republic was not built to endure self-loathing.

One need only look to the Judiciary's treatment of contempt to understand the importance of institutional self-respect. The Judiciary offers a revealing mirror for Congress. Both govern through persuasion and restraint, drawing strength not from punishment or arms but from public confidence in the fairness of their process. Contempt of court invites sanction because defiance of judicial authority threatens the rule of law itself. Judges punish contempt not to defend personal dignity but to preserve the conditions under which justice can be done. Order must precede verdict. A courtroom without discipline becomes theater, and law collapses into noise. History offers examples where contempt went unchecked and the institution faltered beneath the weight of its own leniency.

The Chicago Seven trial of 1969 stands as the clearest illustration of what happens when an institution refuses to defend its own authority. The courtroom drama reached new audiences through Aaron Sorkin's 2020 film *The Trial of the Chicago 7*, which captured both the chaos of the proceedings and the peril of a judge losing command of his chamber (Sorkin, 2020). Judge Julius Hoffman presided over one of the most turbulent trials in American history. The defendants—antiwar activists accused of inciting riots during the 1968 Democratic Convention—treated the courtroom as a stage for protest. Hoffman, an aging jurist shaped by another era, struggled to maintain order. His reluctance to enforce discipline in real time allowed defiance to spread. Defendants mocked the court, taunted the bench, and turned testimony into performance. Hoffman delayed punishment, hoping restraint would invite respect, but delay encouraged escalation. The trial became a national spectacle—part protest, part farce—broadcast as evidence that judicial authority itself had collapsed. When the convictions were overturned on appeal, the episode left a lasting impression (Schultz, 2009). A court

The Long Unraveling

that abandons its own dignity surrenders more than control; the surrender erodes the moral ground on which justice depends.

Earlier in the century, the Sacco and Vanzetti trials revealed the same danger from the opposite direction (Watson, 2007). Judge Webster Thayer's open contempt for the defendants—two Italian immigrants and self-proclaimed anarchists—tainted the proceedings and turned a local murder case into an international symbol of American injustice. His bias from the bench destroyed confidence in the verdict and burdened the judiciary with a legacy of doubt.[*] Seven decades later, the O.J. Simpson trial inverted the lesson. Judicial leniency replaced judicial arrogance, and spectacle replaced order. Lawyers performed for cameras, witnesses sparred for airtime, and the nation learned again how quickly authority dissolves when respect for process gives way to performance.

Congress now faces an analogous peril. The legislative chamber, like a courtroom, relies on shared respect to sustain deliberative purpose. Members once guarded that respect with formality and restraint. Debate could be fierce, but the stage remained sacred. Today, many treat the floor of the House or Senate as a platform for outrage rather than governance. The microphones reward

---

[*] The Sacco and Vanzetti case of the 1920s became a parable of justice undone by judicial contempt. Presiding Judge Webster Thayer blurred the boundary between authority and bias, belittling defense counsel in open court and mocking the defendants in private conversation. Contemporary reporters described him as a man "impervious to the ethical standards expected of one who presides in a capital case" ("Radicals: Thayer Flayed," 1927). His behavior provoked international outrage and led Massachusetts Governor Alvan T. Fuller to convene an independent review. The Lowell Committee ultimately upheld the verdict but censured Thayer for "a grave breach of judicial decorum." The scandal, once front-page news across the world, illustrated how quickly public faith erodes when an institution's guardians mistake ridicule for control (Watson, 2007).

volume, not persuasion. The camera invites posturing, not statesmanship. Contempt of Congress, when practiced by its own members, requires no opposing party to enforce disorder. The punishment arrives through displacement—by executive decree, judicial improvisation, or administrative sprawl. When legislators scorn their own institution, other branches fill the vacuum they leave behind.

The cure does not lie in nostalgia for a golden age but in professional pride: mastery of procedure, respect for colleagues, and public displays of legislative competence. A court restores order through the gavel. Congress must do so through conduct. Members who defend the dignity of the Chamber do not seek moral purity; they seek survival of the Republic's first branch. A legislature that mocks itself teaches the nation to do the same, and a people who no longer respect their Congress will soon find someone else to govern them.

Death of a Newsman

The final element of the Republic's unraveling lies in the disappearance of the printed newspaper—the disciplined institution that once mediated between citizen and state. As Andrey Mir argues in *Postjournalism* (2020), newspapers are dead. What has vanished is not information, but mediation. The age of the editor has yielded to the age of the feed. In the new digital order, "citizen journalism" and what Mir calls "random acts of journalism" have stripped professional journalists of their monopoly on news coverage and "enabled alternative agenda-setting" by individuals who operate outside the discipline of editorial institutions (Mir, 2023). The democratization of news production is a recent—yet not unprecedented—development in modern history that has accelerated the collapse of newspapers and the erosion of professional journalism. Mir captures the deeper constitutional consequence when he writes that the post-journalism era "embodies the shift from 'representative democracy' to 'direct democracy' in news mediation." Editorial distance collapses. Judgment gives way to immediacy. The new media environment transfers editorial authority from professional intermediaries to the crowd itself, a shift that weakens the very distance that once protected judgment from passion.

Professional journalism in the United States grew out of a moment when the country struggled to balance democratic expansion with the need for disciplined public information. Newspapers reached vast audiences during the early twentieth century, yet no formal method existed to prepare the men and women who shaped public opinion. A movement toward professional education emerged in response to that gap. Democracy widened faster than journalistic norms could stabilize. The Progressive Era produced journalists such as Ida Tarbell, whose investigations of Standard Oil demonstrated how evidence-driven reporting could expose corporate abuse and strengthen democratic life (Gorton, 2020). Tarbell's generation revealed both the promise and the danger of a powerful press. Muckraking uncovered wrongdoing, yet the adversarial nature of that work underscored the need for standards that protected fact-gathering from political manipulation (Baldasty, 1992).

The University of Missouri answered that need in 1908 by founding what the institution identifies as the first journalism school in the world (University of Missouri). Walter Williams, the school's founding dean, believed that journalism required disciplined preparation comparable to law or medicine. His "Journalist's Creed" reflected that conviction and helped establish a professional ideal for a rapidly democratizing media environment (Williams, 1914). The Missouri model—rooted in civic purpose, factual rigor, and editorial judgment—encouraged universities across the country to build programs that trained reporters for a democratic republic.

The graph in Fig. 8 visualizes that institutional rise from a single school in 1908 to more than one hundred programs today. The curve draws on milestones preserved in the Missouri School of Journalism archives. The trend reveals the construction of a professional infrastructure that supported the American press for much of the twentieth century. That infrastructure produced the editors and reporters who shaped the civic habits examined throughout this chapter. The graph marks the expansion of a craft that once provided the Republic with a mediating institution capable of slowing emotion and disciplining public argument.

The graphs in Figs. 9 and 10 then show the sharp contraction of that world. The decline of circulation and the erosion of advertising revenue represent not only the loss of business models but the weakening of the professional foundation first imagined by Williams and sharpened by reformers such as Tarbell. Today, a blog with little to no professional education in writing, much less in journalism, can grab a keyboard and an Internet connection and become a digital journalist. The result is a civic environment guided by speed, indignation, and algorithmic incentives rather than the trained judgment associated with a professional press.

The institutional rise shown in Fig. 8, followed by the collapse traced in Figs. 9 and 10, marks the long arc from professionalization to dissolution. Thus, the news cowbell remains loud and news remains abundant, yet the content carried by that noise offers more volume than information—a pattern familiar from many democratic expansions in history. The scale of that collapse is unmistakable. As Fig. 9 shows, daily newspaper circulation has fallen from nearly 60 million copies in 1960 to roughly 21 million today—a contraction that tracks the unraveling of editorial authority itself.

The Long Unraveling

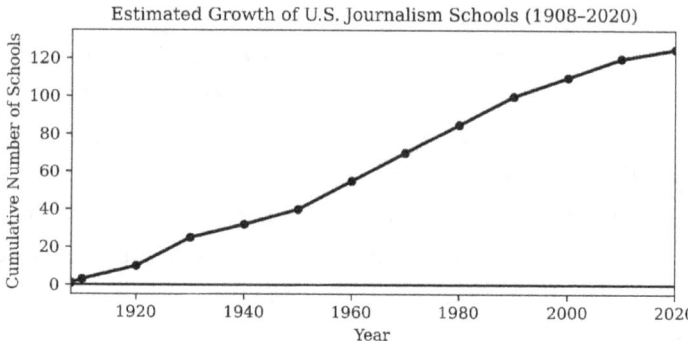

Figure 8. Growth of U.S. Journalism Schools, 1908–2020 (Estimated). The first formal school of journalism opened at the University of Missouri in 1908. Subsequent growth reflects the nationwide professionalization of reporting in the twentieth century. Values represent decade-level estimates based on documented program openings, ACEJMC accreditation records, and historical scholarship in *Journalism & Mass Communication Quarterly*. Because no complete census exists for the full period, the plotted line uses conservative interpolation anchored to known institutional milestones.

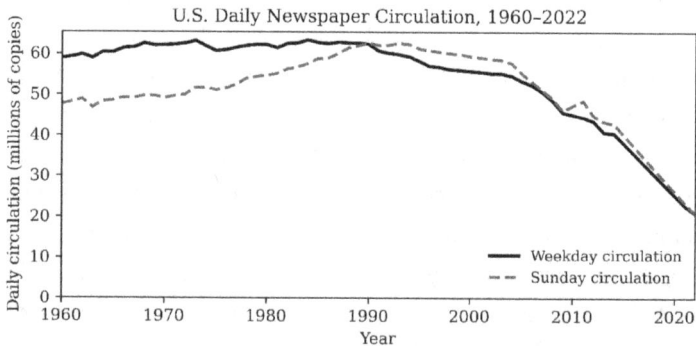

Figure 9. Decline of U.S. Daily Newspaper Circulation, 1960–2022. Total weekday and Sunday circulation fell from nearly 60 million copies in the mid-twentieth century to just over 20 million today. The contraction marks the transition from editor-driven press to decentralized, digitally mediated ecosystem. Data from Pew Research Center (2024).

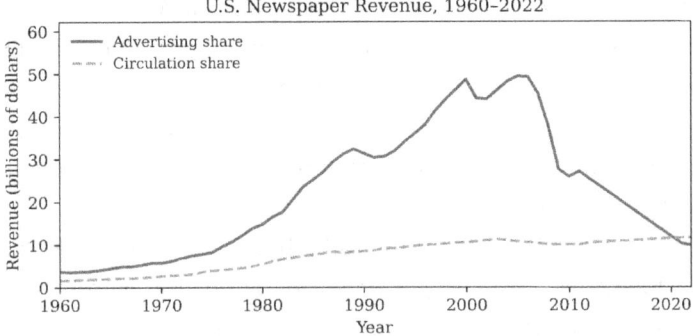

Figure 10. Advertising vs. Circulation Revenue Shares, 1960–2022. Advertising once accounted for the overwhelming majority of newspaper revenue. Since the early 2000s, that model has collapsed. As advertising shrank and subscription-based models expanded, the economic logic of news shifted away from broad public persuasion toward digital activation—an environment where anger outperforms accuracy. Data from Pew Research Center (2024).

Mir's analysis identifies the transformation that now defines political communication. A top-down press—hierarchical, advertising-funded, and more republican in temperament—has been replaced by a bottom-up press—participatory, subscription-based, and more democratic in impulse. The difference between the two extends beyond business models into deeper civic psychology. The top-down press speaks to the public, while the bottom-up press speaks through the public. The first seeks agreement; the second seeks reaction. Advertising media of the twentieth century sought to keep readers content because irritation threatened the interests of advertisers. Anger, pessimism, and outrage, therefore, undermined advertiser interests and undercut the business logic of mainstream newspapers. By contrast, subscription-supported and engagement-driven digital media—today's press—depend less on persuasion and more on activation, and activation thrives on anger and indignation. The digital press demands clicks. As Mir argues, anger sells better than happiness when advertisers no longer stand in the middle, and outrage motivates more clicks than understanding (Mir, 2020). The revenue data reinforce this shift. Figure 10 reveals the long decline of advertising's share of newspaper income and the corresponding rise of subscription dependence—an economic realignment that rewards outrage over restraint and carves out both the editor and the advertiser.

American history has featured both archetypes of journalism. The top-down press, supported either by political patronage or commercial advertising, relies on centralized authority. Early partisan papers of the eighteenth and early nineteenth centuries pursued explicit political goals. Later, as technology and demographics shifted, advertiser-funded newspapers emerged and pursued a quieter goal of stability. In both eras, editors shaped the flow of information to protect either a party's doctrine or a consumer's confidence. The bottom-up press reverses that model. Funding comes from the audience through subscriptions, memberships, or digital engagement, and the collective audience assumes the role of editor. The agenda no longer descends from a boardroom or party office but forms through the aggregation of individual reactions. For Mir, the news becomes a referendum, where reader attention, not editorial judgment, determines significance (Mir, 2020). The result is a system guided not by institutional standards but by emotional gravity—stories rise or fall according to the weight of collective outrage or affirmation rather than their news value.

The Editor Disappears

In his book, Mir also traces the history of the newspaper, a history that mirrors the political evolution of democracy itself. Early newspapers were elite publications—expensive, subscription-based, partisan, and financed from the top down. They served as instruments of political organization rather than vehicles of public information. The emergence of the penny press in the 1830s—Benjamin Day's *New York Sun* (1833), James Gordon Bennett's *Herald* (1835), and Horace Greeley's *Tribune* (1841), among others—broke that model. The one-cent price democratized access to news just as the Jacksonian era democratized access to politics.* Advertising revenue replaced party patronage, and mass readership replaced elite subscription (Baldasty, 1992).

The shift carried mixed consequences. The penny press embodied the promise of an open republic: voices multiplied, literacy expanded, and a national public sphere took shape. Yet the commercial incentives that broadened access also rewarded sensationalism over deliberation. News drifted toward entertainment, and the discipline of reasoned debate began to yield to the economics of attention. This news democratization at the turn of the nineteenth to the twentieth century carried many of the polarizing effects that we are now seeing in the digital era. Mir describes how market forces entered the civic bloodstream long before the digital algorithm did (Mir, 2020).

The digital revolution represents a second democratization of the news. The early Internet of the 1990s and 2000s fostered the Viral Editor—a collective, human-driven network in which millions of bloggers performed the editorial function once reserved for professional gatekeepers (Mir, 2023). That phase required bloggers to compose, reflect, and write at a pace that still resembled the deliberative habits sustaining earlier democratic discourse. The

---

* The Jacksonian era (roughly 1828–1848) is widely regarded as the first major democratization of American politics. Under Andrew Jackson, expanding political participation, new party networks, and a rapidly growing press produced a more popular and emotionally charged style of politics than the elitist style of the early Founders (Howe, 2007; Wilentz, 2006).

bottleneck remained human. The major change came with the rise of social-media platforms in the 2010s. Human curation gave way to algorithmic optimization—and unprecedented speed. Algorithms learned to privilege engagement by systematically amplifying emotional intensity over evidentiary weight.

Under such conditions, the digital environment turns each user into both judge and defendant. Platforms transform civic conversation into moral performance. "Social media," as Mir notes, "increasingly serve not to facilitate the simple exchange of written information but to sort out everyone's attitude toward the most pressing issues of the day." He goes on to write that the "wrong response to someone's hard-fought truth is punished by reciprocal aggression and various forms of ostracism." Mir then contrasts the two phases he identifies, noting that "the Viral Editor required from everyone participation in content selection," whereas "the Viral Inquisitor demands from everyone solidarity with the most widely held views of others." Politicization and polarization are embedded in the digital media process (Mir, 2023). The deliberative pause that once separated thought from reaction has vanished, replaced by an infrastructure that converts reflex into content.

The Demagogue Returns

The danger of this second era of news democratization lies not only in the polarization of the People into angry digital tribes but also in the renewed exposure of the electorate to demagogues—a fear the Founders treated as existential. Alexander Hamilton opened *Federalist No. 1* with a warning about "ambitious demagogues" who mislead the People by exploiting their passions and prejudices. James Madison carried that concern into *Federalist No. 10*, where he described leaders "of factious tempers" who inflame communal passions, and into *Federalist No. 63*, where he warned that the People, "stimulated by some irregular passion," may empower destructive figures they later condemn. Ivan Berend's *Populist Demagogues and the New Authoritarianism* (Berend, 2020) provides a political corollary to Mir's media theory. Across centuries, each technological acceleration in communication has produced a corresponding rise in demagoguery—a renewal of the Founders' fears. Berend's comparative study traces how figures such as Andrew Jackson, Huey Long, Joseph McCarthy, and Donald Trump have exploited new media environments that flattened hierarchy and amplified emotion (Berend, 2020).

Consider how new media have repeatedly widened the path for demagogues. Andrew Jackson, known as "the People's President," harnessed the revolutionary party press of the 1820s and 1830s—a newly nationalized print network—to wage a relentless campaign against bankers, judges, and Eastern elites. His alliance with loyal editors turned political anger into a daily mobilizing force at a geographic scale never before seen. Huey Long, nicknamed "The Kingfish" and elected as both Governor and U.S. Senator from Louisiana, used the new technology of radio in the 1930s to enter private homes with fiery sermons about a rigged economy and a corrupt establishment. The intimacy of the medium made his populism feel personal. Joseph McCarthy, the infamous senator from Wisconsin, seized on the expanding reach of postwar television, transforming congressional hearings into a national spectacle where accusation itself became political theater. Finally, Donald Trump—whose supporters have revived "the People's President" moniker to echo Jackson—mastered social media, collapsing the boundary between message and governance by turning provocation, grievance, and personal insult into presidential practice. Each, in his era, perfected the demagogue's art.

Each leap in communication technology has shortened the distance between leader and follower. The common thread, as Berend argues, is that new media democratizes access to the audience and replaces representation with identification—the emotional bond of a crowd for the deliberative bond of a constituency. Such environments, which the Founders understood intuitively, favor demagogues who claim authenticity over accuracy. A leader need not silence opponents when followers voluntarily filter information to confirm their worldview. The architecture performs the exclusion. The digital media system enforces conformity not through overt censorship but through disappearance—by quietly removing dissent from the feed. In such moments, the demagogue's cowbell overwhelms competing voices.

Thus, the tragedy of the newspaper's death lies not only in economic decline but in the collapse of a civic rhythm. The daily edition forced a pause—a morning beginning, an evening review, a moment between event and interpretation. I remember my mother opening the paper at the breakfast table, the sharp snap and rustle of newsprint stretching between her hands, a sound that marked the start of the day. That sound has vanished. The digital feed abolishes that rhythm and floods the mind with a continuous stream—minute by minute, second by second—of partial truths and tribal affirmations. The Republic loses a cadence that once encouraged daily civic reflection.

The printed press, for all its exclusivity, imposed a necessary and important delay. Reading the paper created a separate moment—a pause in the day that framed news as a civic duty. Producing that paper required gathering, editing, and proofing, a deliberate friction that slowed emotion and sharpened judgment. The digital, algorithmic press eliminates that friction. Each event becomes an opinion in real time. Outrage travels faster than evidence, and by the time correction appears, belief has hardened into identity.

Rebuilding the Republic requires more than nostalgia for paper and ink. The past is the past, and no amount of sentiment will recover the civic rhythm the printed press once offered. The goal is not restoration of a bygone era but the reinstitution of a structure that balances freedom of expression with responsibility of expression. That balance will not emerge through censorship or corporate control but requires cultivating a slower, more deliberate mode of consumption—a civic habit that reintroduces friction into how citizens encounter information. Madison argued in *Federalist No. 63* that republican government depends on "the cool and deliberate sense of the community." Through the Constitution, with its myriad checks, balances, and deliberate delays, the Founders built time and distance into the system to restrain impulsive passions. A modern media structure must do the same, encouraging citizens to read before reacting, verify before sharing, and listen before judging.

The death of the newspaper symbolizes the end of an era when language slowed thought long enough for reason to intervene. The rebirth of republican virtue will begin when citizens once again learn to govern their own attention rather than yield it to digital algorithms. As Mir and Berend remind us—and as Madison warned—the Republic survives only when reflection outruns reaction.

Rosenberg's account of cognitive burden also explains the scarcity of compromise. Compromise demands patience with ambiguity, recognition of partial truths, and acknowledgment that adversaries hold a legitimate place in the constitutional order. Such acts require mental energy—the willingness to hold rival claims in tension. As I argue in *The Art of the Compromise* (Page, 2024), civic maturity often begins with the ability to remain "of two minds," long enough for judgment to rise above instinct. When emotional saturation rises, the reservoir of energy required for that work drains quickly. The comparison engine narrows the field of available possibilities. The mind chooses simplicity over complexity. The nation loses the patience required for the slow work of persuasion.

Madison designed a structure capable of restraining the speed of passion. Rosenberg identifies the psychological pressure now pressing against that structure. Mir describes a media ecosystem that accelerates passion faster than a constitutional filter can absorb. The modern world assigns far greater cognitive weight to the citizen than the eighteenth century ever imagined, while the constitutional supports built to carry that weight have weakened under the force of immediacy and emotionally charged information. The central question for this generation concerns the renewal of republican safeguards—whether a modern republic can reinforce those supports, widen the distance between impulse and authority, and rebuild the barriers that once slowed faction to a manageable pace. The challenge can be stated plainly: are Americans willing to accept more republic and less cowbell?

A durable republic rests on architecture rather than democratic virtue. Madison, as Ricks demonstrates in *First Principles* (2020), understood more clearly than other Founders that liberty depends on structure rather than sentiment. Madison trusted design, and he built a national frame strong enough to resist the turbulence he knew would come. The twenty-first century inherits that frame, yet contemporary pressures demand new forms of restraint. The American Republic grew strong because institutional boundaries shaped democratic energy rather than indulging democratic impulse. Future strength will require a renewed commitment to structural guardrails—the kind that channel passion, protect dissent, and prevent momentary majorities from converting emotion into lasting power.

In Sum

American self-government has lived, since the Founding, at the tension point between democratic impulse and republican restraint. In this chapter, we have traced how modern institutions have weakened that balance. Reformers pursued transparency after 1968 and opened a nomination system that once filtered ambition through deliberation. The new structure rewarded momentum over mastery and encouraged candidates who thrived on performance rather than preparation. Jimmy Carter mastered that structure first, but later figures—Reagan, Obama, and Trump—proved that the method outlasts the moment. The democratization of primary selection produced new forms of legitimacy, yet the process itself drifted away from the republican design that once steadied national leadership and, over time, intensified political polarization.

Congress followed a similar path. The House that governed much of the twentieth century—slow, procedural, internally diverse—yielded to a streamlined structure after 1994 that centralized power, accelerated conflict, and transformed lawmakers into permanent candidates. The era of insecure majorities replaced the era of durable coalitions. Members arrived in Washington as partisans first and legislators second. The permanent campaign silenced the habits that once supported deliberation. Governance has become a continuation of electoral combat by other means, turning institutional disagreement into performative conflict and further exacerbating polarization.

A culture of scandal hardened the shift. Oversight and accountability, once instruments of constitutional balance, became weapons of partisan competition. Watergate supplied the catalyst, but the decades that followed have criminalized politics and transformed ethics investigations from remedy into ritual. The confirmation of Robert Bork marked the turning point in the judiciary. Senator Ted Kennedy's attack against Bork redefined moral accusation as a political strategy. Bork's defeat did not merely sink a nominee; the defeat altered the incentives that shaped who would seek high judicial office and how senators would judge them. Later confirmation battles—Thomas, Garland, Gorsuch, Kavanaugh—revealed the end state of a process no longer anchored by restraint.

The final pillar of the unraveling emerged from the collapse of the printed press. A republic that once depended on the editorial discipline of newspapers now contends with a digital environment that amplifies emotional reaction over reflective judgment. The age of the Viral Editor evolved into the age of the Viral Inquisitor, and the civic pause that once separated news events from news interpretation has largely disappeared. Demagogues—the fear of James Madison and Alexander Hamilton—flourish when the distance between impulse and action narrows. That pattern holds from Andrew Jackson's party press to Huey Long's radio addresses, from McCarthy's televised hearings to Trump's social media presidency. Each innovation accelerates passion faster than institutions can absorb the mob's emotions and polarization stretches thinner with every cycle.

Across these domains—presidential selection, congressional procedure, executive accountability, judicial confirmation, and public communication—the Republic has moved toward greater democratic immediacy and away from the republican mechanisms that once moderated collective passion. These reforms never had malicious intent. Each sought to correct a failure of the previous generation. Yet the combined effect produced a system less capable of cooling political temperature and more vulnerable to the very forces the Founders feared. Faction has become identity. Transparency has become spectacle. Participation has become performance. The civic architecture designed to encourage citizen reflection now amplifies mob reaction.

The Founders anticipated such pressures. They understood that democracy, untethered from structure, tends toward haste, division, and demagoguery. The constitutional design, therefore, built obstacles—staggered terms, indirect elections, bicameralism, federalism, and the separation of powers—to discipline democratic energy and to elevate judgment over impulse. The next chapter turns to those mechanisms and examines how Madison, Hamilton, and their colleagues engineered a republic—the Republic, our Republic—capable of surviving faction, ambition, and public passion. Their insights offer not only a reading of American history but also a warning drawn from the many democracies that unraveled when structure failed to restrain fervor.

The Long Unraveling reveals how a republic shifts when well-intentioned reform forgets well-structured design. The next chapter begins the work of rebuilding by returning to the design itself.

CHAPTER 3

The Well-Constructed Republic

I N COLLEGE FOOTBALL, the cowbell stands as the noisemaker—and some would say the weapon—favored by Mississippi State fans. In 2002, two friends and I drove to Starkville on a long-running mission to visit each Southeastern Conference (SEC) road venue where the Tennessee Vols played. Starkville lived up to the city's name. The place was stark. The landscape thinned as the highway narrowed, and a town carved from pine and red clay appeared—spare, weathered, and strangely endearing. Planning for the trip required an unusual step. We could not book a hotel in Starkville. Instead, we had to book one across the border in Alabama because Starkville offered too few places for the large traveling Tennessee crowd to stay.

What Starkville lacks in scenery, Davis Wade Stadium more than compensates for with noise. Mississippi State fans bring cowbells—thousands of them. The tradition dates to the 1930s, when students adopted the cowbell as a symbol of good fortune and transformed the device into what one columnist describes as "an ear-splitting slice of hell" (Forde, 2025). Cowbells ring through warm-ups, timeouts, defensive stands, and each decisive moment of the game. The metallic surge surrounds the field. Opposing coaches have long argued that the clang disrupts communication and forces quarterbacks to rely almost entirely on hand signals, even after the SEC imposed partial restrictions in 1974 and again in later revisions to the conference's artificial-noise regulations—restrictions that never extinguished the tradition because Bulldog fans kept bringing the bells (Clay, 2019).

My friends and I sat high in the bleachers that afternoon, and the lesson arrived long before the first kickoff. The game relied on structure—hash marks, sidelines, downs, penalties, officiating crews, replay booths, and a field whose boundaries no cowbell could move. Yet the fans still wielded power. Their noise could not sack a quarterback or intercept a pass, but the noise could alter momentum, timing, and psychological clarity. The players had to develop mechanisms to communicate through the clang. They operated inside a frame designed to absorb the crowd's energy without surrendering control of the game itself.

This Mississippi stadium offered a crude analogy—crude, but clarifying for this book. A democracy resembles the crowd: energetic, emotional, impulsive, and loud. A republic resembles the field: structured, bounded, and protected by rules that prevent the crowd from overwhelming the game. The cowbells are not the center of football, yet players ignore those clanging bells at their peril. Democratic noise behaves in the same way. Democratic noise surrounds public life, and the Constitution forces that noise to move through representatives, procedures, and limits before passion can take the shape of power. Players and coaches operate with an additional, unseen layer of strategy—silent adjustments, coded signals, and coordinated movements that escape the crowd's attention. Madison described a similar dynamic within a republic.

Representatives filter and refine public sentiment, turning democratic heat into considered judgment rather than impulsive force.*

Madison understood that dynamic. He studied Greek leagues, Swiss councils, and Dutch provinces, each of which fell into paralysis or collapse when faction or sovereignty claims overwhelmed shared institutions (Ketcham, 1990; Ricks, 2020). He built a national frame that widened the distance between impulse and authority. Representation slowed the velocity. Bicameralism forced reconsideration. Independent courts guarded boundaries. Federal supremacy steadied the larger frame when local majorities pursued exclusion rather than equality. The Madisonian design did not silence democratic noise; the design filtered the cowbell's blast into something a country could govern with.

Modern research reinforces Madison's insight. Shawn Rosenberg, a political psychologist and democratic theorist, shows how democratic participation taxes cognitive capacity and strains the mental habits required for deliberation (Rosenberg, 2019). The author Andrey Mir, who is a media scholar, journalist, and critic of digital capitalism, demonstrates how contemporary media accelerates emotion and compresses judgment into nanoseconds, transforming citizens into what he describes as participants in a system where

---

* Analogies, such as our cowbell here, fracture when pushed too far. Cognitive scientists describe analogies as temporary scaffolding—useful for highlighting structure and contrast, yet dangerous when treated as precise models. Dedre Gentner depicts analogy as a tool for "structural mapping" rather than literal equivalence (Gentner, 1983). George Lakoff's research shows that metaphors illuminate one dimension of a concept while obscuring another (Lakoff, 1993). The stadium comparison follows that pattern. The interplay between crowd noise and on-field structure mirrors only a narrow slice of democratic life, yet the contrast clarifies Madison's central argument. Passion surrounds politics, and republican architecture disciplines that passion without extinguishing the democratic force behind it.

emotional immediacy eclipses reflection (Mir, 2020). The cowbell grows louder each year. The psychological weight on the citizen grows heavier, and the distance Madison built into the frame grows thinner under the Pressure of digital devices that deliver outrage directly into the palm of one's hand.

A well-constructed republic* is the only mechanism capable of converting democratic noise into durable policy. The chapters that follow trace those guardrails across moments when the cowbell grew deafening—secession, the 1876 election dispute, McCarthyism, and the long struggle for Civil Rights. Each episode reaches the same conclusion. Democratic passion produces heat, sometimes righteous and sometimes reckless. The Republic absorbs that heat, redirects that energy, and converts turbulence into constitutional work.

The Starkville analogy remains the simplest way to frame the contrast. The crowd brings the cowbells. The Republic brings the rules. The country endures because constitutional rules outlast democratic noise.

What a Republic Is

Coach Bingham taught eighth-grade civics in a squat brick building that smelled of pencil shavings, floor wax, and adolescent ambition.

---

* The choice of "well-constructed" is deliberate. The phrase echoes Madison's opening line in *Federalist No. 10*, the essay many historians regard as the clearest articulation of the republican remedy to faction. Madison opens the essay by arguing that "a well-constructed Union" provides the strongest defense against the violence of faction. The phrase summarizes his belief that constitutional design, rather than democratic virtue, offers the most reliable safeguard for republican stability.

More Republic, Less Cowbell

His classroom sat two doors down from the gym, which meant whistles and sneaker squeaks leaked into lessons with surprising regularity. Male teachers in the 1980s rarely kept their formal titles. The culture of the era transformed them into "Coach," whether they taught government, geometry, or driver's education. The chalkboard ruled the front wall, and Coach commanded that board as if democracy depended upon his capitalization.

I sat in the back row and delivered more grief than a teacher deserved. I brought none of Judd Nelson's cinematic charisma from *The Breakfast Club*. Rather, I carried awkwardness, nervous energy, and a smart-mouthed confidence completely out of proportion to my social standing. I was a nerd with opinions and very little grace. Coach weathered those interruptions with a patience rarely found among adults charged with explaining the Republic to thirteen-year-olds.

One morning, he wrote three words on the board: democracy, direct democracy, and republic. He underlined each word as if drawing boundaries around three distinct civilizations. When he turned back toward the classroom, his expression carried the seriousness of a man who recognized the long shadow cast by definitions. Coach loved football, but he loved these distinctions more. He was a great teacher. My recollection comes from memory, not notes, but the lesson has never faded.

"Democracy," he began, "means rule by the People." He paused and scanned the room. He went on to explain that "the phrase means more than popular participation. Democracy relies upon majority rule. A majority shapes policy. A minority accepts those decisions, not because the minority agrees with the majority, but because a commitment to peaceful self-government outweighs the frustration that follows a hard political loss." Coach spoke with the plain moral confidence of a teacher who believed the Constitution could be learned in stages, with teaching preceding full understanding.

The Well-Constructed Republic

That pause invited trouble. I stepped directly into the gap.

"So a majority could vote on everything?" I asked, eager to unveil my dazzling eighth-grade brilliance. "Lunch menus? Football plays? Homework?"

Coach raised one eyebrow, a gesture that communicated toleration rather than anger. His reply felt gentle but firm, the verbal equivalent of guiding a kid back into the correct lane.

"Not exactly," he said. "That description matches direct democracy, not democracy in the broader sense."

He returned to the chalkboard and wrote with careful strokes. "Direct democracy means the people vote on each law. Citizens gather and decide each question themselves." He tilted his head slightly, as if inviting us to imagine a New England town meeting, the kind Madison studied meticulously when he dissected ancient and modern democracies before the Constitutional Convention (Feldman, 2017; Ricks, 2020). Direct democracy, Coach explained, demanded constant participation. Governance becomes a permanent meeting rather than a system of representation.

A kid behind me muttered that direct democracy sounded like detention disguised as government. The image of constant voting—ballots each week, maybe each day—struck me with surprising force. My wisecracks collapsed under the weight of that picture. Coach caught the shift in my expression and gave a small, knowing nod, the kind a teacher offers when a student finally grasps a point that chalk alone cannot deliver.

"Which brings us," he said, "to a republic."

He wrote the final word deliberately. Classroom noise faded. Chalk dust hovered in the afternoon light. Coach stepped back from the board with the kind of respect usually reserved for scripture.

"A republic," he said, "means the People choose representatives who deliberate and vote on their behalf. A republic accepts majority rule, yet limits majority power. A republic acknowledges popular sovereignty, yet protects minorities from majorities that might attempt to legislate punishment." His emphasis reached toward Madison's central concern: factions, inflamed by passion, might seize authority and wield that authority against dissent.

Madison analyzed those dangers with piercing clarity, warning that direct democracies and small republics often collapsed under demagogues and sudden movements of passion (Ketcham, 1990). A larger republic, spread across a wider sphere, diluted factional heat and strengthened liberty. One key to Madison's insight was the call to enlarge the sphere—a Madisonian phrase that now carries familiar weight. Madison argued that a broad republic could succeed where smaller republics of the Ancients had failed. The more than 230-year record of the American Republic stands as substantial evidence that Madison's judgment was sound.

Coach Bingham did not cite Madison that morning. He did not mention Athens or the Venetian assemblies that Madison studied. Yet his plainspoken definitions mirrored the logic Madison carried into Philadelphia in 1787. Majority rule supplied the engine of collective decision. A republic placed that engine behind deliberate barriers: representation, slower procedures, and constitutional restraints. Those boundaries protected the People from the heat of their own passions.

Only years later did I recognize the depth inside that classroom moment. The United States spoke in the language of democracy while building a republic meant to restrain democratic excess. Majority rule guided public life, yet constitutional design slowed domination through staggered elections, bicameralism, judicial review, and firm protections for dissent. The architecture reflected Madison's early worry that majority power, left unchecked, could harden into majority oppression—a danger he traced from the ancient democracies he studied (Feldman, 2017).

Coach Bingham could not have known that his chalkboard definitions would follow me long after adolescence receded. The awkward kid in the back row eventually realized that the lesson offered a doorway into the American character. Three words on a board carried three visions of self-rule, each pointing toward the same constitutional question: how can a free people govern without burning the foundations of their own freedom? The journey began in that classroom, but the deeper struggle belonged to Madison, who wrestled with that question long before anyone handed me a civics textbook.

Why Democracies Fail

James Madison entered the Philadelphia Convention in the summer of 1787 as a slight, soft-spoken Virginian who carried disproportionate intellectual weight. Later generations attached the phrase "Father of the Constitution" to his name, but the title merely recognized the labor he had already completed before delegates assembled. Philadelphia became the birthplace of the new American Republic, yet the design that emerged inside the Assembly Room had been forming in Madison's study for years. He arrived with the Virginia Plan in hand—an agenda forged through relentless historical inquiry. He guided debates with calm authority and preserved the record that historians now depend upon.*

---

* For more than a century, scholars treated Madison's *Notes on the Constitutional Convention* as a precise and impartial transcript of the debates. That confidence changed after historian Mary Sarah Bilder conducted a meticulous forensic study of Madison's manuscript—analyzing handwriting, ink composition, page substitutions, and chronological mismatches. Bilder concluded that Madison repeatedly revised the *Notes* long after 1787, sometimes decades later, to strengthen particular arguments or soften positions that no longer aligned with his later political identity (Bilder, 2015). The resulting portrait is not a fraudulent record, but a curated one—part diary, part reconstruction, and part retrospective justification. Bilder's

Madison did not go to Philadelphia searching for abstract theories. He went with a sober awareness that the American experiment had reached a point of crisis. The Articles of Confederation revealed a government drifting toward paralysis. States quarreled, public creditors lost patience, and foreign rivals sensed weakness. Madison recognized that republics rarely collapse through a single dramatic blow. They decay through fragmentation, faction, and the slow erosion of common purpose. He rejected the old belief that small democracies safeguard virtue while large republics invite tyranny. He turned instead to history with the concentration of a physician extending a scalpel. His method was unsentimental: study political death to design political life. He conducted an autopsy of the free governments of the past—a graveyard the Founders knew from their education in the rise and ruin of the Ancients. Madison was steeped in the democracies of the Ancients.

Two winters before the Philadelphia Convention, James Madison secluded himself at Montpelier with trunks of European books purchased by Thomas Jefferson. That pattern—immersion followed by selective departure—was not idiosyncratic. Thomas Ricks describes the intellectual rhythm of the Founding generation as a continual return to Greek and Roman examples, followed by deliberate departure from them when experience demanded new forms (Ricks, 2020). Madison became the most thorough practitioner of that habit. Candlelight, French texts, and Latin histories became a working laboratory. Madison read not to praise the Ancient's constitutional beauty but to expose the reasons free

---

analysis did not diminish Madison's achievement. Rather, the analysis revealed a human hand shaping the record of a fragile moment in American history.

governments faltered. Ralph Ketcham called the result "a dispassionate and relentless study" that left Madison "as well informed on the workings of confederate governments as any man in America" (Ketcham, 1990). Noah Feldman treated that period as the turning point in Madison's intellectual life, the moment when curiosity transformed into constitutional engineering (Feldman, 2017).

Madison titled his study *Notes on Ancient and Modern Confederacies* (Madison, c. 1786), yet the manuscript extended well beyond confederacies in the narrow sense.* He examined aristocratic councils, direct democracies, commercial republics, and imperial leagues. Madison did not search for a model to imitate. He searched for a pattern and found one. Free peoples join together, share authority, hesitate to surrender power, and eventually fail when common institutions lack the force required to secure obedience.

The pattern revealed itself quickly. The Lycian Confederacy balanced voting power with proportional contribution yet collapsed

---

* Madison never published *Notes on Ancient and Modern Confederacies*, and scholars have long debated the reason. The most persuasive explanation points to Madison's own concern about how unfinished the manuscript remained. The *Notes* began as background research for the Philadelphia Convention, and the pages mix summaries, excerpts, translations, and hurried reflections rather than polished arguments. Madison's later writings indicate that he saw the manuscript as a private analytical tool rather than a work ready for public judgment.

Several historians, including Jack Rakove (1998) and Mary Sarah Bilder (2015), suggest that Madison feared premature publication might invite attacks from political opponents who would seize on partial or speculative passages to undermine the broader constitutional project. Madison also believed that an authoritative account of republican design should emerge from the Constitution itself rather than from preparatory notes that exposed the scaffolding behind his thinking. The result is a document that shaped the Convention more than the historical record—a scholar's notebook that remained in the drawer until long after Madison's death.

before Roman expansion. The Amphictyonic Council promised unity through culture and religion yet became an arena for Athenian and Spartan manipulation. Swiss liberty endured through accident of geography more than institutional strength. The Holy Roman Empire carried ceremonial grandeur while lacking the cohesion required for decisive action. Each case illustrated a variation of the same failure: confederacies that treated member states as independent sovereigns assembled diplomatic committees, not governments. Voluntary obedience lasted only under rare harmony or overwhelming danger—conditions that never endure. Direct democracies offered civic energy without internal restraint. Confederacies offered restraint without genuine force. Neither form provided a path for a durable union.*

Two examples struck Madison with particular force. The Achaean League joined Peloponnesian cities in a balanced federal structure that combined equal representation, a shared currency, and coordinated military command. Local magistrates retained control over internal affairs, while a federal senate governed matters touching the entire alliance. Madison admired the symmetry achieved by that arrangement. He also recognized the vulnerability beneath the surface. Member cities obeyed federal decrees only when local inclination aligned with collective demand. Roman envoys exploited that discretionary obedience, whispered to individual cities about wounded sovereignty, and steered the league toward division. Feldman argues that the Achaean collapse struck Madison because the federation's predicament mirrored the

---

* The Soviet Union's late-stage collapse followed the same structural logic Madison identified in ancient confederacies: a central authority dependent on voluntary compliance cannot survive sustained stress.

American crisis under the Articles almost exactly (Feldman, 2017). Ketcham reached a similar conclusion, noting that Madison regarded the Achaean League as both the most promising ancient model and a sobering warning about the limits of a voluntary union (Ketcham, 1990). An at-will union echoed the constitutional theory the South invoked in 1861, a theory that mistook a federal republic for a dissolvable compact.

The Dutch Republic provided the sharpest modern example. Seven provinces formed a loose union after winning independence from Spain in the seventeenth century. Each province guarded its sovereignty with fierce pride. Delegates met in the States General, yet every major decision required unanimity. That unanimity rule guaranteed provincial veto power and prevented coherent national action. The federal treasury depended on voluntary provincial contributions, naval strength suffered, and foreign monarchies learned to manipulate Dutch politics by courting individual provinces rather than addressing the union as a whole. Madison saw a direct parallel. The Dutch Republic displayed what the United States would become if structural reform failed: admirable in reputation, proud in achievement, and paralyzed whenever coordinated national action became necessary.

Madison carried these warnings into Philadelphia. He did not seek a revival of Greek democracy or Swiss federalism. He sought a republic that commanded allegiance from states and citizens alike. A large and diverse territory would dilute faction by multiplying interest. A central government with authority to act directly on individuals, not merely through state legislatures, would cure the structural failures of the Articles. A bicameral legislature would reflect both the People and states while securing national authority. A national treasury, judiciary, and executive would deny future Americans the humiliations suffered by the Dutch and the Achaeans. Madison mined the past not for templates, but for proof that liberty required new architecture. The Constitution would assemble those fragments into a working whole.

The Constitution grew from that discipline. Madison placed no faith in the supposed purity of small democracies and no confidence in the voluntarism that defined loose confederacies. The failures he cataloged gave him a sober purpose that liberty demanded structure. The lessons drawn from those ruins shaped the frame of mind he carried into Philadelphia, a mindset determined to build a republic capable of enduring storms that had destroyed others. History did not disprove his conclusions. Later centuries extended his autopsy into the modern age.

Why Direct Democracies Fail

James Madison studied the democracies of the ancient world with the rigor of a man determined to build something sturdier. He read Greek histories line by line and examined the constitutions of the Italian republics and northern European city-states. He had already seen how momentary majorities pressed collective will through passion rather than judgment. Ancient assemblies often acted with enthusiasm while failing the larger community. Direct democracy inspired loyalty but failed to contain passion. Madison reached the same conclusion again and again. Scale does not moderate conflict on its own. Institutions must intervene to convert popular energy into governable outcomes.

Modern attempts have confirmed that pattern. Reformers have attempted to scale the Athenian ideal into contemporary life, and each effort has encountered the same structural limitations Madison identified in 1787: ambition, faction, immediacy, and the human tendency to favor impulse over steadiness. The record presents two revealing modern tests—one in a small republic where referenda flourish within a constitutional framework, and one in a large state where popular initiatives have hardened into paralysis.

Switzerland appears at first glance to be the strongest example of direct popular rule (Fossedal, 2018). A nation of roughly nine million residents casts frequent votes on referenda, popular initiatives, and constitutional amendments. Many observers cite Switzerland as proof that direct democracy can flourish under modern conditions. The deeper structure, however, tells a different story. Switzerland functions as a confederated republic anchored by a professional parliament, a collective executive, and a federal system that filters national passion through twenty-six cantons—regional political units with their own laws, traditions, and governing authority. Direct votes operate inside a constitutional frame built to restrain sudden majorities rather than indulge democratic impulse. Federalism, local custom, linguistic diversity, and a small population create stability that a continental nation the size of the United States could not reproduce. Switzerland echoes Madison's republic more than Athens's assembly. Modern advocates of direct democracy often point to Switzerland as a counterexample to Madison, yet the Swiss structure quietly confirms Madison's insight: durable self-government depends on filtration, distance, and institutional restraint. Switzerland's experience is often invoked as a model, but it succeeds only where scale remains limited and institutional filters remain strong.

California, with a population of roughly thirty-nine million residents, provides the opposite lesson. Reformers during the Progressive Era—roughly 1890 to 1920—sought to weaken party machines and corporate interests by creating direct channels of popular lawmaking—a move towards more democracy. The California Legislature adopted the mechanisms of popular initiative, referendum, and recall—tools that allow citizens to propose laws, overturn legislation, and remove elected officials without legislative mediation—in 1911 under Governor Hiram Johnson, a reformer who believed that direct legislation would restore public control over a government dominated by railroad barons and entrenched political brokers (Bowler & Donovan, 2000; Gerber, 2011). Progressive leaders promised that direct voting would weaken special interests and strengthen citizen participation.

The long-term result unfortunately confounded those expectations. A small number of wealthy individuals and well-funded organizations gained the resources to draft statutory language, hire signature-gathering firms, and frame ballot measures outside the representative process. Voters confronted complex and highly technical proposals presented through broad emotional appeals. Budget mandates embedded themselves in the constitutional text that no legislature could adjust fast enough to economic cycles. Periodic surges of public anger produced rigid fiscal obligations without negotiation or refinement. California demonstrated that direct democracy does not escape faction. The initiative process draws faction into the center of state government and denies elected officials the authority to filter public judgment or build durable compromises. Debra Bowen, a former California Secretary of State, captured the paradox with unusual clarity. Reforms designed to restrain elite power opened a new channel for well-funded actors, prompting Californians to ask, "How much have we really progressed?" (Bowen, 2011).

Smaller experiments reveal the same limits. Reformers in other nations attempted to cure democratic frustration by widening direct participation, yet the same structural weaknesses reappeared. Iceland's post-crisis crowdsourcing effort in 2011, for example, generated thousands of proposals but never matured into a governing structure (Landemore, 2020; Siddique, 2011). Digital-democracy advocates have made similar promises, envisioning online referenda, blockchain voting, and a perpetual Athenian assembly delivered through handheld devices (Morozov, 2012). None of these projects has produced political stability at scale. Real-time

The Well-Constructed Republic

participation accelerates public emotion, collapses deliberative distance, and magnifies factional impulse. A digital assembly increases velocity rather than judgment.

The absence of durable, large-scale direct democracies since Madison's day does not establish an iron law, yet the pattern remains unmistakable. Assembly-style governance survives only in small communities shaped by shared history and strong personal ties. New England town meetings endure because their scale softens conflict. Those conditions disappear when the population grows, interests diverge, or the complexity of a modern state enters public life.

Madison recognized those limits before the United States existed. He believed that a durable republic required distance in time and space between public opinion and public action—not as aristocratic insulation, but as democratic stewardship. Representatives could refine and enlarge the public view, an elegant phrase that captured Madison's conviction about human nature. A republic balances passion with judgment. Direct democracy trusts passion alone. Modern experiments such as progressive-era California have strengthened Madison's warning rather than softened the danger.

Contemporary debates often drift toward the rhetoric of direct democracy with nostalgic confidence, as though a purer form of popular rule might ease the frustrations that accompany representative life. The appeal reflects a longing for agency rather than a sober reading of history. No large society has solved the problem Madison identified challenges with direct democracies. Scale amplifies passion, and passion requires structure. A republic steadies that energy through institutions that filter, slow, and refine democratic will. By contrast, direct democracy offers immediacy but rarely sustains endurance. The post-1968 shift toward more democratic presidential nominations demonstrated the same tension, as greater immediacy magnified factional heat rather than strengthening broad coalitions. The desire for more democracy—more cowbell—

carries an undeniable force, yet that force rarely strengthens a nation's capacity for self-government.

Madison recognized the popular appeal of direct rule, yet he also understood the danger of unmediated passion. The Republic he helped design was strong enough to carry liberty across conflict and change. Modern experiments continue to confirm his judgment that democratic authority must be channeled rather than unleashed. A free community draws strength not from the intensity of collective emotion, but from institutions that convert judgment into governance. The next section turns to how a properly balanced republican structure performs that work when factions strain the constitutional order.

How Guardrails Work

James Madison entered the Philadelphia Convention prepared to turn theory into design. Months of study had convinced him that a durable republic required more than abstract principles; a durable republic required a national structure capable of managing conflict rather than succumbing to conflict itself. Madison arrived with a clear objective: to replace a failing confederation with a constitutional frame strong enough to unify a diverse people while still protecting local attachments. Where many delegates feared central power, Madison feared unrestrained faction. His focus centered on translating those concerns into institutions—mechanisms that could steady public life, prevent regional breakdown, and transform revolutionary energy into lasting governance. That design combined a bicameral legislature, separated powers, federalism, an independent judiciary, and a national executive capable of acting directly on individuals rather than through states alone. That design combined a bicameral legislature, separated powers, federalism, an independent judiciary, and a national executive capable of acting directly on individuals rather than through states alone.

The Well-Constructed Republic

Shays's Rebellion, which erupted just before the Convention and which many historians regard as a catalyst for the delegates' gathering, illustrated why those guardrails mattered (Richards, 2014).* The uprising did not signal civil collapse, yet the episode revealed the fragility of the Confederation's authority under the loose arrangement of the Articles. A small band of disaffected farmers in western Massachusetts shook public confidence in republican order because the weak national government lacked the power to respond. Madison saw not only disorder but a structural defect. A government unable to protect the nation from internal unrest could not preserve liberty (Ketcham, 1990). A weak center invited collapse from within and vulnerability from abroad.

Madison sought a structure capable of lasting beyond the storms, such as Shays's, that had shaken the Confederation. A strong federal system would preserve state identity while supplying the strength that only national authority could provide. Ralph Ketcham (1990) described Madison's project as an effort to "overcome pettiness and give effect to, not just preach about, 'the general and permanent good of the community'." Such an achievement required a republic rather than a direct democracy. Majorities, in Madison's view, did not deserve unbounded authority, and no electoral margin could stand as a permanent proxy for the common good. Minority communities required protection. Layers of

---

* Shays's Rebellion (1786–1787) was an armed uprising of indebted farmers in western Massachusetts protesting economic hardship, tax policies, and the lack of responsive government under the Articles of Confederation. The state's difficulty suppressing the unrest—and the absence of effective national authority—heightened elite concern about the fragility of republican order and helped catalyze the Constitutional Convention. See Richards (2014) for a more detailed history.

representation and constitutional distance created space for judgment to temper passion. Noah Feldman (2017) observes that Madison came to believe that reason had to be built into the constitutional structure itself—secured by enduring institutions rather than entrusted to voluntary restraint. Unlike other Founders, who placed hope in civic virtue, Madison, as Thomas Ricks argues, trusted structure more than character and believed that liberty would survive not through moral exhortation but through a design strong enough to withstand human frailty. Motivation to do good fades with time; a structure that disciplines power and steadies judgment endures.

Madison's boldest proposal grew from that conviction. He urged the Convention to adopt a federal negative—the authority of the national government to veto state laws (Feldman, 2017). Many delegates considered the proposal too sweeping. Madison regarded the device as the logical answer to the central flaw he identified in the failed confederacies he had studied. A national referee could prevent parochial majorities from converting local prejudice into binding authority. Uniformity was not his aim. Protection against factional abuse was. The federal negative would have supplied the ultimate guardrail for a continental republic by shielding the Union from democratic volatility at the state level.

Madison lost that fight in 1787. The federal negative was voted down. Delegates refused to grant Congress a blanket veto over state laws. Madison accepted the setback yet never relinquished the principle behind the proposal. A durable republic required a mechanism strong enough to halt local majorities when those majorities threatened fundamental rights. Without such a safeguard, the local authority could calcify into local tyranny. Madison argued that a republic worthy of the name needed protection against that danger, even when the remedy demanded a national check on regional power. The federal negative died in Philadelphia, yet the underlying principle—national supremacy in defense of constitutional liberty—would return in another form as an important guardrail.

History eventually supplied the mechanism Madison could not secure in Philadelphia, although the transformation unfolded at a glacial pace in political time. The Civil War and Reconstruction reshaped the federal order more deeply than the delegates imagined. The Fourteenth Amendment introduced new constitutional language—"no state shall deprive any person of due process or equal protection"—and that language soon carried the force Madison had hoped to secure. Through *incorporation decisions** beginning in the late nineteenth and early twentieth centuries, the Supreme Court interpreted the Amendment as a national restraint on state governments, a modern embodiment of the federal negative Madison had envisioned decades earlier (Curtis, 1986). The judiciary assumed the role Madison once hoped the national legislature would play and converted the promises of Reconstruction into structural protections for vulnerable citizens.

The *incorporation doctrine*, developed through a century of Supreme Court decisions, gradually bound state governments to the guarantees of the federal Bill of Rights. Thomas Ricks observes in *First Principles* that the abuses that followed the Civil War—Jim Crow statutes, racial violence, and segregationist laws—confirmed

---

* The incorporation doctrine developed gradually as the Supreme Court of the United States interpreted the Fourteenth Amendment to apply selected provisions of the Bill of Rights to the states through the Due Process Clause. Early cases include *Chicago, Burlington & Quincy Railroad Co. v. Chicago* (1897) and *Gitlow v. New York* (1925), with most core liberties incorporated during the mid-twentieth century. For a comprehensive account, see Curtis (1986).

More Republic, Less Cowbell

Madison's fear that unchecked state sovereignty could become a sanctuary for injustice and that federal supremacy would emerge as the only durable remedy (Ricks, 2020). The development of the *incorporation doctrine* unfolded unevenly, yet the trajectory remained unmistakable. A republic must protect individual liberty when local majorities refuse to do so, and American history offers repeated reminders that such refusals arise with troubling regularity.

The Civil Rights Movement revealed the full force of the principle Madison foresaw. State majorities used statute, police power, and administrative rules to build and preserve a racial caste system (Wilkerson, 2020). Those political coalitions acted with purpose. They won elections, drafted constitutions, and enforced segregation as a democratic expression of local will. Madison would have recognized the danger immediately. A democratic process can produce grave injustice when majority power follows prejudice rather than principle. The Civil Rights Act of 1964 and the Voting Rights Act of 1965 brought federal authority into the struggle not to defeat democracy but to defend republican liberty. Congress and the federal courts intervened to protect citizens whom local governments excluded from basic rights.

The federal negative that Madison once proposed appeared in a different form—federal marshals escorting children into schoolhouses and federal registrars reopening polling places that local officials had closed. The American Republic's guardrails began to turn the tide against institutional racism nearly a century after the Civil War, when constitutional structure finally caught up with moral promise. The Constitution does not promise immediate justice. It commits the nation to the harder work of approaching justice over time. The aspiration to form a more perfect Union presumes imperfection at the start—and endurance in the effort.

Madison feared that democratic power, when unrestrained by structure, could consume the liberty democracy claimed to protect.

Pure democracies, he warned in *Federalist No. 10*, "have ever been spectacles of turbulence and contention" (Madison, 2016). His answer centered on a republic designed to channel public passion rather than obey public passion. Local identity remained secure, yet no locality held the authority to define justice for the entire nation. A national framework built on those principles preserved the Union through conflict and created the constitutional space required for future generations to correct racial injustice, expand citizenship, and strengthen individual rights. Amendments and judicial interpretation transformed Madison's structural choices into broad protections for Americans who lacked regional power. The design remained imperfect, yet the design revealed Madison's clearest insight: republican structure restrains faction, and the preservation of liberty depends on citizens willing to honor that restraint.

Why Minds Strain

Democracy asks a great deal from each citizen. The design assumes that human beings will weigh claims fairly, consider rival arguments, tolerate ambiguity, and discipline the passions that rise when public life grows tense. The Founders expected that many citizens would struggle with those demands. Washington and Adams, in fact, feared the speed of public passion more than the strength of kings. Their warnings were both moral and structural. They believed a republic could survive many storms, but not a citizenry that surrendered reflection to emotion.

Modern research has sharpened this fear. Political psychologist Shawn Rosenberg argues that liberal democracy places a heavy cognitive burden on the public—a burden that grows heavier in an age shaped by digital speed and viral spectacle. His widely discussed paper *Democracy Devouring Itself* concludes that liberal democracy expects citizens to think abstractly, reason across differences, and remain patient with slow and imperfect institutions (Rosenberg,

2019). Many individuals struggle to meet those expectations. The Founders sensed the same danger, though they spoke in a different vocabulary. Alexander Hamilton gave the clearest expression of that concern during the Constitutional Convention in Philadelphia:

> "All communities divide themselves into the few and the many. The first are the rich and well born, the other the mass of the people. The voice of the people has been said to be the voice of God; and however generally this maxim has been quoted and believed, it is not true in fact. The people are turbulent and changing; they seldom judge or determine right. Give therefore to the first class a distinct, permanent share in the government. They will check the unsteadiness of the second, and as they cannot receive any advantage by a change, they therefore will ever maintain good government" (Yates, 1821).

Hamilton's word choice might rankle modern ears with his well-documented aristocratic certainty, yet his argument rests on a broader point. Individuals blessed with steadier temperaments, deeper experience, or stronger civic discipline have no guarantee of drowning out the noise of democratic passion—the mob's cowbells. Madison echoed Hamilton's concern in *Federalist No. 55*: "Had every Athenian citizen been a Socrates, every Athenian assembly would still have been a mob" (Madison, 2016).

Rosenberg's claim and Hamilton's warning point toward the same landscape. Democratic life demands a discipline that many citizens cannot consistently sustain, and the resulting gap between democratic requirements and democratic capacity becomes the ground where demagogues gain traction. Rosenberg does not treat this gap as an indictment of the common citizen. He does not treat citizens as idiots. His concern centers on the sheer volume and velocity of information in the modern world.

The Founders lived in a different environment and spoke with a different inflection. Hamilton and several Federalists believed that

The Well-Constructed Republic

the common citizen often lacked the steadiness required for public judgment. Thomas Jefferson rejected that view. In an 1820 letter, he wrote, "I know no safe depository of the ultimate powers of the society, but the people themselves: and if we think them not enlightened enough to exercise their controul with a wholsome discretion, the remedy is, not to take it from them, but to inform their discretion by education" (Jefferson, 1820). Rosenberg advances a similar faith in human ability. His argument does not rest on claims about intelligence. His concern centers on the cognitive strain produced by an information environment that overwhelms the very discretion Jefferson hoped education would strengthen.

Rosenberg grounds this argument in psychology rather than partisanship. Liberal democracy depends on habits that require sustained mental discipline: tolerance for uncertainty, openness to unfamiliar perspectives, acceptance of procedural defeat, and recognition that rights belong to adversaries as much as allies. Those habits demand stamina—the capacity to hold multiple ideas in tension without collapsing into resentment. Under economic stress, cultural anxiety, or informational overload, many citizens retreat from that complexity toward simpler categories. Clarity replaces nuance. Belonging replaces deliberation. The public landscape hardens into a contest between a righteous "us" and a threatening "them." The Founders intuitively understood this challenge, too.

The appeal of that simplification carries considerable force. Rosenberg draws a sharp contrast between democratic and populist impulses. Democracy and populism occupy different worlds in his analysis. Democracy asks citizens to think; populism asks citizens to feel. Democracy slows reaction; populism accelerates reaction. Democracy treats disagreement as a necessary tool of self-government; populism treats disagreement as evidence of betrayal. Rosenberg does not argue that democracy has collapsed.

Rosenberg argues that democratic life imposes cognitive and emotional demands that many citizens cannot sustain. The turbulence described in Chapter 2 reveals the same dynamic Rosenberg identifies, as waves of democratic frustration have outpaced the public's capacity for judgment and created openings for leaders who feed passion rather than filter democratic emotion. When those demands rise beyond capacity, citizens search for leaders who promise unity, clarity, and decisive action—leaders who validate anger rather than guide judgment. Such moments leave citizens vulnerable to demagogues.

Madison anticipated this problem without today's vocabulary of psychology. He feared the surge of passion, the faction "adverse to the rights of other citizens," and the speed with which that passion could seize the national legislature (Madison, 2016). His remedy was structural. He enlarged the Republic so that contending factions would collide and counteract one another. He filtered public opinion through representatives who could refine and elevate public sentiment before that sentiment became law. Madison assumed limited capacity in the citizenry and built a constitutional design that turned those limits into a safeguard rather than a weakness. Madison designed the Constitution to confound and frustrate the majority.

The Viral Clip

Rosenberg's argument aligns with Madison's diagnosis. Madison worked to slow the passions that destabilize democracies; Rosenberg explains the cognitive mechanism beneath those passions. Democratic life demands patience with ambiguity, yet the modern environment saturates citizens with immediacy. Madison slowed politics through representation. Modern communication accelerates politics through perpetual reaction. The constitutional firebreak that once separated passion from power now thins under the

The Well-Constructed Republic

heat of instantaneous social media. The distance Madison built has shrunk, while the emotional load carried by each citizen has grown heavier.

Andrey Mir's analysis of post-journalism underscores that shift. Mir argues that digital media no longer organizes public life around news information but around emotion, affirmation, and perpetual reaction (Mir, 2020). His account strengthens Rosenberg's claim that modern communication channels intensify the very passions Madison sought to restrain. The events traced in Chapter 2—riots, political eruptions, and the rapid mobilization of anger—demonstrate how those passions move through a modern public sphere stripped of the filters Madison considered essential. These modern pressures confirm the fear Madison carried into Philadelphia. Passion without filtration overwhelms judgment, and judgment without filtration cannot sustain a republic.

These pressures change how individuals process political information. Human cognition leans toward patterns and comparisons, searching for categories that simplify choice. When complexity overwhelms capacity, the mind gravitates toward sturdy narratives and familiar identities. Our cognitive comparison engine—an ever-active mental mechanism—begins to sort rapidly rather than deliberate carefully. Friends and neighbors become members of rival camps. Ambiguous events become moral judgments. A single image, stripped of context, circulates through millions of minds and ignites faction before a single fact can settle.[*]

---

[*] An early illustration came during the 2004 Democratic primaries, when a short, audio-distorted clip of then-presidential candidate Howard Dean's rallying "scream" spread across television and the early web. Glenn Reynolds later noted that the clip's viral reach shaped a national judgment about Dean's temperament long before journalists reported the distortion or

Rosenberg's and Mir's research clarifies why those reactions now arrive with greater speed and intensity. Mir argues that the crisis extends beyond the decline of newspapers and reaches into the collapse of professional journalism itself. Modern politics unfolds not through measured exchanges of letters, editorials, or speeches, but through images that bypass deliberation and the Press corps that once filtered public emotion. A short video can summon a political judgment long before analysis begins. When those clips accumulate, emotional weight saturates the public mind. Citizens feel as though the nation is spinning beyond control, and that sensation fuels an appetite for leaders who promise swift correction. The hunger for simplicity grows, and the capacity for patience withers.

None of this suggests a decline in intelligence. Rosenberg and Mir make no claims of inferiority or moral regression among modern American citizens compared to earlier generations. Their arguments concern cognitive load and market pressures, respectively. When democratic life accelerates, when information multiplies, and when institutions lose the capacity to filter passion, citizens confront demands that exceed normal limits. Social media magnifies those pressures. Each citizen now carries a digital smartphone and participates in a perpetual referendum on national emotion while sipping morning coffee. Madison worked to scatter influence across geography; modern platforms collapse geography into a single screen. Citizens no longer deliberate across distance—citizens react

---

distributed the full recording (Reynolds, 2006). As a conservative, I never found Dean's politics persuasive, yet as an American, I remain troubled by a political culture where a single viral clip carries more weight than the content of a person's character. The moment revealed how a single image or brief soundbite can produce a factional narrative faster than verified facts can reach the public.

within seconds. To Rosenberg, the psychological consequences are immense.

Rosenberg also observes that populist narratives succeed because those narratives relieve cognitive burden. Populism promises a clear "us" and a clear "enemy." Mir identifies a similar shift in the media environment. Top-down journalism once framed national life around an external adversary—most famously the Soviet threat. Bottom-up digital media now seeks a constant internal antagonist—a designated "them." Platforms feed on anger by turning fellow citizens into rivals, because outrage sustains attention. Populist narratives supply certainty where a republic presents doubt, unity where a republic presents disagreement, and speed where a republic presents delay. Such narratives resonate because they reduce the mental labor required for democratic life. The overwhelmed mind seizes slogans and symbols as refuge: chants like 'Lock her up!'—heard repeatedly at rallies during the 2016 presidential campaign (Moody, 2016)—become viral mnemonic shorthand that lowers cognitive burden without the need for a more burdensome full narrative. Neither Rosenberg nor Mir grounds these warnings in claims about reduced intelligence; both argue that contemporary complexity exceeds what many citizens can manage without mental exhaustion.

The Founders feared similar pressures, although they spoke in the idiom of passion, virtue, and self-command and never imagined a digital age. Despite technological change, human nature remains the same. Rosenberg writes in the language of cognitive psychology; Mir writes in the language of post-journalism. Both reach the same conclusion: democracy rests on habits that require cultivation, not assumption. A republic does not collapse because citizens disagree—whether disagreement travels through digital signals or quill-pen ink. A republic collapses when citizens lose the capacity, or the will, to disagree within the boundaries of reason and restraint. When citizens retreat into camps that promise emotional refuge rather than reflective judgment, the Republic feels the strain.

The point is citizen's have not dumb. They are overwhelmed. Figure 11 illustrates a structural imbalance that has widened over the course of American history. The Cognitive Capacity Index (CCI) rises gradually from the Founding through the nineteenth century, reflecting slow gains in literacy and schooling, accelerates during the twentieth century with the expansion of mass education and documented improvements in abstract reasoning, and then flattens as those gains yield diminishing returns. This trajectory is consistent with research on long-term cognitive trends, particularly the Flynn Effect, which identifies substantial twentieth-century improvements in test performance on abstract reasoning tasks but offers limited evidence for continued acceleration in recent decades (Flynn, 1987, 2007; Trahan et al., 2014).

The CCI serves as a proxy for the population's trained ability to process abstract, symbolic, and decontextualized information, drawing on long-run trends in literacy, formal schooling, and twentieth-century gains in abstract reasoning commonly associated with the Flynn Effect. The Information Load Index (ILI) approximates the volume, velocity, and fragmentation of information confronting the average citizen, incorporating historical changes in communication media, publication frequency, and information transmission speed. The shaded region highlights the post-1970 period, when information growth accelerates faster than cognitive capacity. Both indices are theoretical reconstructions rather than direct historical measurements.

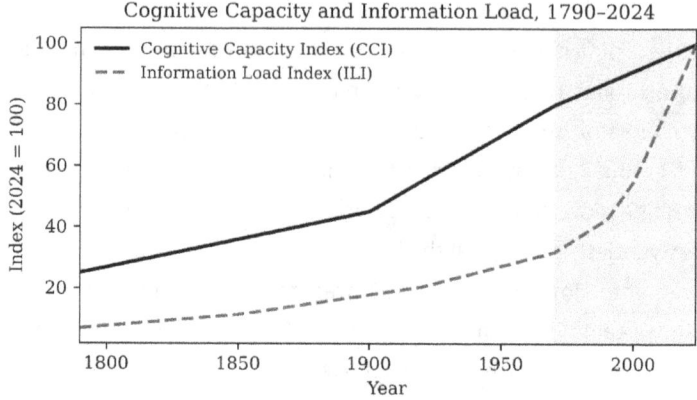

Figure 11. Cognitive Capacity and Information Load, 1790–2024. This graph compares two constructed indices normalized to a common baseline (2024 = 100).

The ILI, by contrast, grows modestly in the early republic—when information was locally bounded, slow-moving, and largely redundant—but rises sharply with the advent of mass print, electronic broadcast media, and, later, digital networks. Studies of information consumption show that while time spent with media increases only gradually, the volume and intensity of information exposure grow rapidly as communication technologies compress transmission time and multiply channels (Bohn & Short, 2012; Hilbert & López, 2011). After roughly 1970, institutional mediation gives way to direct cognitive exposure, shifting the burden of sensemaking from systems to individuals. The figure does not imply declining intelligence or civic virtue. Instead, the graph visualizes a growing mismatch between human cognitive adaptation—which progresses incrementally—and the exponential growth of information environments that modern democratic citizens are expected to navigate without comparable institutional buffering. In such conditions, slogans like "Lock her up" thrive because such demagoguery lower the cognitive cost of participation, offering certainty and emotional release without the burden of sustained deliberation.

The Founding Test

The strain modern democracies place on the mind clarifies why the Republic depends on structure rather than sentiment. Theory alone cannot reveal the full measure of republican safeguards. The American story gained definition when constitutional design confronted actual pressure. Moments of democratic turbulence—Shays's Rebellion, secession, the 1876 crisis, McCarthyism, and Jim Crow—pressed against weak points that surface whenever majorities move faster than judgment. Those episodes reveal how structural design absorbs forces that overwhelm more immediate forms of self-rule. The sections that follow trace those storms and reveal the structure of how a federal republic, rather than a simple democracy, carries a diverse nation through conflict without surrendering national purpose—more republic, less cowbell. The discussion of the next few sections represent case studies to demonstrate the Madisonian structure at work.

The story of more republic begins with the nation's founding. The early Confederation balanced thirteen sovereign democracies on a fragile frame with no executive authority, no national judiciary, and no dependable mechanism for collective action. State legislatures responded to local pressures with a speed that delighted immediate constituencies and alarmed leaders who had just fought a revolution. Relief laws favored debtors, printing presses flooded communities with devalued paper currency, and commercial disputes hardened into regional quarrels. The structure encouraged rapid swings in state policy driven by short-term emotion rather than enduring judgment. The Articles of Confederation had become a failure. The Articles lacked sufficient federal power.

The Well-Constructed Republic

James Madison watched the turmoil with growing alarm. Surveying the Articles of Confederation, he concluded that "the present System neither has nor deserves advocates" (Madison, 1787). As earlier sections in this book have noted, he studied the behavior of the state democracies with the same intensity that previous generations reserved for military campaigns. One biographer describes Madison during these years as "the best informed man in America on the principles of government," drawing lessons directly from the legislative turbulence that followed independence (Ricks, 2020). Madison recognized a pattern: small electorates, compressed geography, and waves of public anger produced the "mischiefs of faction," eruptions that overwhelmed long-range policy and left no space for durable judgment (Ketcham, 1990; Madison, 2016). His genius lay in discerning structure where others saw chaos and in designing a republic strong enough to transform civic emotion into constitutional endurance.

Shays's Rebellion confirmed the nationalists' fears.* As historian Leonard Richards documents, armed farmers marched on courthouses, state governments hesitated, and the Confederation Congress possessed no mechanism to respond (Richards, 2014). Feldman notes that Madison reached his breaking point during these months, concluding that a loose alliance of democratic states could never secure a continent-sized republic (Feldman, 2017). The violence in Massachusetts capped a long sequence of democratic

---

* Historians commonly use the term *nationalists* to describe Madison, Hamilton, Washington, and other leaders during the 1780s who argued that the Articles of Confederation lacked the authority necessary for national stability. Gordon Wood (2011), Ralph Ketcham (1990), and other historians outline the nationalist coalition and critique the state-level democratic turbulence.

whirlwinds and persuaded Madison that only structural reform could steady the nation.

The Philadelphia Convention opened in May 1787 with Shays's crisis fresh in memory. Delegates carried regional grievances and written instructions from home, and many bore their own experience with democratic turbulence. Washington enforced strict rules of secrecy, barring public reporting and private disclosure so that delegates could revise positions without external pressure. Madison supported those measures because he believed constitutional design required distance from the emotional swings that had shaken the states. The delegates created a chamber for reflection rather than reaction—an environment where long-term architecture could outweigh the immediacy that had destabilized the Confederation.

The Constitution that emerged bore little resemblance to the state democracies that had produced the earlier volatility. A bicameral Congress reflected two forms of political identity—the People and the states—through different electoral rhythms. The executive carried independent authority rather than serving as a legislative instrument. The federal judiciary guarded constitutional boundaries and preserved the architecture that delegates hoped would steady a continental nation. These adjustments were not to the Articles; these guardrails were built for endurance as a new form of government.

The delegates understood the scale of the country they hoped to hold together. A continental republic demanded a wider sphere because faction behaves differently across great distances. Citizens in Boston faced different pressures than farmers in Virginia or merchants in Charleston. Madison argued that a large republic would dilute destructive passions by forcing competing groups to negotiate rather than dominate—a claim he articulated most clearly in *Federalist No. 10* (Madison, 2016). The Constitution filtered democratic energy through institutions built to slow, steady, and refine public judgment. Gordon Wood describes the resulting framework as a counter-democratic achievement that channeled popular power into durable forms (Wood, 2011). Jack Rakove likewise argues that republican structure, not spontaneity, offered the only workable path for a continental democracy marked by severe regional differences (Rakove, 1998). Madison's logic in *Federalist No. 51*—ambition balanced by ambition—captured the rationale for a republic built to withstand pressure.

The early Republic proved the point. Federal authority stabilized the currency, facilitated a national market, and negotiated from a position of strength abroad—achievements that would have been impossible under the Articles (Feldman, 2017; Wood, 2011). These gains did not rise from democratic surges. They rose from a constitutional architecture that absorbed conflict without breaking. Shays's Rebellion faded, but the lesson endured: democracies formed at a narrow scale struggled to manage sudden anger, while the larger Republic created space for disagreement without dissolution (Rakove, 1998). The Founding became the first demonstration that structural restraint could preserve popular government across a continent. Later generations—from Reconstruction through the Civil Rights era—would stress the system with far greater force, yet the core architecture held. The Philadelphia Convention supplied the blueprint for endurance, and the young nation began proving Madison correct. A republic, not democracy alone, carries the American experiment forward.

The Secession Test

Secession—perhaps the gravest test of Madison's Republic—was democracy's claim against republican sovereignty. Regional majorities attempted to elevate local preference above the national covenant, and the conflict forced the country to confront a question the Framers never settled. Could the Union survive when state

More Republic, Less Cowbell

conventions asserted a sovereignty greater than the sovereign People of the United States? Were "we, the states" greater than "we, the People"? States' rights framed the legal argument; slavery drove the moral and political confrontation. Secession delivered the test Madison feared most, and Article IV, Section 4—the Constitution's guarantee of protection against "domestic Violence," drafted in response to Shays's Rebellion—provided the constitutional ground Abraham Lincoln needed to resist disunion (Ricks, 2020).

Madison's Constitution never fully resolved the tension between state power and federal power. Instead, Madison designed a republican structure strong enough to confront that conflict and, when required, to summon the federal authority Lincoln later defended at Cooper Union when he argued that "right makes might" (Lincoln, 1860).* Southern conventions followed a similar logic in reverse. Delegates, armed with local majorities, voted to leave the

---

* Lincoln delivered this line during the Cooper Union Address in New York City on February 27, 1860, a speech crafted to demonstrate that the Founders opposed the expansion of slavery and that moral clarity required national resolve. Near its close, Lincoln shifted from constitutional argument to moral appeal: "Let us have faith that right makes might, and in that faith, let us, to the end, dare to do our duty, as we understand it."

The speech reshaped Lincoln's national standing. Eastern newspapers praised the address, Republican leaders took notice, and Lincoln emerged from the event as a serious presidential contender. Many historians regard Cooper Union as the moment that lifted Lincoln from regional prominence to national leadership (Goodwin, 2009).

In contrast to Lincoln, Thucydides' account of the Melian Dialogue—set during the Peloponnesian War in 416 BCE—offered the ancient world's starkest formulation of power politics: justice applies only among equals, and strength defines outcome. The original claim that might makes right. Lincoln's claim that right must make might inverts that logic entirely, embedding moral authority within constitutional force rather than leaving justice hostage to power alone. The distance between those two propositions marks the distance between empire and republic.

The Well-Constructed Republic

Union through procedures that resembled ordinary democratic practice. Elizabeth Varon's *Disunion!* traces how that confidence developed over decades, as Southern leaders embraced the rhetoric of withdrawal whenever national politics turned against regional interests (Varon, 2008). The Civil War would ultimately decide whether local majorities could outweigh national majorities—and whether the Union itself was merely a compact of convenience. Lincoln won the presidency with clear Northern support and no Southern electoral votes, confirming a sectional fracture that democratic procedures alone could not repair. A political order governed solely by shifting majorities would not have survived that strain—and history records how narrowly the United States escaped that fate.

Yet the Republic held—if only by force—because the Constitution created more than a voluntary partnership. Madison learned from Shays's Rebellion that a government unable to answer an insurrection could not endure. The Constitution, therefore, armed the new Republic with the authority the Confederation lacked: national power that reached individuals rather than operating through states. Doris Kearns Goodwin shows how Lincoln relied on that structure when he argued that no state could dissolve the national bond formed by the People acting in their collective capacity (Goodwin, 2009).* The Union survived—although a devastating civil war

---

* As I argue in *The Art of the Compromise* (Page, 2024), the American Union does not function as an at-will association. The Constitution contains no exit clause—no analogue to Brexit, no provision resembling the withdrawal rules that govern the European Union, and nothing comparable to the secession formulas that structured the Soviet Union. The Framers created a national people, not a compact among sovereign states, and the Constitution therefore binds the Republic to a perpetual union. Secessionist claims in the nineteenth century contradicted the architecture established in 1787 and ignored the absence of a constitutional path for

was required to enforce the constitutional order—because the republican frame located the People's sovereignty above the passions of state assemblies. Those assemblies claimed to speak for "the South," yet those claims excluded millions of enslaved Americans. Whatever mandate Southern leaders asserted rested entirely on the preferences of a small class of White elites.

The crisis deepened once Southern leaders claimed democratic—and not republican—legitimacy for secession. Their conventions and referenda spoke in the language of popular authority. The American Republic answered with national force directed by a president who treated the Union as perpetual. Eric Foner's *The Second Founding* (2019) explains how Lincoln's stance preserved the authority required to wage the war and then reconstruct the nation around a broader definition of citizenship, equal protection, and national belonging. A plebiscitary system does not grant a single executive the stabilizing authority required for that task. A republic does.

The conflict echoed an earlier storm. Jon Meacham's *American Lion* (2009) describes Andrew Jackson confronting nullification in the 1830s with unambiguous resolve. That confrontation—now known as the Nullification Crisis—foreshadowed secession. Jackson rejected the doctrine of state sovereignty, asserted national supremacy, and was prepared to enforce federal law by arms if required. Lincoln later invoked Jackson's arguments throughout the Civil War (Goodwin, 2009). Jackson did not resolve the sectional

---

withdrawal. Lincoln emphasized this point repeatedly. Southern states had not merely entered rebellion; they attempted to secede through state conventions that claimed democratic legitimacy. Southern leaders believed those votes supplied legal authority to leave the Union. Lincoln argued, correctly, that the Constitution granted no such authority.

The Well-Constructed Republic

divide, yet his response demonstrated what a republic could supply: national authority strong enough to restrain regional majorities and to preserve time for constitutional development.

Lincoln used the time Jackson purchased and expanded the constitutional logic Jackson had advanced. The Civil War forced the nation to confront the foundational compromise of slavery—an institution preserved in 1787 because the delegates feared disunion more than injustice. The conflict produced a constitutional transformation. The Thirteenth, Fourteenth, and Fifteenth Amendments expanded national authority and achieved in practice the federal negative Madison hoped to secure in Philadelphia. Foner describes these amendments as a refounding—a reconstruction of the constitutional order that introduced federal guarantees of citizenship, due process, and equal protection (Foner, 2019). Those guarantees remained largely dormant in the nineteenth century, but the Reconstruction Amendments supplied the foundation that would later animate the incorporation doctrine and the Bill of Rights, moving our nation closer to a more perfect Union.

The Confederate gamble rested on a faith in democratic passion—the belief that White-only state majorities could dissolve a Union they no longer favored. A strengthened republic proved otherwise. A constitutional architecture built for endurance absorbed the greatest rupture in American history. Reconstruction reshaped the national creed and fortified the Constitution against entrenched injustice. The Republic did not emerge unscarred, yet the Republic did emerge intact and more faithful to the principles that gave the nation shape—all men are created equal. A repaired Union did not guarantee stability, however, and the decade that followed delivered a new test of whether republican structure could restrain democratic turmoil.

The 1876 Test

Little known in modern American history lessons (Baier & Whitney, 2021), the presidential election of 1876 represents a fragile moment nearly as consequential—if not as monumental—as the Civil War. The contested election arrived during national exhaustion. The country carried fresh scars from the war, and Reconstruction faced persistent resistance across the former Confederacy. Federal troops protected new gains in citizenship and voting rights for formerly enslaved Americans, while political violence surged in several states. The return of civil conflict remained possible. The cowbell's ring of democracy once again threatened the stability of the Republic.

The contest between Republican Rutherford B. Hayes and Democrat Samuel J. Tilden collapsed quickly into chaos. Modern Americans remember the uncertainty surrounding Bush–Gore in 2000, but the crisis of 1876 reached deeper. Louisiana, South Carolina, and Florida submitted competing Electoral College certifications. Rival officials in each state claimed authority to speak for the electorate. The Twelfth Amendment outlined how Congress should count electoral votes, but that amendment did not anticipate a moment when states would present contradictory slates. Congress confronted a constitutional problem without an established remedy. The crisis revealed a central truth of the American design: a constitutional text cannot resolve each collision in democratic life, and the Republic depends on representatives and institutional structure to guide the nation through moments the Framers could not predict. Yet, the structure held.[*]

---

[*] A revealing contrast appears in two other extremely close presidential elections. After the narrow Kennedy–Nixon contest of 1960, Richard Nixon

Partisan divisions hardened. Democrats argued that Tilden had won a clear majority. Republicans pointed to paramilitary violence that suppressed Black* voters and compromised state elections. Organizations such as the Red Shirts in South Carolina and the White League in Louisiana used intimidation and targeted violence to drive Black citizens from polling places—a pattern documented by Eric Foner in his study of Reconstruction's political struggles (Foner, 2005). Bret Baier's *To Rescue the Republic* (2021) describes the tension inside both parties. Each side feared manipulation. Each side

---

declined to pursue extensive legal challenges despite documented voting irregularities. Nixon later suggested that prolonging the dispute risked a constitutional crisis and permanent damage to public confidence. That decision was consistent with a party-centered system in which elite gatekeeping and reputational buffering preserved future political opportunity; indeed, Nixon would secure his party's nomination and the presidency eight years later (Milkis, 1995; Polsby, 1983).

By contrast, the disputed Bush–Gore election of 2000 unfolded within a fully democratized, candidate-centered system shaped by post-1968 reforms. In that environment, electoral legitimacy flows directly from mass participation, and defeat is more likely to be interpreted as personal repudiation rather than contingent loss. Scholars have noted that this shift weakens party mediation and strengthens incentives to contest outcomes through judicial channels, a path that had become increasingly normalized in modern election law (Aldrich, 1995; Pildes, 2016). The contrast suggests that institutional design—not merely individual temperament—shapes whether losing candidates accept electoral defeat or seek further adjudication.

* The early chapters of this book refer to "formerly enslaved Americans" when describing the decades immediately following emancipation. That language reflects the historical moment shaped by the Civil War and Reconstruction. As the narrative moves into the twentieth century, I adopt the terms *Black Americans* and *White Americans*, following the conventions used by leading historians of the period. The term *Black*, capitalized, acknowledges a shared historical experience, a cultural identity forged through struggle, and a political community that sought full citizenship during the long campaign for Civil Rights.

More Republic, Less Cowbell

believed that the stakes reached beyond a single contest. Congress responded by creating an Electoral Commission—five senators, five representatives, and five Supreme Court justices—a republican structure designed to provide institutional balance during a moment of constitutional uncertainty (Kuntz, 1969). Americans later witnessed a similar ambiguity in Bush–Gore, yet the Republic endured both crises because republican architecture channeled indeterminacy into an orderly process—imperfect, contested, and slow, yet strong enough to bend public passion toward a solution acceptable to the public.

Republics, more than democracies, can handle such ambiguity. Ambiguity does not break a republic. Ambiguity defines a republic. Democratic impulses rush toward immediacy; republican architecture turns uncertainty into space for judgment. Modern scholars of constitutional design—including Sartori (1997), Lijphart (1999), Linz (1990), and Manin (1997)—each argues that layered institutions manage uncertainty more effectively than direct popular rule.

As a result, the 1876 Electoral Commission awarded the disputed electoral votes to Hayes by an 8–7 margin. Many Americans felt betrayed, yet the country accepted the outcome because the decision moved through a recognizable republican form—an openly constituted process grounded in congressional authority rather than raw partisan force. Institutional process carried greater weight than partisan preference. The Republic demonstrated that disappointment need not threaten national cohesion when the dispute moves through a structure capable of containing political emotion.

The compromise that followed—the agreement that ended Reconstruction and withdrew federal protection for formerly enslaved Americans—marked a painful step backward. The nation had taken two steps forward through the Civil War and the Reconstruction Amendments, only to surrender part of that progress in 1877. That retreat cleared the way for what came to be known as *Jim Crow*: a regime of state and local laws, customs, and enforced social norms

The Well-Constructed Republic

designed to reassert racial hierarchy after emancipation. The term itself, borrowed from a degrading minstrel caricature,* captured both the cruelty and the intent of the system. Jim Crow disenfranchised Black citizens, segregated public life, sanctioned violence through law and neglect, and rendered constitutional guarantees hollow in large regions of the country. Foner (2019) describes the 1877 compromise as an abandonment of the Republic's most vulnerable citizens, a judgment confirmed by the rapid consolidation of Jim Crow rule across the South. Republican progress rarely advances in straight lines. Madison understood that human nature and faction could bend even the strongest design, and Lincoln reminded the country that moral purpose requires patience as well as resolve. The bill for that bargain would come due in the twentieth century.

A republic grows through durable gains rather than flawless moments. The country faced not only the obligation to protect formerly enslaved Americans but also the Pressure created by a defeated South struggling under military occupation and political exclusion. From a modern vantage point, the suffering of White Southerners can appear morally irrelevant. Yet history offers

---

* The term *Jim Crow* originated not as a neutral descriptor but as the name of a degrading minstrel character popularized in the 1830s by white performer Thomas D. Rice. Performed in blackface, "Jim Crow" caricatured Black Americans as ignorant, lazy, and subhuman, reinforcing racial stereotypes for mass audiences in the antebellum North and South. By the late nineteenth century, the term migrated from stage performance into political language, becoming shorthand for the legal and social regime that enforced racial segregation and Black disenfranchisement after Reconstruction. The adoption of a theatrical slur as the label for a governing system was not incidental. The slur reflected the moral logic of the regime itself: a deliberate effort to normalize inequality, trivialize citizenship, and render constitutional rights performative rather than real. See (Lott, 2013)

repeated warnings—Weimar Germany, humiliated by the Versailles settlement chief among them—about the dangers of humiliation without reintegration. The Compromise of 1877 opened the door to Jim Crow, but a renewed civil war would have shattered the Union and fractured the continent. Hindsight simplifies moral judgment. The deeper truth rests in the Madisonian calculus, where moral advance arrives unevenly and constitutional growth must contend with human limitation. Progress rather than perfection preserves a constitutional frame strong enough to carry future generations toward fuller justice.

Even this flawed settlement revealed the strength of the republican structure. The country resolved a contested election through institutional design rather than force. Congress created a process that required negotiation across branches, and the nation accepted a result that disappointed millions. A direct democracy could not have contained the passions of 1876. A republic could. The structure restrained panic long enough to prevent the collapse of national authority and the reopening of sectional conflict. The Republic survived another storm—imperfectly, yet decisively—because republican architecture can diffuse conflict, manage ambiguity, and carry a divided nation through moments when fear outweighs clarity. Yet, the next storm—McCarthyism—would test the frame in an entirely different way, when national anxiety gathered not around ballots or armies but around suspicion, accusation, and the politics of fear.

The McCarthy Test

Democratic passions can surge with remarkable speed, yet the Republic was built to withstand such surges. Few moments have tested that design as sharply as the early 1950s, when fear of Soviet infiltration created a national climate in which accusation carried more weight than verification. Thomas Ricks observes that the

The Well-Constructed Republic

Founders anticipated such pressure—not the Red Scare specifically, but demagoguery. Madison warned that "enlightened statesmen will not always be at the helm," and Jefferson cautioned that "bad men will sometimes get in" and manipulate public sentiment for personal gain (Ricks, 2020). Senator Joseph McCarthy exploited the moment of anxiety, giving rise to the infamous phenomenon that soon carried his name.

McCarthy directed Cold War anxiety toward diplomats, scholars, and civil servants—targets whose reputations guaranteed public attention and outrage. Historian Richard Hofstadter later described this style of populism as the "politics of resentment," a mode of politics anchored in suspicion rather than deliberation (Hofstadter, 2012). Among McCarthy's most prominent targets were General George C. Marshall, the architect of the Allied victory and the future Secretary of State. McCarthy, offering no evidence, claimed that Marshall had "with great stubbornness and skill...always and invariably serve[d] the world policy of the Kremlin"—a remarkable charge given Marshall's record. The claims were false and later dismissed by military historians and the Eisenhower administration, yet such accusations inflicted real reputational damage during the early 1950s (Roll, 2020; Stoler, 2021). Polls from 1953 revealed broad public sympathy for these accusations—even the most extraordinary ones—because the accusations matched the anxieties of the moment. McCarthyism embodied the democratic instinct for speed during national unease, and McCarthy supplied that speed with theatrical confidence. Media coverage amplified his charges, creating a feedback loop that modern digital readers would readily recognize. As Andrey Mir (2020) observes, mass attention rewards provocation.

The republican structure resisted the democratic surge that carried McCarthy to prominence. The Senate's scale, procedures, and longer terms insulated the Chamber from the daily turbulence of public fear. McCarthy's conduct during the Army–McCarthy hearings breached those expectations of restraint. His interruptions, accusations, and intimidation strained the body's traditions, revealing the limits of a politics sustained by spectacle and demagoguery. David Oshinsky observes that the hearings displayed not only McCarthy's methods but also the institutional boundaries he attempted to bend to his will (Oshinsky, 2019). McCarthy was exposed as a sheep in wolf's clothing. The moment called for a response rooted in constitutional rhythm rather than partisan retaliation.

That response emerged from a coalition of republican actors who understood that democratic enthusiasm alone could not resolve the crisis. Dwight D. Eisenhower refused to elevate Joseph McCarthy by entering a public feud, choosing instead to protect the Army and allow Senate procedures to expose McCarthy's conduct. Eisenhower grasped a core republican lesson: demagogues draw strength from confrontation with legitimate authority. By refusing to share the stage, he denied McCarthy the stature he sought and allowed institutional process to drain spectacle from accusation. At Eisenhower's direction, Richard Nixon, then vice president, quietly encouraged Senate Republicans to defend their institution rather than indulge a momentary populist wave—an approach later scholars would describe as institutional containment rather than performative opposition.

In the Senate itself, resistance took a different form. Margaret Chase Smith delivered her *Declaration of Conscience*, warning her party against riding to victory on what she called the "Four Horsemen of Calumny—Fear, Ignorance, Bigotry, and Smear." Just moments before the speech, Smith encountered Joseph McCarthy on the Senate subway. "Margaret, you look very serious," he remarked. "Are you going to make a speech?" Smith answered plainly: "Yes—and you will not like it." She delivered the address that afternoon (U.S. Senate Historical Office, 1950).

The Well-Constructed Republic

Conscience alone, however, did not end McCarthy's influence. A few years later, Arthur V. Watkins, a Republican from Utah, chaired the Senate's select committee charged with evaluating McCarthy's conduct. The response turned on hearings, cross-examination, and documented evidence rather than counter-spectacle—an approach that mirrored the deliberative mechanisms the Framers believed necessary when democratic passion threatened institutional norms. As Ellen Schrecker observes, this methodical process helped restore constitutional order as public hysteria began to recede (Schrecker, 1998).

Television brought the Army–McCarthy hearings into homes across the country. The medium that amplified McCarthy's rise also revealed the recklessness beneath the performance. When Army counsel Joseph Welch confronted McCarthy—"Have you no sense of decency, sir?"—the rebuke carried moral force precisely because the public could see McCarthy's behavior unfiltered (Oshinsky, 2019). Yet televised revelation alone could not correct the imbalance. The Republic had to act through its institutions. Eisenhower withheld public comment but supported the Senate's internal mechanisms; Nixon advised party colleagues to defend the Chamber's authority; and Watkins shepherded a process that separated accusation from evidence. The republican structure, not the popular audience, delivered the decisive judgment.

In December 1954, the Senate voted 67–22 to censure McCarthy. The author Sam Tanenhaus underscores that McCarthyism thrived on democratic energy and could only be halted by a republican institution capable of slowing that energy long enough to assess the facts (Tanenhaus, 1998).* McCarthy lost the spectacle that sustained his influence the moment the Senate reclaimed the tempo of constitutional deliberation. The episode illustrates Madison's design. *Federalist No. 63* envisioned the Senate as a check against "sudden and violent passions" (Madison, 2016). McCarthy's rise revealed the danger; the Senate's response revealed the protection. Careers ended and freedoms suffered, but the Republic endured because the Senate possessed structural mechanisms built to restrain passion and restore deliberation, despite the loud cowbell of McCarthyism and demagoguery. The system bent but did not break.

The McCarthy episode revealed how republican institutions can restrain sudden democratic passion. The Civil Rights era would test the opposite danger: what happens when democratic majorities entrench injustice through stable, enduring control.

The Civil Rights Test

From federal withdrawal in 1877 through the years surrounding both world wars, White voting majorities across the South believed their choices protected community order, even as those choices

---

* The commentary by Sam Tanenhaus is noteworthy, given the animosity he documented between Chambers and McCarthy. Whittaker Chambers—an ex-Soviet spy who defected in the 1930s—became a central figure in the Alger Hiss case, a clash that helped ignite the early Cold War anxiety McCarthy later exploited. Chambers viewed McCarthy as reckless and intellectually shallow, warning that McCarthy's methods threatened to discredit legitimate concerns about communist espionage. Tanenhaus's biography of Chambers therefore illuminates both the emotional terrain that fueled McCarthyism and the sharp divide between a genuine witness to Soviet infiltration and a politician who rode public fear toward personal power.

The Well-Constructed Republic

hardened racial separation. The region sustained that confidence for generations. White voters relied on referenda, legislative sessions, and state constitutional rewrites—such as Mississippi's 1890 convention—to preserve segregation through law (Foner, 2019; Perman, 2001). Those measures expressed the preferences of White communities and ignored the dignity of Black neighbors forced to live under the resulting order. Democratic majorities constructed a racial hierarchy designed to endure, a hierarchy Isabel Wilkerson describes as a caste system engineered to outlast individual lifetimes (Wilkerson, 2020). White voters controlled legislatures, courts, sheriffs, and party primaries. That control guaranteed the survival of the order through institutional continuity. No state ballot would have dismantled Jim Crow because those who benefited from the structure supervised the machinery of state democracy.

The Reconstruction Amendments created a national promise grounded in equal citizenship. Federal withdrawal through the 1877 Compromise drained that promise of force. Courts narrowed the Fourteenth Amendment through restrictive interpretations. State governments developed new instruments of exclusion. Poll taxes, literacy tests, grandfather clauses, and White primaries restored political dominance to those who had defended slavery and then defended segregation. Eric Foner describes the post-Reconstruction settlement as a "counterrevolution," a deliberate attempt to reassert racial hierarchy under the appearance of legal order (Foner, 2019). The loud ring of cowbell majorities achieved through procedure what earlier generations had pursued through violence. However, the Republic had not yet spoken its final word.

The twentieth century revealed both the limits of small democracy and the strength supplied by a large republic. In response to the failures exposed by Jim Crow, the Supreme Court gradually revived the Bill of Rights through the incorporation doctrine, applying fundamental liberties against state governments through the

Fourteenth Amendment. Rights once directed solely at federal action became national guarantees that no state could abridge. In effect, the Court supplied what Madison had sought unsuccessfully at the Constitutional Convention: a functional federal negative capable of restraining state abuses when local majorities hardened into injustice. That judicial shift would become indispensable to the Civil Rights Movement.

The need for incorporation arose from an earlier constitutional failure. In the late nineteenth century, the Court had legitimated racial hierarchy through the doctrine of "separate but equal." The phrase entered American constitutional law in *Plessy v. Ferguson* (1896), which upheld a Louisiana statute mandating racially segregated railroad cars. Writing for the majority, Justice Henry Billings Brown concluded that segregation did not violate the Equal Protection Clause so long as the state provided facilities that were nominally equal. In practice, equality existed only on paper. The doctrine authorized racial separation across public life, sanctioned gross disparities in education, housing, and public accommodations, and supplied legal cover for the Jim Crow regime that followed the collapse of Reconstruction (Klarman, 2004).

The National Association for the Advancement of Colored People (NAACP), founded in 1909, emerged as the leading national organization dedicated to securing equal citizenship for Black Americans through litigation and public advocacy. NAACP leaders recognized that state ballots would never correct state injustice because those who benefited from segregation controlled the levers of state authority. Thurgood Marshall—chief counsel of the NAACP Legal Defense Fund and the future first Black Justice of the Supreme Court—guided a strategy grounded in constitutional principle and empirical evidence. Marshall and his colleagues filed challenges county by county across the U.S. and documented unequal conditions with precision (Klarman, 2004). That strategy culminated in the landmark Civil Rights victory of *Brown v. Board of*

Education (1954). More Republic had begun to quiet the cowbell of segregation, although the nation still faced substantial work.

Chief Justice Earl Warren's unanimous opinion in *Brown* rested on the Equal Protection Clause rather than regional sentiment. Warren emphasized both citizenship and the psychological and civic harms created by enforced separation. In his memoir, Warren (1977) later described unanimity as essential to the ruling's national authority. The decision marked a national interpretation of constitutional duty that state legislatures shaped by Jim Crow would never have delivered. *Brown* also demonstrated how a judiciary armed with the Fourteenth Amendment and incorporation could act as the functional equivalent of the federal negative Madison sought in Philadelphia. A court shielded from electoral retaliation performed exactly what Madison hoped republican structure would allow: restraint of faction and protection of rights against determined majorities. The decision fortified the Republic and pried loose another brick from the wall that upheld the fiction of "separate but equal."

Widespread resistance followed. Southern legislators issued the *Southern Manifesto* in 1956, a congressional declaration signed by nineteen senators and seventy-seven representatives that pledged to use "all lawful means" to block desegregation and condemned *Brown* as a "clear abuse of judicial power" (Green et al., 2010). Southern governors campaigned on defiance, and Southern school boards adopted delay as doctrine. Democratic majorities across the region supported obstruction because segregation preserved the local hierarchy that those voters defended at the ballot box. The confrontation revealed a truth familiar to the Founders: majorities often possess a strong appetite for violating fundamental rights when those violations reinforce regional power. Majority rule alone can deliver tyranny over a minority—the central fallacy of pure democracy.

More Republic, Less Cowbell

Federal authority stepped in where Southern legislatures refused to honor constitutional duty. President Dwight Eisenhower sent the 101st Airborne Division to Little Rock in 1957 after Governor Orval Faubus blocked the integration of Central High School. Historian Stephen Ambrose notes that Eisenhower viewed enforcement of judicial authority as a federal obligation, even when Southern voters rejected desegregation (Ambrose, 2014). Eisenhower acted under constitutional duty rather than regional sentiment. His response demonstrated Madison's design in practice: a national government strong enough to restrain local majorities when those majorities attempted to nullify constitutional rights.

Most importantly, Congress codified *Brown v. Board of Education* through the Civil Rights Act of 1964 and the Voting Rights Act of 1965. Southern delegations did not author those statutes. A national coalition, shaped by the moral reckoning that followed World War II, delivered legislation aimed directly at the racial order Jim Crow had preserved for nearly a century. The victory arrived slowly, but its meaning was unmistakable: the Republic at last began aligning its laws with its creed, converting the promise that "all men are created equal" from a rhetorical inheritance into an enforceable national obligation—choosing progress through law over the illusion of moral perfection.

President Lyndon Johnson understood the political cost. Shortly after signing the Civil Rights Act, he told his aide Bill Moyers, "Well, I think we may have lost the South for your lifetime—and mine" (Kaiser, 2023). A Southern man shaped by a racially segregated culture, Johnson nonetheless recognized that Civil Rights legislation would fracture the Democratic coalition and accelerate the South's realignment toward the Republican Party. He accepted that consequence because the nation required a national answer to a national wrong. The time for progress had arrived. The Civil Rights Act dismantled the final legal supports of "separate but equal," and the Voting Rights Act removed the last formal barriers denying Black citizens full participation in American political life.

The Voting Rights Act delivered the sharpest structural correction in the century after Reconstruction because the statute targeted the machinery of exclusion directly. The Act prohibited tactics designed to suppress minority participation and placed jurisdictions with entrenched patterns of exclusion under federal oversight. Critics warned of federal intrusion into state authority. Supporters pointed to the constitutional obligation to secure voting rights when state institutions violated those rights. Michael Klarman argues that the Act finally ended nearly a century of voter suppression maintained by White majorities in the South (Klarman, 2004).

Republican structure—not state democracy—moved the American experiment another step toward a more perfect union.

Harnessing the Noise

If the reader will forgive me for a moment, I want to divert our discussion to gain insight through an analogy to enhance our understanding of these republican tests we have just discussed. The diversion centers around a perhaps unusual topic—the U.S. Apollo moon program—documented in the engaging book *Apollo, the Race to the Moon* (Murray & Cox, 1989). The engineers who designed the F-1 engine for the Saturn V rocket in that daring program faced a problem that no amount of optimism could wish away. The F-1 was the most powerful single-chamber liquid-fueled rocket engine ever built, and its power exposed a flaw that nearly doomed the Apollo program before leaving the ground. When fuel and oxidizer met at the injector plate and ignited inside the combustion chamber, pressure waves formed. Those waves fed on themselves. Oscillations amplified. Engines tore themselves apart in milliseconds.

This phenomenon—combustion instability—was not a minor defect but a systemic one. Early design efforts focused on prevention. If the oscillations could be avoided entirely, the problem would vanish. Engineers tried smoother flows, tighter tolerances, cleaner geometries. No solution worked. The instability was not an anomaly but a natural consequence of extreme energy density. The noise could not be engineered away.

One team took a different approach. Instead of asking how to suppress oscillations, they asked how to survive them.

Their insight was counterintuitive. If instability was inevitable, then stability had to come from structure, not silence. They abandoned the illusion of perfect calm and focused on damping—allowing oscillations to begin, then absorbing and dissipating them before they could cascade into failure. The chose not to eliminate the noise of cowbells but to channel that noise when it arose.

To test that theory, the engineers built a test stand designed to do precisely what no engineer wants a system to do. They intentionally induced instability. They detonated small explosive charges—dynamite—inside the combustion chamber to trigger pressure waves at will. They forced the engine into its worst behavior, again and again, while measuring how the engine responded. Only under those induced extremes could they see what worked. Baffles, cavities, and injector modifications emerged not as ways to prevent oscillation, but as ways to manage the tumult. The final engine design did not eliminate noise. Their design harnessed noise. Stability came not from suppressing energy, but from channeling it.

The F-1 flew because the engineers accepted a hard truth: complex, high-energy systems cannot be made safe by pretending turbulence will not arise. They can only be made safe by structures strong enough to endure the violence.

That lesson extends well beyond rocketry. Each of the constitutional tests examined in this chapter tells the same story in political form. The Founding confronted faction and refused to outlaw dissonance, choosing instead to extend the sphere. Secession revealed the cost of allowing a moral instability to grow unchecked until war became the only damping mechanism left. The crisis of 1876 demonstrated how informal norms could absorb electoral shock when formal rules ran thin. McCarthyism showed that democratic energy, when left unstructured, can consume itself—and that republican institutions exist to slow, not silence, public passion. The Civil Rights struggle forced the nation to confront whether majority rule without constitutional enforcement amounted to justice at all.

In each case, the Republic endured not by eliminating political noise, but by relying on institutional mechanisms capable of absorbing conflict and channeling energy. The temptation in moments of political stress is typically the same: quiet the cowbells. Suppress the voices. Short-circuit the process in the name of efficiency or unity. That temptation misunderstands both democracy and engineering. Noise is not a flaw to be erased. Noise is a signal that energy exists. The task of republican design is not to deny that energy, but to shape it—through structure, restraint, and time—so that the energy produces lift rather than destruction.

The Saturn V did not reach the Moon because its engines were silent. The spacecraft reached the Moon because the designers built a system that could withstand the noise they knew would come.

So too with the American Republic.

In Sum

This chapter has explored the tension between democratic passion and republican design, a tension that animated Madison's deepest fears. Madison worried that concentrated democratic power—especially when shaped by emotion, immediacy, and factional identity—could overwhelm constitutional architecture and consume the liberty a republic aims to preserve. The Founders answered that danger with distance, layers of representation, staggered terms, and a national frame large enough to diffuse political heat before legislation or executive authority changed direction. These devices were not ornamental. These devices formed the core of the American experiment.

Modern political life presses against those stabilizers with unprecedented force. Media environments accelerate anger. Outrage travels faster than deliberation. Citizens receive more political stimulation in a single day than earlier generations encountered across a season. Rosenberg's analysis of cognitive strain helps explain the Pressure placed on voters and institutions (Rosenberg, 2019), while Mir's description of the Viral Editor captures the speed of democratic emotion in a post-journalism age (Mir, 2020). A structure built for measured tempo now faces a permanent storm.

The Trump presidency has revealed that pressure with unusual clarity. Trump did not create the present polarization, and Trump did not emerge as the final consequence of modern cowbell politics. Trump, however, belongs to a long line of demagogues the Founders expected to arise from time to time (Square, 2024). The Framers worked diligently to shield the People from leaders who excel at performance rather than restraint. In the era of Trump, the Left gains no wisdom from panic, and the Right gains no strength from celebrating demagoguery. A republic requires steadier judgment than either impulse provides.

Trump approached the constitutional order with a style shaped by improvisation, personal instinct, and public display. That style collided with the Madisonian expectation that authority would move through measured channels. In his first term, Trump voiced open frustration with those channels, describing the Constitution's architecture as "archaic" and poorly suited to executive action (Borger, 2017). Agencies resisted. Courts rejected expansive claims. Congressional majorities limited presidential ambition. Scholars studying Trump's first term have identified repeated

The Well-Constructed Republic

clashes between presidential desire and institutional guardrails (Driesen, 2024; Millemann, 2017). Those clashes have not destroyed the Republic—as many on the Left have claimed. Those clashes confirmed the continued relevance of republican machinery designed to restrain demagogic energy before that energy reshapes authority.

Trump's presidency reveals neither a story of collapse nor a story of triumph. The tenure exposed both strengths and weaknesses within the constitutional structure. A demagogic style, amplified by modern media, reached the Oval Office, yet constitutional design slowed the pace of unilateral action. Schlefer (2025) argues that the period demonstrated a deeper institutional resilience—resilience rooted in legal continuity, civic infrastructure, and constitutional friction.

That resilience should not invite complacency. A constitutional design that restrains executive power primarily through friction will strain when democratic energy accelerates faster than institutional mechanisms can absorb. Excess democratic pressure—not one individual, not Trump—now tests the constitutional frame (Nord et al., 2025). Trump is not the danger. Too much cowbell is. The American system today suffers less from the presence of Trump—as many critics on the left contend—than from an excess of unfiltered democracy, a quieter distinction but a more consequential one.

The next chapter moves to that diagnosis. The Republic faces a democracy problem: too many direct pressures on representatives, too little space for deliberation, too little insulation from factional surge, and too much expectation that leaders respond instantly rather than govern responsibly. We, thus, next outline reforms aimed at strengthening republican distance in a world that rewards immediacy. Madison's architecture still stands. The task ahead involves renewing a proven system—nearly 250 years in operation—within a constitutional republic.

More Republic, Less Cowbell

Renewal does not begin with silencing the cowbells. Renewal begins with strengthening the structures that once absorbed their sound. The American Republic historically relied on three such mediating institutions: the Chamber, a legislature designed for deliberation rather than immediacy; the Pipeline, a political pipeline that formed leaders before elevating them, and the Press, professional journalists that filtered information instead of amplifying impulse. When those institutions weaken, democratic energy has nowhere to go but straight into authority. The chapter that follows turns to that work of renewal for the Chamber, the Pipeline, and the Press.

CHAPTER 4

The Cowbell Reform

D RUMS THUDDED IN THE summer heat of 1783. Months of unpaid wages had pushed soldiers from the Pennsylvania Line to the edge of mutiny, and several hundred marched into Philadelphia demanding relief. They surrounded the State House and held the delegates of the Confederation Congress under a silent threat. The Articles of Confederation provided no national army, no federal police, and no mechanism to compel protection. The urgency in the streets drowned thoughtful judgment inside—an early cowbell moment when noise overwhelmed structure. Alexander Hamilton and a small committee appealed to the Pennsylvania Executive Council for assistance. President John Dickinson and the council hesitated, uncertain that their own militia would fire on fellow soldiers. With no assurance of safety, the delegates adjourned, gathered quietly the next morning, and slipped out of the city under escort. They reconvened at Nassau Hall in Princeton, a day's ride away, and resumed the nation's business from exile.

Richard B. Morris, the Gouverneur Morris Professor of History at Columbia University and a leading scholar of the nation's founding era, describes this episode as a turning point in American

The Cowbell Reform

constitutional development—a moment when national leaders confronted the reality that Congress could not deliberate freely while operating inside a jurisdiction controlled by a single state (Morris, 1988).

In June 1783, several hundred Continental Army soldiers—unpaid, frustrated, and convinced Congress had abandoned them—surrounded the building where the Confederation Congress met in Philadelphia. Pennsylvania's Executive Council refused to protect the legislators. Alexander Hamilton urged Congress to evacuate quietly, and James Madison recorded that members slipped out a side door and fled the city under threat. Congress reconvened in Princeton, then Annapolis, then Trenton, before finally settling temporarily in New York. The episode convinced Madison that the national legislature required a seat of government under exclusive federal control so no state or local force could ever again intimidate representatives or shape national policy through proximity. The federal city that emerged in 1790 is, in many ways, the institutional child of that humiliation (Ferling, 2016; Rakove, 2019).

Delegates carried that lesson into the Constitutional Convention four years later and embraced the logic of a federal district under exclusive congressional authority. The Residence Clause—the basis for the District of Columbia—created a neutral seat of government so that national decisions would not rest on the resolve of a single governor, a single militia, or a single crowd. The aim was not insulation from the People, but insulation from sudden pressure—protection that preserves the breathing room republican government requires.

Modern America no longer enjoys that buffer. Digital crowds arrive faster than soldiers on cobblestones, and outrage travels farther than any marching column. Pressure lands in an instant. Members track factional temperature rather than substantive text. Cameras, feeds, and algorithmic alerts pull representatives toward performance and away from negotiation. The Founders did not fear citizens; the Founders feared stampedes. The mutiny of 1783 never vanished. The form changed from muskets in the street to lenses in the Chamber and algorithms in each citizen's pocket.

This chapter follows the lesson the delegates learned in 1783: republican government survives only when structure steadies passion. This chapter looks at reforms to the Chamber, the Pipeline, and the Press. The Chamber must recover the distance and discretion that allow committees to function as genuine workshops rather than stages. The Pipeline must once again produce candidates who command durable majorities instead of mobilizing narrow factions. The Press must rebuild an informational center capable of anchoring public judgment amid constant noise. A republic does not endure by amplifying passion. A republic endures when institutions restore the space in which reason can govern.

Too Much Democracy

We begin with reform of the Chamber. The revelation that the United States now endures too much democracy may sound strange, but that challenge now defines public life. A healthy republic does not deny democratic energy, and a healthy republic does not suppress democratic passion. A healthy republic channels democratic force through stabilizing structure—distance, representation, scale, and time. When those guardrails weaken, the promise of republican design begins to unravel. Demagogues rise. Extremism blocks compromise. Impulse displaces deliberation. Citizens experience politics as a continuous referendum rather than steady governance. That description identifies government in the U.S. today.

The problem did not begin because Madison and the other Founders failed to anticipate modern technology—though they surely did. The problem did not arise because republican institutions remained trapped in eighteenth-century design. Technology has changed, yet human nature has not. As we have documented in the previous chapters, the problem emerged because modern reforms—well-intentioned but short-sighted—dismantled too many republican devices that once moderated democratic pressure. The 1994 restructuring of committee power in the House accelerated leadership control. The reforms that followed 1968 made primaries more democratic in theory but more factional in practice. In the twenty-first century, professional journalism has lost the economic base that once supported verification, filtration, and contextual reporting. These shifts promised openness, but these shifts instead delivered speed—and that speed has overwhelmed republican machinery.

Polarization offers one of the clearest signals of that imbalance. I do not treat polarization as a perfect measure of national political health because polarization is only a barometer—a way to assess how difficult compromise has become. As I argued in *The Art of the Compromise* (2024), the Republic never aimed to produce harmony or consensus among the citizenry. Americans are a cantankerous people. The Republic aimed instead to create the conditions where representatives could negotiate differences into legislative progress. The goal has never been unity. The goal has been workable compromises, the hallmark of our Constitution and our Republic.

Polarization is thus a symptom, not a cause, of this shift, and the graphs that follow help illuminate this change. They do not appear as curiosities. They function as diagnostic instruments—evidence that the stabilizing machinery of the Republic no longer absorbs democratic pressure.

The first graph in Fig. 12 demonstrates how public life has stretched away from the political center. Affective polarization offers the clearest signal that the stabilizing machinery of the Republic now operates under strain. The graph shows the American National Election Studies (ANES) Feeling Thermometer (2024). The data reveals a nation that applauds one's own faction while directing sharpened hostility toward the opposing side. Rival-party feeling has eroded since the 1980s, slipping to roughly half of the earlier level. The emotional gap between partisans has widened into a chasm. The distance shown in the figure is not merely psychological. The distance shapes voting behavior, narrows negotiating space, and accelerates the centrifugal forces that Madison feared. Cowbells chime the noise of polarization.

The second graph in Fig. 13 reveals a more acute problem. Congress once operated as the central negotiating table of the Republic. Members traded amendments, forged partial victories, and accepted incremental gains. Committee expertise mattered. Cross-pressured districts—where voters held overlapping and often conflicting political commitments—forced legislators to assemble coalitions broader than their immediate faction. Today, a deeper strain emerges inside Congress. DW–NOMINATE, a long-running data series developed by a group of political scientists (Lewis, 2025), uses congressional roll-call votes to estimate the ideological position of each member on a liberal–conservative scale. The pattern is unmistakable. The scores show that the ideological overlap that once supported bipartisan bargaining has nearly vanished. The Republican Conference has moved sharply rightward, the Democratic Caucus has drifted leftward, and the gap between the two has expanded into a structural barrier. Congress has become more polarized than the public they serve—a dangerous situation. The graph captures not only partisan difference but the disappearance of the middle ground where negotiation once occurred. Congress has not only polarized; Congress has forgotten how to bargain. The Chambers have surrendered the slow work of negotiation to the faster, narrower logic of leadership-driven dealmaking—the tyranny of the deal.

The Cowbell Reform

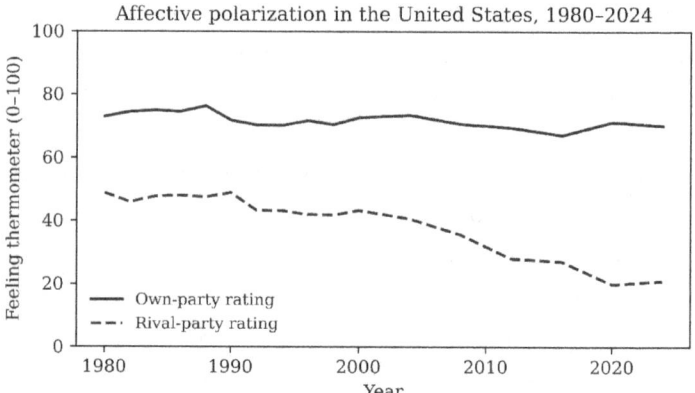

Figure 12. Affective Polarization in the United States, 1980–2024 (ANES Feeling Thermometer). Americans now rate their own party warmly while rating the rival party increasingly coldly. Rival-party feeling has fallen from the mid-40s to near 20 on the 0–100 scale. Own-party feeling has remained high and relatively stable. The widening gap between these measures reflects affective polarization—a growing emotional distance between partisans that complicates coalition-building and narrows the space for political compromise. Data Source: ANES, Feeling Thermometer Time Series, 1980–2024.

The graph in Fig. 13 reveals a simple truth with profound consequences. Democratic energy now accelerates faster than republican structure can absorb. Pressure builds among citizens, yet the more dangerous pressure accumulates inside Congress. The machinery inside the Capitol walls that once moderated the democratic tempo outside those walls no longer slows the surge. Polarization among Americans may frustrate civic life, yet polarization among representatives poses a direct threat to the Republic.

More Republic, Less Cowbell

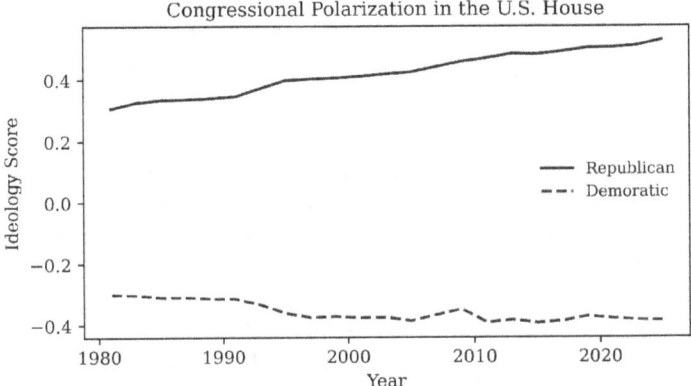

Figure 13. Congressional Polarization in the U.S. House, 1980–2026 (DW–NOMINATE Scores). The ideological distance between the parties in Congress has widened dramatically. Republican members have moved steadily rightward, while Democratic members have moved modestly leftward. The dotted line shows the resulting polarization gap, which has grown to levels that earlier Congresses never approached. The collapse of ideological overlap removes the bargaining space that once allowed legislators to negotiate amendments, trade concessions, and assemble cross-party coalitions. The graph shows how Congress has lost the structural habits required for compromise. Data in Lewis (2025).

That imbalance frames the proposed reforms in this chapter. Polarization is not the underlying disease, particularly among the People. Polarization is the fever—the visible symptom of a deeper structural illness. That illness lies in three domains that once steadied the Republic: the Chamber that organizes collective decision-making, the Pipeline that elevates candidates, and the Press that shapes public judgment. In other words: the Chamber, the Pipeline, and the Press. These domains form the focus of the reform agenda that follows—reforms designed to restore republican stabilizers and quiet the cowbells that now overwhelm the system.

The Cowbell Reform

Chamber, Pipeline, Press

The Chamber, the Pipeline, and the Press once provided friction—useful friction—that slowed impulses and broadened coalitions. Each domain now accelerates factional intensity.

> *The Chamber*: Congress now depends on leadership bargaining, with significant Executive encroachment, rather than committee deliberation and member-driven expertise.

> *The Pipeline*: Primaries reward narrow groups mobilized in low-turnout contests, producing candidates shaped by intense factions rather than broad coalitions.

> *The Press*: Contemporary media amplifies speed rather than verification, rewarding outrage over judgment and narrowing civic understanding.

The Republic requires renewed machinery. The graphs above, particularly Fig. 13, reveal where the machinery falters.

A historical context for this modern crisis exists. The technology of today may differ, yet the People have not changed. People are people. The Founders would have recognized the pattern, not because the Republic has returned to the Articles of Confederation, but because they understood how quickly democratic passion can outrun institutional restraint. They witnessed legislatures that lurched from one crisis to the next, policies that shifted faster than institutions could absorb, and public pressure that built without the buffers a republic requires. The Constitution corrected those weaknesses, and the design remains sound. The danger arises not from the structure itself but from the gradual removal of the guardrails that give the structure force. Modern reforms—noble in intention but misguided in effect—have pushed public life toward greater immediacy and away from the republican moderation the Constitution expects.

Chapter 1 examined the nation's anxieties with close attention. Chapter 2 traced the long unraveling that accompanied modern changes in party structure, journalism, and digital communication. National parties weakened. Primaries replaced internal deliberation. Journalism moved from gatekeeping to amplification. Digital platforms removed the last remaining filters. Institutions designed for reflection now operate inside an environment designed for reaction.

Chapter 3 reminded us that the Republic has weathered greater storms. Nullification, secession, assassinations, economic collapse, and urban unrest each tested the guardrails in earlier eras. The Republic absorbed those shocks because the Republic maintained distance, scale, staggered terms, and layered representation. Committees provided expertise. Federalism supplied buffering zones. Institutional architecture converted democratic energy into workable outcomes. The Republic has survived constitutional vibrations before, and the Republic will survive this moment as well.

Modern reforms and digital technology have stripped away too many of the devices that once steadied the Republic. Leadership structures within Congress have replaced the negotiating table with messaging campaigns. Transparency rules—well-intentioned—have exposed each stage of deliberation to an audience that rewards spectacle rather than settlement. The sunshine of open democracy has become the spotlight of political performance. Changes in the primary process, designed to make candidate selection more democratic and more responsive to the will of the People, have inadvertently empowered factions rather than coalitions. The Press, unprepared for the digital revolution, shifted from society's verification to the demagogue's velocity. These shifts carried democratic appeal, yet democratic appeal often obscures structural consequence. More access did not produce more stability. More immediacy did not produce more accountability.

The Cowbell Reform

Yet a turning point toward reform remains possible. The Republic does not require sweeping reinvention. The Republic requires the restoration of guardrails that have been neglected, weakened, or deliberately removed. The instincts of contemporary reformers have misread the moment. They call for more democratic participation—more primaries, more referenda, more transparency, more immediacy. Those instincts carry democratic appeal, yet they accelerate the centrifugal force. They exacerbate polarization. More voice does not guarantee more governance. More immediacy narrows the space for bargaining. More transparency rewards the camera, not the negotiating table. Critics shout about corruption, elites, or gridlock, yet those accusations rarely offer structural remedies. The old saying is that a fool can tear down a house, but only a craftsman knows how to rebuild one. The Republic needs craftsmen, not demolition crews. I do not claim mastery in the architecture of government, yet I stand on the shoulders of giants—James Madison in particular—in the recommendations that follow.

The Republic does not require a new philosophy. The Republic requires renewed machinery—machinery that restores the republican wisdom that once steadied the American experiment. Citizens must once again sit at the feet of Madison and listen.

The remainder of this chapter turns to those devices of repair. The argument moves through three arenas where the Republic has thinned—the Chamber where laws are shaped, the Pipeline through which leaders are chosen, and the Press that binds a shared civic world. Renewal begins where these structures regain their strength. Such reforms do not quiet citizens or restrain political passion. They restore the breathing room that allows passion to settle into judgment. They do not diminish democracy. They steady the Republic so that our democracy can endure.

The Chamber Unravels

As a brief review, Congress once moderated democratic energy through a structure designed to slow, filter, and refine public demands. Prior to 1994, committees formed the core of that structure. Members accumulated experience across years of service. Committee chairs acted as institutional stewards who shaped oversight, managed legislative tempo, and protected the Chamber's capacity to negotiate. Legislation moved through hearings, markups, revisions, and bargains. The House resembled a workshop. The workshop produced law. Members—though the idea may seem remote in today's polarized environment—often placed the institution ahead of party. That workshop operated at a meaningful remove from the passions swirling outside the Chamber. Washington stood far from its constituents, and professional journalists shaped the informational bridge between Congress and the public. The distance strengthened deliberation. The distance steadied the Republic.

The Founders built that distance deliberately, as we noted, through the Residence Act of 1790 by placing the District of Columbia on the Potomac River under federal control. Congress was meant to think before the nation reacted. Geography supplied the distance the Constitution required for representatives to deliberate without interference.

That geography no longer provides the buffer the Founders assumed. The digital age has erased the functional distance between the District and the public. Real-time broadcasting and algorithmic amplification have turned the federal city into a transparent arena. No digital refuge exists. As we have discussed, research on the "C-SPAN effect" shows that televised proceedings increase emotive rhetoric and reduce deliberative behavior. Commentary from institutional observers echoes the same point: cameras shift incentives from negotiation to performance (Gennaro & Ash, 2023). Mediaecology scholars, beginning with Neil Postman's critique of television culture, have warned that modern communication systems impose entertainment incentives on political speech, accelerating spectacle at the expense of deliberation (Kovach & Rosenstiel, 2011; Postman, 2005). Congress now operates under constant visibility. That visibility rewards performance, not governance.

A broad body of political science reinforces these patterns. Research on partisan identity formation shows how emotional sorting intensifies division and narrows the space for agreement across party lines (Mason, 2018). Studies of congressional agenda control reveal how House leaders have shifted floor time away from consensus bills and toward conflict bills, converting the Chamber into a venue for partisan clarity rather than negotiated governance (Harbridge, 2015). Scholars tracking institutional decline have shown how leadership-drafted omnibus bills, and weakened committees have eroded regular order (Mann & Ornstein, 2006).* Work on primary electorates explains why visible compromise now carries political risk, as members respond to incentives that reward confrontation more readily than problem-solving (Anderson et al., 2020). Research on governing networks demonstrates that durable policy once emerged from relationships formed inside committees and across parties, not from speeches aimed at audiences outside

---

* "Regular order" refers to the traditional committee-centered legislative process in which bills are developed through hearings, markups, amendments, and committee reports before reaching the floor (Mann & Ornstein, 2006). Regular order disperses agenda-setting power, builds member expertise, encourages cross-party negotiation, and allows legislation to be shaped incrementally rather than dictated by leadership. The erosion of regular order concentrates authority in party leaders, reduces deliberation, and replaces legislative bargaining with take-it-or-leave-it votes.

the Chamber (Grossmann, 2014). Historical accounts of mid-century politics illustrate how quiet, cross-institutional bargaining once steadied national governance (Donaldson, 2014). Even case studies of major bipartisan reforms, such as the 1986 tax overhaul, show that success depended on committee craftsmanship rather than televised performance (Murray & Birnbaum, 1988). Taken together, this scholarship reveals a simple conclusion: as digital communication accelerates and democratic pressure intensifies, the institutional foundations that once steadied the Republic have continued to fracture.

The committee workshops have become a stage. A stage rewards certainty and applause, while a legislature requires uncertainty, bargaining, and revision. The House cannot fulfill its constitutional role while operating as a broadcast studio for identity politics and real-time outrage. The Republic that Madison designed expects the Legislative Branch—the first branch among equals—to convert democratic noise into republican law. That conversion requires committees with authority, members with time, and a chamber built for bargaining rather than spectacle.

In the pages that follow, I do not offer these repairs as a lone steward—only as a careful observer. These pages stand on the shoulders of scholars who mapped the congressional institution long before its modern decline—Mann and Ornstein (2006) on the broken branch, Harbridge (2015) on agenda control, Mason (2018) on identity hardening, Grossmann (2014) on governing networks, Donaldson (2014) on backstage coalition craft, Anderson et al. (2020) on the politics of rejecting compromise, and Murray and Birnbaum (1988) on committee stewardship. Their work traces the fault lines that now shape the Chamber. The recommendations that follow draw strength from their insight.

Diagnosing the Chamber

The first reform is to rebuild the House's committee system. My early admiration for Newt Gingrich shaped my understanding of political leadership. In the 1990s, Gingrich brought intellectual energy to a party hungry for direction. He organized a fractured minority, crafted a national message, and transformed a back-bench grievance into a governing force. The Contract with America in 1994 demonstrated what disciplined strategy, clear goals, and relentless mobilization could deliver within an unwieldy institution. That achievement deserved respect then, and that achievement deserves respect now. Yet time has revealed a harder truth. The same methods that propelled a minority into power also weakened the institution that victory was meant to serve. The shift from institutional stewardship to perpetual insurgency accelerated polarization inside the Chamber (Mann & Ornstein, 2006). My admiration for Gingrich remains complicated because I also recognize that the reforms he instituted in 1994—centralizing leadership power, elevating confrontation as a governing tool, and weakening the committee system—trace a long, gradual path to the polarization now embedded in the House nearly thirty years later.

Nothing in this history suggests malice. Gingrich did not seek to permanently weaken Congress. He sought to win. He sought to break a long-standing majority—Democratic control of the House, which had remained uninterrupted from 1955 to 1994, a span of forty years (Fig. 5).* He sought to replace drift with direction. Those

---

* Journalists in late 1994 confronted a transformation that felt seismic. "Republicans rode a tidal wave of voter discontent to capture both the Senate and the House last night, ending a four-decade Democratic dynasty in Congress" (Balz, 1994b). The next day, the same paper described the result

goals required discipline, messaging coherence, and procedural control. The problem emerged after the victory. The habits of insurgency became the habits of governance. Gingrich-style floor combat replaced committee work. Confrontation overshadowed deliberation. The Chamber evolved into a stage designed for partisan clarity rather than legislative craftsmanship. Laurel Harbridge documented how House agendas shifted toward conflict bills rather than consensus bills during this period, amplifying division even when policy agreement was possible (Harbridge, 2015). She later showed, along with collaborators Anderson and Butler, how primary voters began punishing legislators who attempted cross-party bargaining, further incentivizing the combative style Gingrich had normalized (Anderson et al., 2020).

The consequences accumulated quietly at first, then visibly, then inescapably. The House forfeited the slow work of legislating for the fast work of messaging, and the balance of power inside the federal government tilted further toward the Executive Branch. The Legislative Branch—long understood as the first among equals—has, since the Gingrich Revolution, increasingly operated as a partisan institution rather than a deliberative one.

---

as an "upheaval that gave Republicans control of the House and Senate for the first time in four decades" (Balz, 1994a). Scholars and official record-keepers likewise mark 1994 as the year Republicans captured the House after a generation of uninterrupted Democratic control. The metaphor is apt: the takeover felt less like a policy adjustment than the reopening of a long-sealed chamber—institutional dust shaking loose after decades of one-party rule. The Gingrich Revolution broke that hold, restored meaningful partisan turnover to the People's House, and reopened the possibility that either party could govern—a pattern confirmed in the decades that followed as control of the Chamber has shifted repeatedly between Republicans and Democrats (U.S. House of Representatives & Office of the Historian). Recall Fig. 5.

The Cowbell Reform

Political scientists describe the resulting pattern as partisan presidentialism: when congressional majorities share the President's party affiliation, the legislature frequently defers to the White House as the party's commanding center; when control is divided, the Chamber defaults to stalemate rather than governance (Howell & Moe, 2020; Sinclair, 2016). The House thus yields ground in both conditions, unsettling Madison's design of coequal branches and transforming Congress from a rival center of power into a deferential one.

The House once held firm as an equal. Today, partisan agreement bends the knee of a servant—Congress yields to the President—or partisan division hardens the back of a fighter—Congress ruled by the opposing party refuses accommodation.

Scholars across the field have traced the institutional consequences of this drift. Public administration scholar Donald Kettl and political scientist Charles O. Jones documented the steady expansion of administrative discretion as Congress delegated broad authority to federal agencies and relied increasingly on executive implementation to resolve policy conflicts (Jones, 2005; Kettl, 2000). Political scientist Terry Moe explained the rise of unilateral executive action and the incentives that encourage presidents to bypass Congress when legislative pathways narrow (Moe & Howell, 1999). Presidential scholar William Howell, in *Thinking About the Presidency: The Primacy of Power*, described how presidents exploit legislative inaction to expand their reach, using orders, memoranda, and administrative guidance to advance policy aims when Congress refuses to act (Howell, 2015). The first branch has slipped toward the margins as the Presidency has grown more agile, more centralized, and more appealing to members who run to the White House when the Chamber slows. Madison would be appalled.

A republic suffers when Congress relinquishes governing authority, particularly to the Executive Branch. The Founders placed the legislature at the center of the constitutional design, not the president. Madison also understood that the branch closest to the People would also be the branch most tempted by faction. That tension required internal structure: committees, rules, norms, chairs, and staff who could channel democratic energy into republican order. The House once operated with that balance. Committees held real authority, as congressional scholars David Deering and Steven Smith have detailed (Deering & Smith, 1997). Members developed expertise. Chairs stewarded their jurisdictions responsibly, a pattern described by Richard Murray and Jeff Birnbaum in their study of committee leadership (Murray & Birnbaum, 1988). Staff provided continuity. Bargaining shaped outcomes. The process was slow, uneven, and often maddening. Yet this slow, uneven, maddening process was the process of a functioning republic.

The contrast becomes clear when returning to an earlier Congress—the Congress chronicled in Richard Birnbaum and Alan Murray's *Showdown at Gucci Gulch* (Murray & Birnbaum, 1988). That Congress wrestled through a full tax-code overhaul in 1986. Committees drafted the architecture. Members defended their jurisdictions with real expertise. Chairs bargained. Coalitions shifted. Negotiators rewrote provisions line by line. The Senate Finance Committee produced a bill that reflected months of hearings, amendments, and tradeoffs. The process angered lobbyists, confounded interest groups, and forced lawmakers to weigh competing claims inside a real deliberative institution. That legislative world was messy, plodding, and mercilessly public. Yet that world showed how a republic functions when Congress behaves as a governing body rather than a partisan weapon: members argued, conceded, revised, and finally legislated. The Tax Reform Act of 1986 still stands as a major legislative achievement, a reminder of what Congress can produce when members engage a genuine deliberative process.

Modern reforms weakened that architecture. Leadership concentrated agenda control through restrictive rules, same-day

The Cowbell Reform

authority, omnibus drafting, and crisis calendars. I remember watching C-SPAN during this period, absorbing the spectacle but not yet grasping the structural changes beneath the changes. Legislative scholar Barbara Sinclair traced the rise of "unorthodox lawmaking," a pattern that accelerated after 1994 as party leaders pulled decisions into their own offices and replaced committee-driven legislating with leadership-drafted substitutes (Sinclair, 2016). Bills have become prebaked rather than forged through member-driven hearings, amendments, and negotiation.

The Rules Committee—once a procedural traffic cop—has evolved into an enforcement arm of the Speaker, issuing far more closed and structured rules than in earlier decades. Same-day authority, rarely used before the mid-1990s, has become routine, allowing major bills to reach the floor with only hours of notice. Regular appropriations collapsed as continuing resolutions and omnibus packages have displaced the committee process. Conference committees have dwindled, often eliminated entirely. Members have learned that influence now flows not from committee expertise but from proximity to party leadership.* Subcommittee chairs have lost independence. Committee markups have narrowed, and opportunities for substantive amendment have shrunk. The

---

* Scholars and journalists have documented a growing connection between fundraising and committee influence since the mid-1990s. Although committee chairs have never been literally "sold," both parties gradually adopted formal fundraising expectations—often called *party dues*—for members seeking influential committee posts or leadership positions. By the early 2000s, these expectations were institutionalized within the Democratic Congressional Campaign Committee and National Republican Congressional Committee, and by the 2010s, several former members publicly acknowledged that fundraising capacity had become a *de facto* prerequisite for chairmanships and other prestigious roles (Kornberg, 2024; O'Donnell, 2016).

Chamber's internal life has contracted into a handful of leadership rooms where major packages are drafted under deadline pressure—rooms are designed to reward message cohesion rather than negotiation or craft (Mann & Ornstein, 2006). The Bush administration reinforced this turn. Karl Rove's well-publicized "fifty-percent-plus-one" strategy treated narrow majorities as sufficient mandate and strengthened the logic of partisan presidentialism already reshaping the House (Hacker & Pierson, 2005).

Rebuilding the House

Scholars across the field have traced the cumulative effects of these shifts. Mann and Ornstein showed how party leaders gradually centralized procedural authority, bypassed committees, and replaced regular order with crisis-driven legislating (Mann & Ornstein, 2006). Gary Cox and Mathew McCubbins have explained the logic behind this consolidation: majority parties tightened internal agenda control to prevent unpredictable outcomes on the floor, strengthening leadership at the expense of committees (Cox & McCubbins, 2005). Frances Lee and James Curry have documented the institutional consequences as committee staff have declined, leadership offices have grown, and lawmakers have relied increasingly on leadership-drafted legislative text (Curry & Lee, 2022). David Rohde's framework of conditional party government offers the deeper pattern beneath these developments: as the parties have grown more ideologically cohesive after 1994, leaders have gained both the authority and the incentive to centralize decision-making (Rohde, 1991). Taken together, these findings describe a single arc. The Chamber has shifted from member-driven deliberation to leadership-managed policymaking. Oversight has weakened as institutional expertise has thinned. The first branch has drifted toward the margins while the presidency has grown more agile, more centralized, and more attractive to members frustrated with gridlock.

The Cowbell Reform

Rebuilding the House requires reversing this drift. Mann and Ornstein offer the clearest guidance on this point. Congress must rebuild the committee system that existed prior to 1994, because committees provide the durable institutional structure capable of translating public preferences into workable legislation (Mann & Ornstein, 2006).

A restored committee system does more than process bills. A strong committee system revives the legislative craft that modern politics has allowed to atrophy. Lee and Curry have shown how weakened committees erode member expertise and shrink the space for cross-party negotiation—two qualities essential to governing a large, diverse republic (Curry, 2022; Curry & Lee, 2022).

Genuine reform therefore begins with committee chairs. Chairs must regain authority over committee agendas. Chairs must direct hearings, shape markups, and negotiate policy within assigned jurisdictions. Chairs must steward institutional memory and defend committee boundaries against the centrifugal pull of leadership politics. Chairs must be selected for legislative skill rather than fundraising prowess. Chairs must be lawmakers, not party financiers.

When chairs regain strength, the Chamber regains strength. Rebuilding the House requires severing the link between committee authority and party fundraising.

The next step involves a rebalancing. A House governed largely through restrictive rules cannot deliberate. When most bills arrive on the floor pre-cooked, closed to amendment, and rushed under manufactured deadlines, members cannot exercise judgment. They can only perform. The Chamber needs more open rules, more debate, and more opportunities for members to propose amendments rooted in constituency knowledge. Harbridge's work demonstrates that opportunities for amendment correlate strongly with legislative productivity and bipartisan coalitions (Harbridge, 2015). Regular order slows the pace, but that pace is the point. A republic requires friction that filters public passion. A republic requires governing rooms, not only performance halls.

A third repair involves restoring knowledge. Congress cannot compete with the presidency without deep expertise. Staff capacity declined dramatically after the 1990s as appropriations for committees and support agencies shrank. Lobbyists filled the void. Grossmann's research on policy networks revealed how the decline of congressional expertise shifted policy drafting toward interest groups and executive-branch actors (Grossmann, 2014). When staff expertise weakens, oversight weakens. When oversight weakens, Executive power expands. Staff growth therefore becomes a constitutional necessity rather than a bureaucratic indulgence. Congress must increase the professional staff who support members and their committees, rather than relying on lobbyists and Executive Branch staffers. A disciplined cadre of professional staffers supporting the Chamber—dedicated solely to members of Congress—must be restored.

A rebuilt House does not require a return to pre-1994 routines or a sentimental reconstruction of an earlier Congress, but authority must flow back through committees. Members must develop expertise, and staff must provide continuity for deliberation to regain footing. Leadership must channel disagreement rather than extinguish deliberation. Political science supports this design. Gary Cox and Mathew McCubbins have shown that excessive centralization in leadership offices suppresses committee capacity and narrows the paths available for member influence (Cox & McCubbins, 2005). Lee and Curry have also demonstrated that leadership-driven chambers generate messaging bills rather than substantive laws, leaving the Executive Branch with greater freedom to define national policy (Curry & Lee, 2020). The goal is not weakened leadership but disciplined leadership—leadership strong enough to coordinate a majority yet restrained enough to preserve committee authority and member participation. A chamber governed entirely from the top evolves into an engine for partisan mobilization, a structure that amplifies division and produces little genuine governance.

The deeper purpose of these reforms concerns the place of the legislature within the constitutional order. The Founders positioned Congress as the first branch because congressional decision-making embodied the central principle of republican self-rule. A strong legislature restrains Executive excess. A strong legislature defines national priorities. A strong legislature provides citizens with a channel for peaceful political contest and organized dissent—mechanisms Madison viewed as essential antidotes to faction. When the House surrenders that role, the Executive fills the vacuum. Power gravitates toward decisiveness, and presidents often interpret legislative silence as legislative permission. The constitutional balance shifts not through formal amendment but through institutional erosion, and each shift strengthens a Presidency already armed with speed, unity, and a national platform

Rebuilding the House—by restoring committees, rebalancing procedure, and reinvesting in expertise—revives Congress as a coequal branch, and properly understood, the first among equals. A republic that seeks balance must begin with the branch designed to hold the center. Madison, however, never relied on institutional capacity alone. He assumed that certain duties would force decision—and that failure to perform them would carry consequence.

Privacy for Deliberation

For the first reform, we must remove cameras from Congress. Face-to-face meetings without cameras matter because governing requires persuasion among peers, not performance before an audience. Cameras in Congress are destroying our Republic with too much democratic access. Research in media studies, behavioral science, and legislative scholarship converges on the same conclusion:

public observation changes how individuals reason and act, shifting behavior toward performance rather than deliberation—a phenomenon known as the Hawthorne Effect.* The Hawthorne studies and subsequent work on evaluation apprehension demonstrate that individuals become more cautious, less candid, and more attuned to audience expectations when they know they are being watched (Mayo, 2004; Rosenthal, 1976). Televised politics alters meaning and message (Jamieson & Birdsell, 1990). Robert Zajonc's research demonstrates that the presence of observers strengthens dominant, rehearsed responses and suppresses exploratory reasoning—a well-established dynamic that helps explain behavior now common in contemporary congressional hearings (Zajonc, 1965). The camera's lens is exposing Congress to the Hawthorne effect with polarizing results.†

---

* The term *Hawthorne Effect* derives from a series of industrial studies conducted at the Western Electric Hawthorne Works in Cicero, Illinois, between the 1920s and 1930s. Researchers found that workers changed their behavior whenever they knew they were being observed, regardless of whether lighting, breaks, or supervision levels actually changed. The findings revealed that the act of observation itself can alter conduct, a conclusion that has since shaped decades of research in psychology, organizational behavior, and social science.

† Some readers may point to the success of police body cameras as evidence that cameras improve accountability. Police cameras, however, monitor discrete encounters for retrospective review. Legislative work demands prospective negotiation, reconsideration, and candid exchange. The camera that protects a citizen during a traffic stop distorts a representative during a deliberative act. A randomized control trial in 2018 in Las Vegas revealed increased arrests and citations by officers wearing body-worn cameras. That pattern suggests a shift in discretionary behavior (Braga et al., 2018): under the watchful eye of a camera, officers may choose formal enforcement over discretionary leniency, a behavioral response consistent with evaluation-apprehension and self-awareness research.

The Cowbell Reform

Complementary research in organizational psychology finds that small-group, in-person exchanges promote trust formation, reduce misunderstanding, and increase collaborative problem solving because facial cues, tone, and shared physical presence help participants interpret one another more accurately and resolve conflict more constructively (Olson & Olson, 2000; Short et al., 1976). Congressional scholars report the same pattern. Public discussions reward message discipline, while private, face-to-face discussions allow members to test ideas, ask sharper questions, and acknowledge legitimate concerns across party lines (Binder, 2014; Lee, 2022; Sinclair, 2016). Together these findings establish a simple legislative truth: candid exploration flourishes only when representatives meet directly, without an audience, and without the lens that converts deliberation into performance.

Congress requires a deliberate return to structured privacy. A legislature cannot sustain genuine deliberation beneath permanent visibility. The reforms proposed in this chapter seek to restore the conditions Madison believed essential for republican self-government: a space where representatives can test ideas, reconsider assumptions, and negotiate without performing for a factional audience.

The path forward centers on three structural adjustments. First, committees should adopt Chatham House–style rules* for early-

---

* The Chatham House Rule was established by the Royal Institute of International Affairs in London to promote candid discussion among diplomats, scholars, and political leaders. The rule permits participants to use the information exchanged but forbids identifying the speaker or their affiliation. The rule's purpose is to encourage open exploration of ideas without the reputational pressures associated with public attribution. The format has become a global standard for sensitive policy dialogue and offers a useful model for early-stage congressional deliberation.

More Republic, Less Cowbell

stage deliberation. Such procedures originated in 1927 to allow the substance of a discussion to be shared while prohibiting public attribution of individual remarks, and without cameras (Royal Institute of International Affairs, 1927). Second, hearings should unfold in phases. An initial private scoping session would allow members to identify contested facts and surface technical concerns without performing for a camera. A second, limited-visibility phase would permit recording only through wide, institutional shots of the room—no close-up feeds of individual members—to reduce performative incentives while preserving transparency. Only then should a fully public session proceed once factual disputes are resolved. Third, Congress should prohibit the conversion of hearing footage into campaign material. Representatives should not transform legislative oversight into partisan audition. These reforms do not hide government from the governed. They restore the structural distance that enables representatives to govern and reduce the noise of the cowbells.

The necessity of these reforms becomes clear once the behavioral consequences of constant observation are understood. A legislature cannot reason under a lens that transforms each hesitation into a permanent artifact. Video clips become handcuffs. Representatives grow bound to the sharpest version of their words rather than to their considered judgment. A republican institution designed for reflection now performs for an audience waiting outside the room—and lingering unseen in the minutes, days, and years that follow.

The evidence for this dynamic extends across disciplines. The first televised presidential debate in 1960 campaign remains the clearest illustration of media's distorting power. Radio listeners concluded that Richard Nixon won the exchange, but television viewers favored John Kennedy. The words did not change. Only the medium changed the meaning (Jamieson & Birdsell, 1990). James Druckman's controlled experiment confirmed the effect that

The Cowbell Reform

television viewers evaluated candidates differently, relied more heavily on personality traits, and even learned different facts from the same debate (Druckman, 2003). A Congress that insists on performing each deliberative act in full view should expect similar distortions. Multi-stage hearings offer a counter to this tendency.

Experience inside Congress offers its own confirmation. Members involved in bipartisan "gangs" routinely note that progress depends on keeping early conversations off camera.* The 2013 "Gang of Eight" immigration negotiators stated openly that televised sessions would have collapsed the coalition before a draft existed (Parker, 2013). The 2021 infrastructure negotiations followed the same pattern (Everett & Levine, 2025; Levine & Everett, 2025). Senate scholars Barbara Sinclair and Sarah Binder observe that gangs form because committees and party leaders cannot offer the privacy required for compromise (Binder, 2014; Sinclair, 2016). A committee structure designed to produce cross-party agreement now produces little beyond televised messaging. Chatham House–style rules would repair that gap.

---

* The Senate's use of the word *gang* predates the "Gang of Eight" in 2013. The label was originally informal—journalists and staff used the term to describe small, cross-party groups that operated outside leadership channels to defuse institutional crises. The language carried a hint of rebellion, suggesting a temporary alliance formed to break procedural deadlock. Political historian Barbara Sinclair noted that these ad-hoc groups emerged as committees lost authority and party leaders struggled to broker agreements in public view. The terminology echoed an older congressional habit of giving nicknames to temporary factions—borrowing from nineteenth-century expressions such as "cabal," "clique," or "knot"—but "gang" persists because the term conveys a sense of rogue pragmatism in a chamber increasingly defined by party discipline. See Sinclair (2014) for a historical overview of these informal bargaining networks.

The pattern extends to committee staff and procedural experts who consistently report that members ask sharper questions, explore more nuanced options, and acknowledge legitimate concerns from the other party when discussions occur off camera (Binder, 2014; Sinclair, 2016). Frances Lee's research shows that partisan competition encourages members to treat public hearings as opportunities for message discipline, not problem-solving (Lee, 2022). Erving Goffman's account of front-stage performance illuminates the same dynamic. As the audience grows, self-presentation hardens (Goffman, 2023). Ethan Bernstein's transparency paradox shows that excessive visibility reduces creativity, candor, and collaborative problem solving (Bernstein, 2012). A phased approach introduces the camera's glare gradually and provides the space for a predictable escalation of publicity that does not suffocate early-stage deliberation.

Federal courts have long recognized this principle. The Judiciary Branch has restricted cameras for nearly a century, reflecting a settled belief that adjudication requires distance from public performance (Canon & Johnson, 1999). The Judicial Conference first prohibited broadcasting in federal trials in 1946 and reaffirmed the ban in 1972, 1996, and most recently 2016. Scholars note that these restrictions reflect long-standing institutional concerns that cameras alter courtroom behavior, intimidate witnesses, and shift judicial proceedings toward performance rather than adjudication (Canon & Johnson, 1999). By contrast, many state and local courts permit varying degrees of camera access, with the O.J. Simpson murder trial—presided over by Judge Lance Ito—standing as the most famous (or infamous) example of televised courtroom spectacle (Zorthian, 2015). Even so, the federal judiciary remains one of the nation's most camera-averse institutions, preserving a zone of deliberative privacy unfortunately long abandoned by Congress. A republican legislature requires the same protection.

The Cowbell Reform

Deliberation cannot flourish under a lens that converts hesitation into a viral spectacle.

The Founders understood the coercive power of public passion. Madison defended the confidentiality of the Constitutional Convention because deliberation demanded space for reconsideration. Delegates needed shade to reason together before facing the nation. A modern legislature that governs beneath permanent illumination has lost that shade. The reforms proposed here—structured privacy, phased hearings, and limits on performative visibility—restore the conditions under which republican judgment can flourish.

Congress does not need more spectacle. Congress needs the freedom to think. Cameras diminish that freedom. Structured privacy restores an atmosphere ripe for deliberation over grandstanding.

Stop Misguided Reforms

The final reform to consider for the Chamber is to stop current misguided reforms that are merely in the name of democracy. Proposals that promise "more democracy" attract intuitive support. Those ideas sound righteous because they draw strength from a democratic instinct, deep within our American psyche, that believes increased democratization strengthens the system. That instinct is misleading. A republic depends on filters, calibration, and time. Several popular reforms would strip away each of those layers. The proposals appear fresh and modern, yet they revive an older pattern. Earlier generations lived through moments when democratic passion surged faster than republican structure could contain the forces unleashed by sudden majorities. Those periods produced volatility, not self-rule.

Congressional term limits offer the clearest demonstration of misguided reform. Reformers in the early 1990s believed entrenched legislators had lost touch with citizens. California voters responded by imposing strict limits on state elected offices. The result proved far weaker than reformers expected. The limits forced near-constant turnover across both state chambers. The reform sounded democratic, but the consequences hollowed out legislative capacity. The legislature transferred institutional knowledge and political know-how from elected politicians to institutional staffers. Unelected foxes effectively ran the hen house. Political scientists who studied Sacramento documented how rapid rotation destroyed institutional knowledge, weakened committees, and shifted expertise to lobbyists and permanent staff who understood the process better than elected officials (Cain & Kousser, 2004; Kousser, 2005). Legislators became short-term visitors in a Capitol increasingly shaped by permanent actors who never faced the voters. Negotiation migrated outside the Chamber. Public accountability deteriorated because meaningful deliberation no longer occurred in public view. California gained fresh faces through term limits, but lost the seasoned judgment a legislature requires. Term limits promise renewal in theory but, in practice, produce institutional decay. Term limits are an anti-republican measure that must be avoided.

Abolishing the Electoral College carries a similar intuitive appeal for a reform that misunderstands the architecture of a republic (Ross, 2004, 2019). Advocates argue that a national popular vote, an alternative to the College, would advance fairness by giving each citizen equal weight. The surface logic attracts support, yet the Republic's deeper structure would fracture. Scholars have shown that a national popular vote encourages candidates to pursue narrow, intense factions concentrated in major population centers rather than broader regional coalitions (Edwards III, 2023). Regional concerns would weaken. The incentives would reward turnout from fervent supporters rather than broad persuasion across diverse communities. Madison's warning in *Federalist No. 10* about the dangers of factional intensity in small republics would reappear on

The Cowbell Reform

a continental scale. The Electoral College—imperfect in imagined and real ways—forces presidential contenders to assemble geographically diverse support. Removing that filter would nationalize each grievance and accelerate the volatility of national media cycles. Electoral College reforms should also be avoided.

Other misguided reforms seek sunshine, or what some advocates describe as total transparency—the belief that every word must be recorded and every negotiation disclosed. The democratic instinct, again, appears noble. Yet observation reshapes human behavior, especially in an age when each moment becomes a permanent digital record. The Hawthorne Effect exerts enormous force in environments shaped by cameras, microphones, and instant publication. The reforms that promise more sunshine misunderstand how human beings reason. Excessive visibility discourages candor and narrows the space for honest exploration. Sunshine reforms should be viewed with a skeptical eye.

Each misguided reform shares a common flaw. The proposals imagine that direct, unfiltered participation produces stronger outcomes in a large, complex republic. Yet, in practice, these well-meaning reforms have proved deeply destructive and have intensified polarization. Democratic energy remains essential, but democratic immediacy dissolves the republican architecture that channels disagreement into durable settlements. Term limits displace expertise. A national popular vote elevates factional intensity. Absolute transparency rewards performance. Each reform narrows the space for serious negotiation.

A republic requires filters that slow judgment and broaden perspective. A republic requires representatives who possess the authority, time, and privacy to govern without the distraction of cowbells. A republic cannot function as a permanent plebiscite. The path toward renewal does not depend on more democracy. The path toward renewal requires stronger institutions—institutions capable of absorbing democratic passion without losing republican form.

A Majority Pipeline

The next reform avenue is political primaries—the Pipeline that elevates candidates. Primaries, particularly presidential ones, are broken, and reform is necessary. The modern nomination pipeline has grown more democratic than the Founders ever imagined. Although the Founders did not foresee modern parties, the Constitutional design relied on local intermediaries—personal reputation, community judgment, and small caucuses—to mediate ambition before candidates reached Congress. That structure endured through much of the twentieth century, imperfect yet stabilizing, and remarkably durable. The 1968 Democratic Convention, however, shattered that stability. The chaos in Chicago revealed a primary process out of step with the country, and the response that followed produced a new structure for choosing national leaders—unfortunately, a less republican structure.

After 1968, the Democratic National Committee created the McGovern–Fraser Commission to rewrite the rules of delegate selection and restore legitimacy to the nomination process. The Commission required open procedures, public notice, and binding selection rules, and those requirements shifted power from party leaders to voters who participated in state-run primaries and open caucuses. The McGovern–Fraser reforms opened the gates, mandating delegate-selection procedures rooted in publicly accessible contests rather than party-boss discretion (Polsby, 1983; Shafer, 1983). Delegates would no longer emerge from party networks and party bosses. Delegates would emerge from primaries that rewarded activists, volunteers, and early mobilizers—more democracy, more cowbell.

The Cowbell Reform

The reform carried a democratic spirit but lacked republican principles. Few observers would object to reducing the influence of party bosses and party elites, yet the reform moved too far, too democratic. Citizens gained a greater voice in nominations, and the process appeared more open and more representative. Yet the deeper logic shifted. A republic designed to filter political passion removed a crucial layer of filtration after 1968. Primaries have become the firehose that feeds the national legislature, and the post-1968 structure has become a major force in the polarization of American politics and cracked the door open for demagogues.

The consequences arrived quickly. Primary electorates have skewed more ideologically than general-election electorates. Participation fluctuates sharply from cycle to cycle. Small bands of motivated voters determine which candidates enter Congress (Hirano et al., 2010). A dedicated minority can remove a broadly popular incumbent by threatening to "primary" a member who displays a spirit of compromise. Parties cannot discipline those members because those members no longer owe their position to the party. Members owe their survival to factions that dominate the primary electorate. Mann and Ornstein have warned for two decades that this dynamic punishes moderation, rewards confrontation, and transforms the Pipeline into a mechanism that selects performers, not legislators (Mann & Ornstein, 2006).

Reform must reverse that pressure. Primaries should require nominees to demonstrate majority support within the party electorate, not mere plurality support. A republican order cannot grow from contests in which twenty-five or thirty percent of party voters impose nominees on the broader party coalition through plurality-based systems. Several institutional designs can restore majority rule. One approach requires an absolute majority to secure the nomination. Another allows voters to rank candidates or express preferences within the party primary, though such voting-system reforms remain contested. A further alternative combines a top-four or top-five qualifying round with a majority-producing final contest.

Each of these structures rewards candidates who build broader coalitions rather than narrow, high-intensity followings. The shared goal is to correct the central flaw of the post-1968 nomination pipeline by asking candidates to appeal beyond the most activated voters and to earn majority approval within the party electorate. In doing so, these reforms restore the mediating function that earlier changes unintentionally removed.*

Some scholars have questioned the degree to which primary electorates differ from general-election voters. Sides et al. (2020) find that primary electorates are not uniformly more extreme across each contest, yet this nuance underscores rather than weakens the case for reform. The structural flaw of plurality primaries does not depend on ideological distance. A fractured field still allows a narrow faction to prevail whenever the broader coalition divides. A majority threshold remains the most reliable safeguard against that vulnerability. This structural vulnerability shapes the incentives inside each crowded primary field.

---

* I personally favor preference-based voting systems, such as ranked-choice voting, within party primaries. Preference voting allows voters to express ordered (or in some forms, unordered preference) choices among candidates, reduces the risk of vote-splitting, and increases the likelihood that nominees command majority support without requiring multiple rounds of voting. For a clear, nonpartisan overview of preference voting and other electoral systems—along with their respective advantages and tradeoffs—see Suzuki (2015).

The Peacock Effect

Today's plurality-based primaries resist coalition-building. Plurality rules reward fragmentation, intensify factional pressure, and generate what one might call the Peacock Effect. The Peacock Effect—rooted in evolutionary and economic theory (Darwin, 1872; Frank, 1985; Tullock, 1971)—describes a competitive spiral in which contestants adopt louder, sharper, and more attention-seeking displays to stand out within a fragmented field. Biologists note that peacocks grow extravagant plumage not because such displays strengthen survival, but because they succeed inside a narrow signaling contest. Political plurality creates the same dynamic. Candidates develop symbolic excess—sharper rhetoric, purer gestures, theatrical confrontation—to attract a small but decisive faction, even though those displays weaken long-term governance.

The Peacock Effect draws on evolutionary and economic models that explain how costly displays can dominate competitive environments even when those displays weaken long-term performance. Charles Darwin first described this mechanism in his theory of sexual selection, where organisms develop extravagant traits that succeed within narrow signaling contests rather than broader survival needs (Darwin, 1872).

Economists have traced similar spirals in markets shaped by asymmetric information and winner-take-all incentives, including plurality-based political primaries. Robert Frank, an economist known for his work on status competition, shows how conspicuous consumption emerges as a rational response inside distorted signaling environments, while Gordon Tullock, a pioneer of public choice theory, demonstrates how rent-seeking behavior flourishes when rewards are decoupled from productive outcomes (Frank, 1985; Tullock, 1971). George Akerlof, a Nobel Prize–winning economist, further shows how low-quality entrants can prevail—and even displace higher-quality competitors—when information asymmetries degrade market signals (Akerlof, 1970).

Plurality primaries recreate those conditions. Fragmented coalitions and asymmetric political information allow narrow factions to elevate candidates who excel at attention-seeking displays rather than durable governance.

Plurality does not merely permit these dynamics; the first-past-the-post system magnifies them. Plurality rules accelerate this spiral because factional candidates can prevail with narrow support while broader coalitions divide, rewarding spectacle over statesmanship (Ross, 2004). When several candidates divide the broad middle of a party, a motivated minority can prevail with a small share of the vote. Tara Ross has argued that plurality voting rests on the weakest form of electoral legitimacy because plurality elevates candidates who never secure majority approval.

The Founders agreed with that principle. They favored majorities—and, when matters were grave, supermajorities—to prevent narrow factions from capturing institutional power. Nowhere in the U.S. Constitution do pluralities prevail—majorities and supermajorities drive our founding document.

Primaries, by contrast, developed outside the constitutional framework. They developed organically. They inherited plurality rules for reasons of administrative convenience rather than constitutional design (McCormick, 1982). Hand-counted runoffs once imposed burdens that many states sought to avoid, particularly before automated counting aids (Alvarez & Hall, 2010). When parties formed at the Founding and later stabilized after the Civil War, electronic counting systems and modern voting theory did not exist, and plurality voting reflected the practical constraints of the era (Benoit, 2004; Lijphart, 1994). Plurality was the best system at the time.

Modern technology and election systems remove that burden. Ranked-choice voting, instant runoffs, and the mathematical

The Cowbell Reform

methods described by Suzuki (2015) enable majority mandates without costly second elections. These systems reverse the downward spiral of the Peacock Effect by encouraging candidates to seek broader approval and to attract second-choice and third-choice support. I do not advocate for a particular voting system—that discussion should be a public debate—but I do advocate for a system, like our Constitution, that prefers majority and supermajority selection rather than mere pluralities. A candidate who relies on a narrow faction cannot prevail when a majority threshold governs the race. This logic connects modern primary reform with the Founders' constitutional philosophy—majorities, not pluralities matter.

The philosophical grounding of this position follows Madison's extend-the-sphere argument in *Federalist No. 10*. Madison sought to dilute factional pressure by broadening the geographic range of the Republic; the majority-based primary seeks to dilute factional pressure by broadening the electoral base. Both strategies widen the base of consent. Majority voting in primaries restores the filtration that the Founders believed essential to self-government and reconstructs a nomination pipeline capable of producing legislators rather than performers. Rebuilding the primary pipeline does not require dismantling the party system. Some reformers have argued for nonpartisan structures that would dissolve or bypass the party system altogether (Schumer, 2014), yet such proposals misread human nature and the logic of republican government. Parties arise because citizens seek coordination, identity, and a means to organize political ambition. A durable republic requires better parties, not their abolition. In our *de facto* two-party system, majority requirements for primary selection uphold the Founders' principles and fulfill Madison's elegant vision for extending the sphere. The remaining question is whether observable patterns align with this institutional logic.

We now look to empirical patterns to reinforce this argument. Primary turnout fluctuates sharply from cycle to cycle, revealing how small bands of motivated voters can shape nomination outcomes. Primary elections also attract a narrow electorate. Participation often ranges between fifteen and thirty percent of the voting-eligible population, a level far below general-election turnout and far too low to confer broad representative legitimacy. Figure 14 illustrates this volatility across presidential primaries from 1972 to 2024, where participation rises and falls in wide arcs rather than following a stable democratic rhythm. The long sweep of data shows turnout dropping by half between 2008 and 2012 and then surging again in 2016—a pattern significant not for the absolute values but for the amplitude of change. A system that permits turnout to swing by fifty percent from one cycle to the next reflects an unstable electorate, one especially susceptible to capture by highly motivated factions and demagogic mobilization.

Such volatility allows a motivated minority to redirect the nomination pipeline toward sharply different ideological outcomes. Polling data shows ideological concentration among primary participants, often distant from the district median, which further exacerbates the issue (Pew Research Center, 2018). These patterns confirm a pipeline that amplifies political heat rather than moderating factional intensity. A republic requires pathways that slow political energy and channel that energy toward deliberation. A primary structure that demands majority support among party voters can restore that pathway, replacing a volatile pipeline with a channel shaped for republican judgment. The Pipeline demands such reform.

A legislature inherits the qualities of the Pipeline that produces its members. A republican chamber requires a republican pipeline. A pipeline shaped by narrow factions will send narrow voices into the Chamber. A pipeline shaped by broad participation will send members capable of governing a vast and varied nation. A republic endures only when the path to office cultivates the habits that republican government demands.

The Cowbell Reform

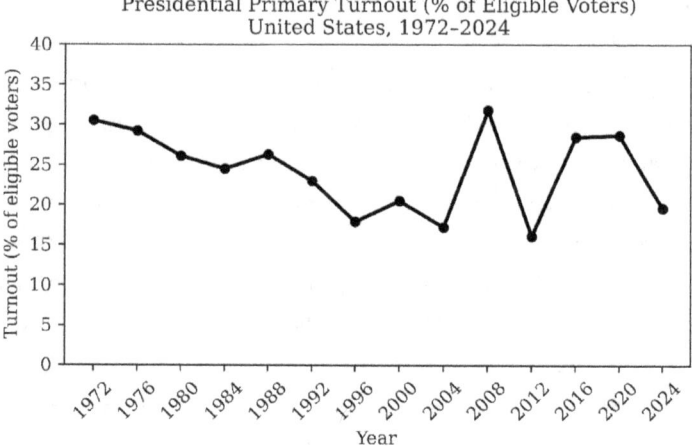

Figure 14. Presidential Primary Turnout as a Share of Eligible Voters, 1972–2024. Turnout in presidential primaries has swung sharply across the last half-century, with voting-eligible population participation ranging from lows near 16 percent to highs above 30 percent. These fluctuations suggest that nomination contests are disproportionately shaped by small, motivated electorates rather than broad, stable participation. Data compiled from Berrang (2012), Ferrer (2023), Geiger (2014), Desilver (2025), and aggregated state results for the 2024 cycle.

The Governing Campaign

A republic was never designed to operate inside the "Permanent Campaign." That phrase, first popularized by Sidney Blumenthal, described the moment when governing time collapsed into campaign time (Blumenthal, 1982). Today, American politicians are continuously campaigning, locked into a cycle of motion without progress. A representative democracy presumes the opposite rhythm—a bounded campaign followed by a season of governing. The modern campaign has reversed that order. Two forces sustain the Permanent Campaign: the scale of money required to run for office and the expanded calendar that requires candidates to raise that money across nearly an entire year. We must reform to move away from the Permanent Campaign and to return to a more productive "Governing Campaign."

The first flaw concerns the sources of political money. The legal framework after *Citizens United* reflects a constitutional judgment that political speech merits broad protection even when that protection complicates the work of self-government (Hasen, 2016). That judgment stands, and reform must respect that framework.*

---

* The Supreme Court's decision in *Citizens United v. FEC* (2010) held that the government may not restrict independent political expenditures by corporations, unions, or associations because such restrictions burden political speech protected by the First Amendment (Hasen, 2016). The ruling did not alter limits on direct contributions to candidates; the opinion addressed only independent expenditures.

Opposition to the decision has been strongest among Democratic officials and activists, who argue that the ruling amplifies the political influence of wealthy donors and outside groups, distorts representational balance, and erodes public confidence in electoral fairness (Lessig, 2018). Republican officials generally defend the ruling as a necessary safeguard for political expression and organizational advocacy, emphasizing that independent expenditures do not constitute quid-pro-quo corruption and therefore fall outside the government's regulatory reach (Smith, 2009). Public opinion reflects this division. Surveys consistently show that Democratic voters overwhelmingly support overturning the decision, while Republican voters remain more supportive of its free-speech rationale (La Raja & Schaffner, 2015).

The ruling thus occupies the contested space between free expression and democratic equity—a space the Constitution protects even when the political consequences are difficult to manage. The quixotic demand that the Judicial Branch overturn *Citizens United* is untenable. Critics who seek durable reform must take the more republican path and pursue a constitutional amendment rather than judicial reversal. Since *Roe v. Wade* (1973), the Supreme Court has too often become the convenient route for resolving constitutional disputes that a republic should settle through the amendment process.

The Cowbell Reform

Free expression cannot hinge on administrative judgments about who speaks too loudly. Yet nothing in *Citizens United* prevents Congress from structuring contribution rules that strengthen local accountability. Scholars have long observed that national donor networks skew representation toward ideologically intense funders, crowd out moderates, and encourage confrontational styles of politics (Barber, 2016; Barber et al., 2017; Bonica, 2013). This dynamic does not remain at the margins. Internal party practices now reinforce this elite funding machine. Investigative research by Issue One shows that party committees require members to raise extraordinary sums to secure leadership positions or influential committee assignments, turning fundraising prowess into an informal qualification for legislative authority (Issue One, 2017). Such incentives replicate the Permanent Campaign inside the legislature itself, replacing deliberative capacity with financial performance metrics.

A structural remedy exists if we choose to channel Madison. I would propose a federal law that permits citizens to donate only to candidates who stand for election within that citizen's jurisdiction—constituent–donor financing. One can only donate to candidates for which one can vote. Therefore, a resident of one congressional district could not finance campaigns in another district, another state, or another region of the country. One Congress member could not donate to another member's campaign to garner favor. Only citizens could donate—no corporations, no political action committees, no institutional intermediaries. Such a rule may emerge

---

Nine jurists should determine what the Constitution permits, not what the Constitution becomes. A self-governing people must claim responsibility for structural reform rather than outsource our republic to judicial decree.

through House rules or may require a constitutional amendment, and if that proves necessary, the amendment would provide a cleaner and more republican path toward restoring accountability in federal elections. This proposed constituents-only financing does not suppress political participation, but the rule does return financial influence back to the local community that bears the consequences of electoral choice. Contributions would once again signal the support of an actual constituency rather than a distant ideological faction. Loopholes would remain—the creativity of the human mind always outpaces the bureaucracy that attempts to regulate it—but such a rule would begin to restore the geographic integrity of representation that the Framers intended.*

With constituent-only financing in place, the second flaw we need to address concerns the length of the campaign itself. The modern primary calendar stretches across the better part of the year because early states have discovered that earlier contests produce influence. Scholars have documented this front-loading dynamic for decades (Mayer & Busch, 2003; Norrander, 2019; Ranney, 1975). Early contests generate momentum; momentum shapes media attention; media attention attracts money. Cohen et al. (2009)

---

* A contribution rule tied to the franchise would not foreclose loopholes. Independent expenditures protected under *Citizens United* would remain available to third-party entities unaffiliated with a candidate or campaign. A well-financed supporter could also attempt to route funds through a local resident with passthrough contributions. Such a transfer, however, would constitute taxable income for the intermediary and place legal responsibility on a known individual within the constituency. Direct contribution limits would continue to cap the amount that residents may give. These examples do not exhaust the universe of potential workarounds—loopholes emerge wherever political creativity meets legal constraint—but a structure anchored in the represented community would introduce transparency and accountability absent from the current nationalized donor system.

The Cowbell Reform

show how this momentum-driven sequence erodes party capacity for deliberation and encourages candidates to campaign long before most citizens begin paying attention.

The modern primary calendar reflects a structural shift that began after 1968, when the McGovern–Fraser reforms transferred nomination control from party organizations to direct voter participation. That democratization reshaped candidate incentives and extended the audition period that precedes the general election. Figure 15 reveals the structural consequences. The earliest presidential primaries have migrated steadily toward January—sometimes even brushing the edges of the holiday season—while the final contests drift only modestly toward midsummer. The result is a nomination window that has stretched rather than contracted. In 2012, the distance between the first and last state primary approached six months, a span that forces candidates into a half-year audition before the general election campaign even begins. The same pattern shapes congressional politics. States scattered their primary dates across the calendar, producing long periods in which incumbents govern under electoral uncertainty. A primary-defeated House member can become a lame duck for nearly half of their final term—an arrangement that undermines authority, blunts legislative ambition, and weakens the representative relationship.

The figure's two curves—the earliest state primary and the latest state primary—display a widening band over time. That band marks the expansion of the primary season and, with that expansion, the steady erosion of the boundary between campaigning and governing. A calendar originally designed for temporary engagement now demands perpetual performance. Candidates must raise money earlier, travel earlier, audition earlier, and sustain visibility long before the electorate turns their attention to national affairs. The structure of the calendar now shapes the structure of political behavior. The primary calendar compels a Permanent Campaign not by choice but by design.

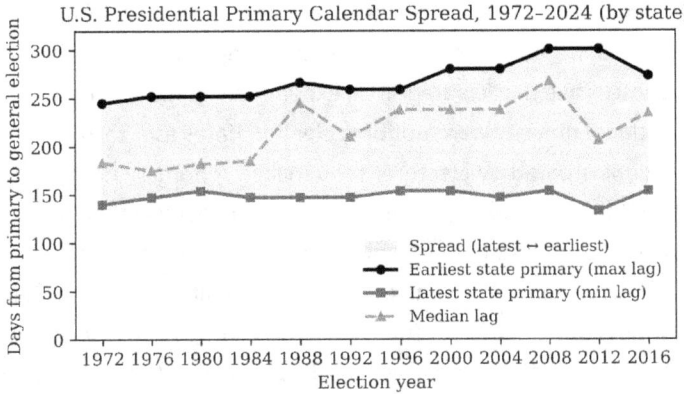

Figure 15. Presidential Primary Calendar Spread, 1972–2024. This figure traces the distance between state presidential primary dates and the November general election across the modern nomination era. The upper curve plots the earliest state primary in each cycle (the maximum lag in days before the general election). The lower curve plots the latest state primary (the minimum lag). The shaded band represents the full range of state-level timing. Data are drawn from *The Green Papers* historical compilation of presidential primary dates, which provides state-by-state records from the post–McGovern–Fraser period through 2024 (The Green Papers, n.d.).

Reform requires compressing the political calendar so that governing and campaigning no longer compete for the same time. Scholars across the ideological spectrum—including Polsby et al. (2008), Mayer and Busch (2003), Steger (2013), and Norrander (2019)—argue that shorter nomination windows limit the outsized influence of early contests, widen representational input, and encourage coalition-building rather than factional appeals. When contests are clustered—or, more decisively, synchronized on the same day—rather than stretched across months, nomination outcomes reflect broader electorates rather than sequential media narratives, reinforcing representation over momentum.

The historical case for synchronization is well established. In his study of nineteenth-century congressional elections, Scott James

The Cowbell Reform

(2007) shows that when races "unfolded sequentially over time," they became vulnerable to "distinctive interstate contagions," as unexpected outcomes in early contests reshaped later races before most voters had participated. That experience ultimately motivated the national move toward uniform election dates as a corrective to distortions created by electoral sequencing. A primary nomination system that permits early states to exercise similar leverage repeats an institutional mistake the Republic has already corrected once.

That principle echoes the logic behind a uniform national Election Day,* adopted to prevent sequential voting from shaping outcomes before the electorate could fully participate (Keyssar, 2000). A shorter nomination season of eight to twelve weeks follows directly from these findings—or, more decisively, a single national primary day. Reform that places primaries in a late-spring-to-early-summer window preserves retail politics, where candidates are tested through direct, local engagement rather than sustained media saturation, while curbing the distortions created by the current ten-month runway.

Yet this reform will not be easy. Parties control the Pipeline. Party organizations control the primary schedule, and courts remain understandably reluctant to dictate internal party

---

* Congress established a uniform national Election Day for presidential elections in 1845, fixing it on the Tuesday following the first Monday in November. Prior to that statute, states selected their own election dates, producing staggered contests that unfolded over weeks. Lawmakers expressed concern that early results could influence later voting, invite strategic manipulation, and undermine the representative character of national elections. The move to a single Election Day sought to synchronize participation, limit sequential influence, and ensure that outcomes reflected a common electorate rather than the cumulative effects of earlier contests (Keyssar, 2000).

governance—a principle affirmed repeatedly in disputes over party rules and associational rights (Issacharoff et al., 2022; Issacharoff & Pildes, 1998). The constitutional framework established by *Citizens United* and long-standing First Amendment jurisprudence renders judicially imposed reform both improbable and undesirable (Hasen, 2016). A republic gains strength when legislatures and citizens confront structural failures directly rather than delegating repair to courts by decree. The Constitution is not a suicide pact. A political system that no longer produces the deliberative space required for republican self-government requires correction through legislative action or constitutional amendment, not judicial improvisation.

The most practical path forward lies in incentives rather than prohibitions. Congress can establish public campaign-matching funds or small-donor amplification programs conditioned on participation in a shortened primary calendar. Such incentives would not compel party compliance, yet they would reshape the cost-benefit structure that currently rewards perpetual campaigning. By aligning financial advantage with temporal restraint, the system would reward candidates who govern rather than audition year-round. Public incentives of this kind reduce political noise rather than amplify the problem—less cowbell, not more—by narrowing the space in which perpetual campaigning can dominate the work of governing.

A shorter primary calendar—achieved through federal legislation, negotiated party compacts, or constitutional amendment—would restore the cadence of a temporary campaign followed by a season of governing. Representatives would again devote more time to legislating than to fundraising. No single pathway guarantees a condensed nomination season, yet several viable mechanisms stand open. The national conversation should therefore shift away from whether reform is necessary—a conclusion increasingly supported by empirical studies of front-loading and primary timing (Mayer & Busch, 2003; Norrander, 2019)—and toward the institutional tools capable of producing a healthier electoral rhythm that reforms the Pipeline.

Reform proposals advanced by organizations such as Issue One further demonstrate how structural incentives can recalibrate congressional behavior. Restrictions on fundraising during legislative sessions, internal rules that sever committee advancement from fundraising performance, and limits on campaign activity while Congress is in session would reinforce the boundary between campaigning and governing (Issue One, 2017). The purpose of this book is not to supply a final blueprint for repairing the primary system, especially since nomination structures arise from party practice rather than constitutional mandate. The purpose is to restore a serious national conversation about structural reform—one that moves beyond reflexive debates over *Citizens United* and toward a recovery of the republican art of self-government. Parties may stand outside the constitutional text, but the nomination processes they control shape the officials who interpret and execute that text. Primary reform therefore warrants the same gravity applied to formal institutions of governance.

The task now is not to ring the cowbell louder, but to dismantle the Permanent Campaign and restore a Governing Campaign through deliberate institutional repair of the Pipeline. The task is difficult, but the authority to act resides—despite the naysayers—with We the People.

Reimagining Representation

The final reform for the Pipeline centers around the representation ratio of one Congress member to constituents, particularly in the House. When the delegates gathered in Philadelphia, the most divided men in the room agreed upon one premise: the House of Representatives would stand closest to the citizens—the House of the People. The first Congress honored that conviction. Each member represented roughly 30,000 people,* a scale that presumed proximity—of neighborhoods, of values, and of memory. A representative might not know each citizen, yet communities would likely recognize themselves in the person who carried their voice to the Congress (Farrand, 1911). The Founding's design reflected an instinctive understanding of human capacity as well as political theory.

Modern districts no longer resemble the Founder's world. A representative now speaks for more than 760,000 residents, more than twenty-five times the scale of the first Congress. Recall where Fig. 2 captures the transformation from the early Republic to the present. That graph climbs steeply over the decades that follow. The jump from 1910 to 2020 reveals the most dramatic change, driven by a frozen House size and a population that has tripled. The Constitution did not shift. Human nature did not shift. The structure alone shifted—and quietly. The scale that once grounded republican governance in local life now strains against human cognitive limits that no institution can ignore.

The limits of human interpersonal relationships appear across disciplines, although the Founders approached these questions without the benefit of modern social science. The 30,000-to-one ratio in the Constitution was not a product of neuroscience, but the ratio was not arbitrary either. George Washington's lone substantive intervention at the Convention urged a smaller House ratio out of concern for public confidence and proximity to the People (Farrand, 1911; Wood, 2011). General Washington's instinct—

---

* Representation ratios varied considerably in the earliest Congresses because apportionment rested on population estimates rather than standardized census counts. Greater uniformity emerged only after the first federal census in 1790.

The Cowbell Reform

grounded in experience rather than theory—aligns remarkably well with what later research would reveal about human social scale and the boundaries of meaningful representation. With time, anthropologists have identified a recurring pattern in social life. Humans maintain stable, meaningful relationships within clusters of roughly 150 individuals (Dunbar, 1992). This pattern, often labeled Dunbar's Number, is not political in origin but emerges from the architecture of the human brain—the neocortex.[*] Building on this number, scientists in social network theory observe a related phenomenon. Social ties cluster; information moves rapidly within groups but slowly across them; and networks saturate long before they approach the population size of a modern congressional district (Granovetter, 1973; Watts, 2004). Popular culture nods to this structure through the "Six Degrees of Kevin Bacon" game—a reminder that even humorous parlor tricks rest on real constraints in how human networks form and connect.

Figure 16 models how a social network—a friend who knows a friend whose friend knows yet another friend—expands when each person can maintain relationships with about 150 individuals. With partial overlap in those 150 ties, the network saturates quickly. Each new degree of separation adds fewer unique individuals, and the cumulative reach levels off near 600 people under a conservative assumption of 25 percent overlap. This number is far short of the 760,000 citizens in a contemporary district. A single representative

---

[*] Dunbar's Number rests on a prosaic biological fact: the neocortex scales social complexity. By comparing neocortex ratios across primates, Robin Dunbar estimated that humans can sustain roughly 147.8 stable relationships—a limit later popularized by Malcolm Gladwell (2006). Monkeys, unsurprisingly, manage fewer. The Constitution, equally unsurprisingly, never mentions neurons.

therefore has an effective social reach of roughly 600 individuals and must work across thousands of 600-person clusters with little shared context and little structural support in a district of 760,000 residents.

To do the math, the naïve expectation behind these numbers assumes exponential expansion. One might imagine that each person's 150 contacts lead to 150 new contacts at each step, but real networks do not behave that way. Friends tend to know the same people, their circles overlap, and each degree of separation introduces fewer new individuals than the last. Network researchers have shown that this overlap produces a geometric pattern that quickly saturates, Fig. 17, rather than exploding into the millions as one might assume (Granovetter, 1973; Watts, 2004). Under a 25 percent overlap, a Dunbar-sized network of 150 strong ties expands to only about 600 unique people before repeating itself.*

---

* This discussion necessarily simplifies a large and technical literature. References to Dunbar's cognitive limits, Gladwell's popular account of "connectors," and the folk metaphor of "six degrees of separation" are used heuristically rather than as precise models. Each concept originates in distinct scholarly traditions—evolutionary anthropology, network sociology, and small-world graph theory—and none maps cleanly onto the others. Nonetheless, the underlying intuition is well supported: human social networks exhibit strong clustering, rapid overlap, and diminishing reach absent brokerage across structural gaps. For more rigorous treatments, see Robin Dunbar (1992) on cognitive constraints in social networks; Mark Granovetter (1973) on weak ties; Ronald Burt (2003) on structural holes; Duncan Watts (1998) on small-world networks; and The *Tipping Point* (Gladwell, 2006) for a nontechnical synthesis. My intent here reflects the limits of exposition, not the absence of a serious theoretical foundation.

The Cowbell Reform

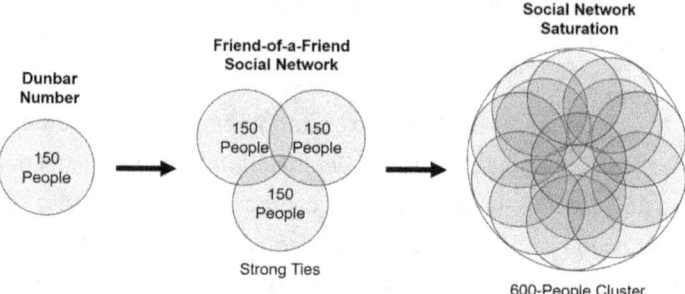

Figure 16. Modeled expansion of social reach as relationships move outward through successive degrees of separation, assuming a cognitive boundary of roughly 150 people as stable ties (Dunbar, 1992) and a 25 percent overlap among people's social networks, consistent with observed network clustering (Watts, 2004). The cluster saturates near 600 unique people, a limit grounded in human cognition.

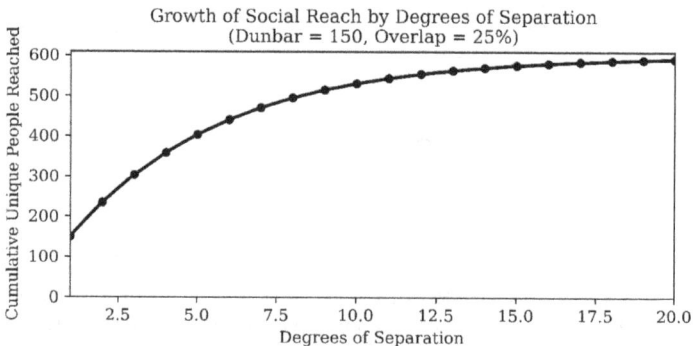

Figure 17. Geometric growth of a social network: overlap among friendship ties causes each degree of separation to add diminishing numbers of new individuals, producing a rapid approach to saturation. Empirical findings support this graph that reachable-but-not-meaningful ties plateau quickly and saturate. Here the assumption of 25% overlap in social networks a strong dominating assumption that can dramatically change the absolute numbers but not necessarily the plateauing and saturating curve.

The familiar "Six Degrees" phenomenon reflects a different structure and is represented in Fig. 18. Strong social networks form tight clusters, yet a few weak ties connect those clusters across greater social distance. These long-range, low-intensity ties collapse social distance even though each person maintains only a small and highly clustered social circle. The distinction between strong and weak ties simply describes the relative intensity of the bond. This pattern explains why personal networks saturate near 600 people even as the broader population remains reachable through a handful of long-range links (Granovetter, 1973). Malcolm Gladwell later popularized this dynamic by describing "Connectors"—individuals who occupy unusually central positions by bridging otherwise separate clusters (Gladwell, 2006).

If we translate Dunbar and people networks to Congress, a single representative must depend on more than 1,200 weak ties to maintain connection with 760,000 constituents, or more realistically a constituent must know one of these 1,200 weak links to connect with their representative. This reliance on 1,200 weak links exceeds the cognitive scale that either the representative or the constituent can sustain. By contrast, under the 30,000-to-one ratio, the required connection is one of 50 weak ties (30,000 divided by 600), a number well within the cognitive range of real social networks for both the representative and the constituents.

District Trustee Reform

Where do these limits lead, and what reform follows from them? The answer is not to abandon scale nor retreat into smaller legislative districts that fracture national coalitions. The answer is to restore proximity without surrendering enlargement. The task is not to choose between Madison and Washington but reconcile them.

The Cowbell Reform

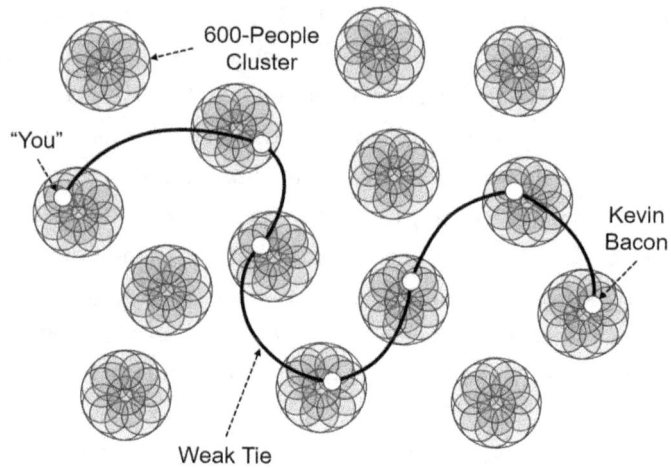

Figure 18. Illustration of "Six Degrees" connectivity. Strong-tie clusters of roughly 600 individuals link to distant clusters through a small number of weak ties. These long-range connectors bridge otherwise isolated social worlds and create the illusion of universal reach across network clusters. Individuals who perform this bridging role—often described as simply Connectors (Gladwell, 2006)—carry the weak ties that collapse social distance. In the diagram, the Connectors appear as white circles and the weak ties as the dark lines linking them.

Begin with a fixed premise. The modern House of Representatives retains its current structure. The ratio of approximately 760,000 citizens per House member remains unchanged. The size of the Chamber remains fixed. The institutional benefits of large, single-member districts—coalition-building, interest aggregation, and national accountability—remain intact.

Now introduce a complementary layer of representation beneath each House member: *Public Trustees of the District*, or more simply District Trustees.

District Trustees would be elected officials representing non-overlapping subdistricts of approximately 30,000 citizens within each congressional district. Each House district would therefore contain roughly twenty-five District Trustees, aligned closely with the representational scale favored by George Washington at the Constitutional Convention. Citizens would vote separately for their House member and their District Trustee—allowing for the possibility that some District Trustees may be in opposing parties to their House member. The two offices would coexist, not compete. The House member would retain full legislative authority. District Trustees would hold none.

This distinction is essential. District Trustees would not vote on legislation, sit on committees, draft statutory language, or travel regularly to Washington. Legislative authority would remain exclusively with the House member. The District Trustee role is representational rather than legislative—anchored at a human scale. District Trustees would reside full time within their subdistricts, where visibility, reputation, and repeated social contact impose pressures that abstraction dissolves, a dynamic long observed in congressional behavior under conditions of proximity and continuous local scrutiny (Fenno, 1978).

District Trustees would live within their communities. They would convene public forums, maintain regular contact with constituents, and serve as structured conduits between local civic life and national governance. They would gather constituent perspectives on legislation, translate concerns into coherent feedback, and maintain continuous communication with the sitting House member while Congress is in session. Representation would once again operate through sustained relationships rather than episodic campaigns. As elected officials embedded in local life, District Trustees would exercise representational authority that professional staff—however capable—cannot supply.

Once each year, District Trustees would convene nationally in a week-long conference hosted by a rotating state and held outside Washington, D.C. These conventions would bring together more than 35,000 District Trustees alongside sitting members of Congress in a closed-door, non-binding setting. The purpose would not be lawmaking. The purpose would be alignment. Representatives and District Trustees would exchange perspectives, identify emerging concerns, and build working relationships before issues harden into factional conflict. Deliberation would precede mobilization. In function, this gathering would resemble the coordinating role once played by political machines, but with legitimacy anchored in elected representation and transparency rather than patronage—preserving the benefits of pre-electoral bargaining while mitigating the corruption incentives that discredited the machines themselves (Golway, 2014; Mansbridge et al., 2012).

This layered structure restores an older republican logic. James Madison described representation as a system of successive filtrations, where public views are refined through multiple stages before becoming law. Enlargement widens the sphere, but filtration preserves judgment. Modern governance retains enlargement while abandoning filtration at the social level. District Trustees restore that missing stage without fragmenting legislative authority and mitigating corruption.

The proposed District Trustee layer restores a function that once existed informally in American politics but never constitutionally. Urban political machines such as Tammany Hall performed this connective work imperfectly and unlawfully, yet the underlying function proved real. Ward captains translated local needs upward, mediated disputes before escalation, and buffered mass democratic pressure before that pressure reached citywide or national institutions. Corruption followed because the Republic refused to perform that connective labor openly and lawfully at scale.

District Trustees recover the function without inheriting the vice. Unlike ward captains, District Trustees derive authority from elections rather than patronage, operate within formal rules rather than party machinery, and remain accountable through regular review rather than loyalty networks. The proposal does not revive machine politics. The proposal formalizes mediation within republican design.

This layer addresses a structural absence that modern reforms never replaced. Citizens today encounter representation either at an inhuman scale or through informal intermediaries who answer to no electorate at all. District Trustees restore human-scale representation as a visible, legitimate component of the governing system. Pressure dissipates locally. Negotiation precedes escalation. National representatives receive filtered demands rather than raw factional intensity.

The historical lesson is not that the Republic needs fewer layers. The lesson is that the Republic needs better ones.

The reform also introduces a structural check on extreme gerrymandering. Gerrymandering thrives when districts are large enough to be socially incoherent. When representation operates at massive scale, mapmakers can assemble fractured communities into artificial constructs optimized for partisan advantage. Scholars have shown that large districts permit high-precision sorting, allowing lines to slice through neighborhoods, institutions, and shared civic life with little resistance (Chen & Rodden, 2013; McGann et al., 2016). Distortion becomes the purpose rather than the byproduct of mapmaking.

Subdistrict-based representation counteracts this tendency. District Trustees depend on coherent local communities for legitimacy. They cannot survive politically if boundaries sever neighborhoods, schools, churches, and civic institutions from one another. The presence of elected officials anchored to small, socially legible districts creates organic resistance to cartographic manipulation. Gerrymandering does not disappear, but its effectiveness diminishes when representation is rooted in lived community rather than abstract aggregation.

Recent scholarship reinforces this design from a different angle. In *Responsible Parties*, Frances Rosenbluth and Ian Shapiro argue

The Cowbell Reform

that democratic stability depends on large districts capable of forcing interest aggregation and sustaining durable governing coalitions (2018). Narrow districts encourage parochialism. Broad districts enlarge the political sphere and discipline factional excess. Madison understood this logic well.

Yet the Founders also understood that enlargement alone was insufficient. Washington warned that representation stretched too far from the People would erode trust and legitimacy. His concern was not legislative efficiency. His concern was confidence. Representation, he understood, requires proximity as well as scale.

The District Trustee reform reconciles these insights. Large House districts remain intact to preserve coalition-building at the national level. Beneath them, a human-scale representational network restores proximity, continuity, and reputational consequence. Enlargement persists without alienation. Proximity returns without parochialism. The republic regains balance.

This proposal may appear awkward at first glance. That reaction reflects modern habits rather than constitutional logic. Expanding the House directly would restore proximity, but at an unacceptable institutional cost. Reestablishing the original 30,000-to-one ratio would require a Chamber exceeding 10,000 members—far beyond the capacity of a deliberative legislature. More importantly, fragmenting representation into districts of that scale would forfeit the benefits of large single-member districts, which force interest aggregation, discourage parochialism, and sustain governing coalitions at the national level (Rosenbluth & Shapiro, 2018). The District Trustee reform recovers the representational advantages of proximity without inflating the Chamber or sacrificing enlargement.

Representation remains socially legible only when relational distance is constrained; beyond that point, formal authority persists while reputational accountability dissolves. The Chamber must remain functional.* This reform leaves Congress intact. It does not dilute legislative authority. It does not fragment national coalitions. It restores representation to a level of social comprehension the Founders intuitively understood and modern science now confirms. Representation becomes once again a lived relationship rather than a statistical abstraction.

Proximity alone, however, does not guarantee responsibility. Structure creates capacity. Consequence creates discipline. The next section turns to the condition under which that restored structure becomes active—when the People's business goes undone.

---

* This discussion raises a counterfactual question rather than a policy proposal: if the House of Representatives remains fixed at 435 members, how far can the citizen-to-representative ratio expand before social accountability ceases to function as a meaningful constraint? Approaching representation as a social network rather than as a purely electoral mechanism suggests that accountability depends on relational distance as much as on formal authority. Research in anthropology and cognitive neuroscience indicates that humans sustain stable, reputationally binding relationships within bounded cognitive limits, often observed near 150 individuals, with additional layers of weaker ties saturating quickly due to overlap (Dunbar, 2010; Dunbar, 1992). Social network theory further shows that as intermediary layers expand, ties become abstract rather than socially constraining, even though formal reach persists (Granovetter, 1973; Watts, 2004). The figures referenced here are illustrative boundary conditions intended to situate modern districts—already far beyond such limits—rather than to define an optimal or desirable scale. Under the District Trustee model, a rough boundary-condition upper limit lies in the range of 3–4.5 million citizens per House member, with 4.5 million serving as a clean illustrative ceiling under the Dunbar-style assumption. The present ratio of roughly 760,000 citizens per representative remains well below this theoretical boundary—potentially good news for future Americans.

The Cowbell Reform

The Budget as a Forcing Function

The Public Trustees of the Districts possess no ordinary legislative authority and exercise no control over the daily work of Congress. Their role is deliberately narrow. The proposal vests in each District Trustee a single, extraordinary power—one suggested by the title *Trustee** itself. Trustees do not govern. Trustees intervene only when trust has failed. What follows when a legislature refuses to perform the one task the Constitution assumes cannot be avoided?

James Madison assumed that certain acts of governance would be unavoidable. Appropriations stood foremost among them. Control of the purse was not an administrative detail; budgetary authority formed the hinge on which legislative power turned. A legislature that could not fund the government could not govern, and a legislature that could not govern could not retain legitimate authority. The Constitution never contemplated a stable equilibrium in which Congress repeatedly failed to pass a budget while authority remained intact. The District Trustee reform addresses this failure not by expanding ordinary power, but by restoring consequence when governance breaks down.

Modern governance has instead normalized precisely that failure. Continuing resolutions, omnibus packages, emergency authorities, and executive improvisation have transformed budget failure from a crisis into a routine. Government continues in degraded form. Salaries are paid. Markets adjust. Blame disperses.

---

* The definition of a trustee is an individual entrusted with limited authority to act on behalf of others under defined conditions, owing a fiduciary duty to preserve continuity, safeguard shared interests, and exercise independent judgment when ordinary mechanisms fail. A trustee does not possess general governing power and intervenes only within the scope and triggers established by law.

Responsibility thins. What once functioned as a forcing mechanism has become a procedural inconvenience. Under these conditions, Madison's logic no longer operates. Factions do not negotiate. Factions wait. The failure is not moral. The failure is structural.

A republic that tolerates indefinite budget failure cannot be repaired through exhortation alone. A legislature that skips its core obligation year after year and retains authority has little incentive to behave differently. Reform must restore a principle the Founders took for granted: authority endures only so long as responsibility is exercised.

The representational structure introduced earlier remains dormant during ordinary governance. District Trustees exist to restore proximity, continuity, and reputational accountability. That structure does not interfere with legislation, nor does it dilute the authority of elected House members. Under normal conditions, the District Trustee layer remains inactive with respect to formal power. Its function is latent.

The forcing function activates only upon failure. If Congress fails to enact a full annual budget by a fixed statutory date, all House members are removed from office simultaneously. No shutdown follows. No continuing resolution intervenes. No executive substitution occurs. Authority transfers automatically and internally. Within each congressional district, the District Trustees convene and elect one of their own to serve as the replacement Representative. The replacement member is seated immediately. A short, fixed deadline follows for budget passage. If failure persists, the replacement process repeats. The cycle continues until a budget is enacted.

This mechanism does not resemble recall. This mechanism does not operate as impeachment. This mechanism does not invite populist upheaval. The mechanism functions as institutional self-repair.

Madison feared legislative abdication more than turnover. The Constitution already permits expulsion, vacancy, and replacement. What the constitutional design does not contemplate—because

The Cowbell Reform

Madison assumed the People would never tolerate it—is a legislature that refuses to perform its most basic duty indefinitely while retaining authority. The replacement mechanism restores the consequence Madison expected without collapsing the regime itself.

Three stabilizing effects follow. First, unavoidability returns. Budget failure now terminates authority. Delay ceases to function as a viable strategy. Completion becomes the only stable outcome. Parliamentary systems achieve a similar effect by tying budget passage to confidence in the government, where failure precipitates collapse or election (Rosenbluth & Shapiro, 2018). The American approach proposed here preserves constitutional continuity while reintroducing the same forcing logic through legislative replacement rather than regime dissolution.

Second, accountability re-enters at a human scale precisely when it matters most. Replacement Representatives emerge from a layer of elected officials embedded in local communities and subject to sustained social pressure. Bargaining occurs among individuals who know one another and remain close to the voters who will judge the outcome. This structure offers a more republican and more measured alternative to snap elections, allowing continuity of governance while restoring consequence. As a safeguard, the framework may permit District Trustees—by supermajority vote[*]—

---

[*] The use of a supermajority threshold reflects long-standing constitutional practice rather than a novel procedural innovation. The Constitution repeatedly reserves supermajority requirements for extraordinary actions that reverse, override, or temper otherwise decisive outcomes, including treaty ratification (Article II, Section 2), conviction following impeachment (Article I, Section 3), expulsion of a member (Article I, Section 5), and the override of a presidential veto (Article I, Section 7). In each case, heightened consensus serves as a safeguard against impulsive reversal while preserving the gravity of the underlying consequence. The supermajority

to reinstate a displaced House member once a budget passes, preserving experienced legislators who ultimately fulfill their obligation while maintaining the primacy of consequence.

Third, accountability remains internal to the representative system. Authority flows upward from smaller republican units rather than downward from courts, executives, or plebiscitary mobilization. The system disciplines itself.

Once the House passes a budget under this discipline, responsibility shifts to the other chamber. Bicameralism requires concurrence, though the Constitution assigns origination to the House. The Senate was designed to refine legislation, not to suspend governance indefinitely. Under this proposal, when a House operating under the replacement mechanism passes a budget, the Senate must vote by a fixed statutory date. Senators retain full authority to amend, revise, or reject the proposal. If the Senate affirmatively overrides the House-passed budget by supermajority vote, the measure fails.* Absent such an override, the House-passed budget becomes law. Senators no longer retain the option to delay. Bicameralism exists to sharpen judgment, not to paralyze the Republic.

Modern politics treats officeholding as a status conferred by election and protected by time. Madison treated officeholding as a

---

referenced here performs the same constitutional function: reinstatement is possible, but only when broad agreement affirms that responsibility has been restored. This structural mechanism will also serve to encourage seated House members to maintain good standing with their District Trustees, particularly during budget season.

* This treatment of Senate override is illustrative rather than definitive. The balance between bicameral refinement and the need for finality in appropriations raises questions that demand national deliberation. The proposal offered here is intended as a starting point for that debate, not its conclusion.

The Cowbell Reform

trust sustained by the faithful execution of duty. This reform makes that distinction explicit. A legislature that governs retains authority. A legislature that refuses to govern yields authority—peacefully, constitutionally, and internally.

No riots follow. No shutdowns ensue. No executive improvisation fills the void. A republic endures because the system insists on completing the work the Republic was created to perform. The Chamber addresses governing failure. The Pipeline addresses candidate failure.

Freelance Campaigns

After the 1968 primary reforms, a new type of candidate emerged—one that no longer needed the party during the nomination process, one that operated more as a freelance political actor than as a party veteran. Reformers did not intend this result. The goal was transparency and participation. The consequence was a structural inversion. The political system now rewards candidates who can assemble campaigns independently of party institutions and approach the general election with personal organizations already in place. Therefore, serious reform of the nomination process must reduce the need for freelance campaigns and restore party-centered pathways to national office because freelance candidates empower demagogues.

The post-1968 primary system did not merely weaken political parties. The primary system reassigned responsibility. Before reform, parties bore the burden of aggregation, vetting, and long-term stewardship. Parties maintained voter lists, trained volunteers, cultivated leadership, and absorbed political risk across election cycles. After reform, that burden shifted to individual candidates. The nomination Pipeline became candidate-built rather than institutional. That inversion altered incentives more deeply than reformers anticipated, because ambition no longer passed through a shared structure before reaching national power. Ambition now constructs a personal pathway—independent of the party machine—and dismantles that pathway once the election ends—hollowing out the party each election cycle.

During the primary phase, candidates operate as provisional political actors largely independent of party structure. Parties provide ballot access, compliance rules, and debate procedures, but parties offer little organizational capacity. Candidates must raise funds, recruit and manage national staff, assemble state-by-state field operations, secure voter data, coordinate volunteers, impose messaging discipline, and sustain turnout efforts without durable institutional support. The party exists primarily as a regulatory shell until the general election arrives.

This arrangement did not arise in a vacuum. Progressive-era reforms dismantled the oft-maligned party machines of the late nineteenth and early twentieth centuries, including organizations such as Tammany Hall and the politics associated with Boss Tweed (Golway, 2014). The corruptions of Tweed-ism were real and corrosive. Patronage, exclusion, and graft deserved reform. Yet those organizations possessed one structural feature now missing from American politics: independence from individual candidates. Party machines endured beyond election cycles. Organizational memory persisted. Candidates who were qualified to govern did not also need to be exceptional fundraisers or charismatic mobilizers. The skills required to raise money and dominate attention were separated from the skills required to govern. The 1968 primary reforms completed the dismantling of party machines and replaced them with freelance candidate organizations—temporary, personality-driven, and often sustained by demagogic rhetoric rather than institutional discipline.

A republic cannot rely on temporary organizations to perform permanent civic work. Parties once existed to absorb political energy and translate that energy into governing coalitions capable of

The Cowbell Reform

enduring beyond a single campaign or a single candidate. That function did not depend on virtue. That function depended on friction. Leaders persuaded internal actors before mobilizing the public. Factions negotiated under rules that rewarded patience, compromise, and durability. Boss Tweed's infamous remark about selecting candidates captures this dynamic in an unsettling form, but the underlying reality remains instructive. The post-1968 primary system stripped away internal negotiation and replaced institutional bargaining with direct competition for attention. The result is not greater accountability. The result is a nomination Pipeline that rewards emotional intensity over institutional responsibility.

Political scientists Steven Levitsky, a leading scholar of democratic erosion, and Daniel Ziblatt, a historian of party systems and democratic survival, describe this shift as the collapse of party gatekeeping. Levitsky and Ziblatt argue that parties historically protected democratic systems by filtering out candidates who thrived on polarization but lacked governing restraint (Levitsky & Ziblatt, 2019). Rosenbluth and Shapiro reach a similar conclusion from a different direction, observing that parties once operated as accountability structures that balanced electoral responsiveness against governing capacity (Rosenbluth & Shapiro, 2018). The modern primary system dissolved that balance. Candidates now prove viability through mobilization rather than stewardship. Legitimacy flows from enthusiasm rather than trust.

Arnold Schwarzenegger, better known for success as a bodybuilder than for politics, once observed that motivation is a poor substitute for routine (Schwarzenegger, 2012). Mobilization and motivation do not equate to stewardship and routine. Motivation feels powerful, but motivation burns quickly. Routine sustains effort over time. That distinction applies directly to political parties and campaigns. Modern primaries reward motivation—anger, enthusiasm, spectacle—but starve routine. Party organizations once supplied routine through voter maintenance, coalition management, and institutional memory.

The term *political machine* has become derisive because of Tammany Hall and late-nineteenth-century corruption, yet the mechanical analogy remains instructive. Machines run on steady inputs rather than bursts of emotion. Systems endure through repetition, maintenance, and reliability. Candidate-built campaigns run hot and fast, then collapse. A republic cannot be governed on adrenaline. Today's parties function less like machines and more like pop-up organizations—assembled quickly around a candidate, optimized for visibility, and dismantled once the electoral moment passes.

Under these conditions, loyalty predictably erodes. Candidates who survive primaries through personal organization rather than party support owe little to party institutions or long-standing coalitions. Consider Alexandria Ocasio-Cortez, who defeated a senior incumbent in a low-turnout primary with minimal backing from party leadership. Having built her own campaign infrastructure and volunteer base, she entered office accountable primarily to a movement rather than to party elites or institutional norms. The same structural logic applies, from the opposite ideological direction, to Donald Trump, who was initially rejected by Republican party leaders but succeeded by constructing a parallel political organization that ultimately subsumed the party itself. Trump did not capture the party machine. Trump replaced the party machine.

These outcomes were not aberrations. These outcomes were predictable consequences of a system that rewards candidates for bypassing parties rather than working through them. When nomination success depends on defeating party stalwarts rather than earning institutional trust, primaries become weapons rather than filters. The threat of being primaried evolves into a counter-insurgency mechanism aimed at enforcing ideological purity and

The Cowbell Reform

punishing compromise.* Party members who lean across the aisle to govern face electoral vulnerability at home, not because constituents reject compromise, but because activist intensity dominates low-participation primaries. A system designed to democratize nominations inadvertently discourages the very behavior that republican government requires.

The reforms proposed here seek to reverse that misalignment. The goal is not to insulate parties from voters. The goal is to realign candidates with party institutions rather than position candidates against them. Stronger party stewardship during the nomination process would reduce the incentive to construct personal political machines and weaken the strategic use of primaries as tools of ideological enforcement. In a counterintuitive but necessary turn, restoring party-centered campaigns would make cross-party compromise more sustainable by reducing the constant threat of internal punishment.

The consequences extend beyond any single election cycle. When candidates must build personal organizations from scratch, time horizons contract. Campaigns focus on moments rather than movements. Volunteers assemble around feelings rather than plans. Moderates free-ride while activists dominate, not because moderates lack conviction, but because nomination rules reward intensity rather than breadth. These pressures do not corrupt

---

* The term *being primaried* refers to an incumbent officeholder facing a serious intra-party challenge, typically from a more ideologically intense faction. Political scientists have identified the threat of primary challenges as a central mechanism through which activist minorities discipline elected officials and deter compromise. See Mann and Ornstein (2016), Klein (2020); Rosenbluth and Shapiro (2018).

democracy through bad faith. These pressures distort democracy through institutional design.

Repair requires acknowledging that participation alone does not create legitimacy. Deliberation creates legitimacy. Parties once provided that deliberative layer by aggregating interests before exposing candidates to the full force of mass politics. Reformers after 1968 removed that layer in the name of openness. The nomination Pipeline now lacks an internal mechanism capable of slowing momentum or testing readiness. No amount of voter education can substitute for institutional mediation. Structural incentives overpower civic aspiration.

Reconstructing the nomination Pipeline does not require a return to secrecy, exclusion, or Tammany Hall. Smoke-filled rooms are not the remedy. Shared ownership is the remedy. Nomination infrastructure must again belong to parties rather than to candidates. Voter data, volunteer training, turnout logistics, and delegate processes should persist across election cycles and remain accountable to party institutions rather than dissolving into personal brands. Candidates should compete within that shared framework rather than constructing parallel organizations designed for a single moment. Such a system does not silence insurgents. Such a system requires insurgents to persuade institutions as well as crowds.

The challenge lies in where authority resides. Political parties are extra-constitutional entities. The Constitution neither defines political parties nor governs their internal structures. That silence leaves party discipline dependent on voluntary institutional norms rather than formal constitutional authority, a condition scholars have long recognized as both a strength and a vulnerability of the American system (Schattschneider, 1942). The reconstruction of the nomination Pipeline therefore depends not on constitutional amendment, but on whether parties choose to reclaim responsibility for candidate selection and enforce norms that privilege stewardship over spectacle.

The Cowbell Reform

Time also matters. Madison understood delay as a stabilizer rather than a defect. The extended republic was designed to slow the conversion of passion into law. The modern nomination Pipeline accelerates that conversion at precisely the moment when media systems amplify outrage and reward spectacle. Reforms that lengthen qualification timelines, restore layered endorsement processes, and shorten the extended primary season would not weaken democracy. Such reforms would strengthen legitimacy by ensuring that authority reflects sustained trust rather than transient excitement while also reducing the incentives of the Permanent Campaign.

Money further complicates the nomination Pipeline. Early fundraising success now substitutes for broad coalition support. Candidates who provoke outrage often outperform candidates who inspire confidence, because financial momentum compounds emotional momentum. Research on campaign finance shows that early resource concentration amplifies ideological extremes rather than consensus builders (Mann & Ornstein, 2016). A nomination pipeline that reconnects fundraising thresholds to party structures would not eliminate small-dollar participation. Such a system would prevent viral reach from replacing institutional confidence as the primary measure of readiness. The constituent–donor reforms discussed earlier align naturally with this repair.

The deeper issue is not nostalgia for a vanished party system. The deeper issue is republican function. Parties once converted democratic energy into governing capacity. The modern primary system dismantled that conversion mechanism and left candidates to perform institutional labor that individuals cannot sustain. The result is a political environment rich in participation and poor in restraint, loud in expression and thin in durability. Parties should not sit on the sidelines during the primary season. Parties should act as active participants, supporting candidates and reducing the infrastructure burdens that now reward demagoguery over governance.

The problem does not end when the primary concludes. The winning candidate often becomes the *de facto* party leader. The candidate's campaign infrastructure becomes the party's infrastructure. The party no longer selects the candidate. In a striking reversal, the candidate inherits the party. Party-centered platforms give way to candidate-centered platforms. Personal brands eclipse institutional identity. Long-term party stability yields to waxing and waning cults of personality driven by primary outcomes rather than shared principles. The modern citizen encounters the presidency less as an office embedded within a governing party than as a personality that temporarily occupies one.

This failure does not stand alone. The nomination Pipeline once slowed politics internally while the Press slowed politics externally. Both institutions have weakened simultaneously. Candidates now move from outrage to amplification without meaningful friction. Rebuilding the nomination Pipeline restores only part of the republic's stabilizing architecture. The next section turns to the other half of that failure, where information systems magnify passion faster than institutions can absorb political pressure.

Reconstructing the Fourth Branch

A republic depends upon institutions that slow judgment, widen perspective, and steady public life. The American press once played that role. For much of the twentieth century, local newspapers and national bureaus formed a loose Fourth Branch of governance. They could not pass laws or command armies, yet the Press shaped the informational environment in which voters and representatives understood their world with integrity and responsibility. Their presence produced a common frame of reference—though imperfect and not without bias. Their absence now accelerates democratic volatility (Schudson, 2008).

The Cowbell Reform

The Press' collapse arrived with startling speed. Advertising revenue evaporated as digital platforms captured the market and dismantled the cross-subsidies that once funded investigative reporting (Levy & Nielsen, 2010). Consolidations gutted metropolitan and regional newsrooms (Abernathy, 2018). Entire counties lost professional reporters, producing what scholars call "news deserts." Social media platforms filled the vacuum with algorithmic feeds optimized for engagement rather than verification (Tufekci, 2015).* Scholars describe this new environment as postjournalism, where emotional mobilization substitutes for factual reporting and where the Viral Editor—an algorithm trained to provoke—replaces the human editor trained to filter (Mir, 2020). The result mirrors the pattern described in our first chapter, where informational acceleration invites the cowbell mob and overwhelms deliberative judgment. A society that prizes reaction over reflection cannot sustain republican governance.

A diagnosis emerges. Modern democracies cannot sustain a professional press on democratic incentives alone. Professional journalism did not arise from the nation's founding but from reforms that followed the excesses of yellow journalism. By the 1920s, newsrooms began embracing norms of verification, editorial independence, and public responsibility. That professional era,

---

* The most famous demonstration comes from a 2014 Facebook experiment that altered the emotional content of users' News Feeds to test whether moods would shift in response. Nearly 700,000 users were unwitting participants. The study showed that small tweaks in the algorithm produced measurable changes in the emotional tone of user posts, offering experimental confirmation that platforms can influence collective behavior at scale (Kramer et al., 2014). In other words, Facebook did not simply measure the weather of public emotion—it ran the climate system for a week.

however, proved fragile and began to erode rapidly as the twentieth century closed. The unofficial Fourth Branch reached its highwater mark during that period, yet its foundations weakened long before the Internet arrived. Market structures reward immediacy, spectacle, and conflict, not verification or deliberation. Though the rise of the Internet bears most of the blame, scholar Robert McChesney and political journalist John Nichols note that when "the Internet came along as a significant force, newspapers were already heading south" (McChesney & Nichols, 2011). Professors Leonard Downie, Jr. and Michael Schudson wrote in a 2009 report that "the economic foundation of the nation's newspapers, long supported by advertising, is collapsing, and newspapers themselves, which have been the country's chief source of independent reporting, are shrinking—literally" (Downie Jr & Schudson, 2009). No commercial model can subsidize slow reporting, document review, and investigative depth when sensational content attracts larger audiences. A strong republic requires a stabilizing informational center that democratic markets cannot naturally produce.

The repair must therefore adopt a republican form. The nation requires a rebuilt Fourth Branch. One reform proposal is community newspapers supported by independent endowments and governed by the logic of civic infrastructure. A newspaper should resemble a library: an institution created for public use, protected against political manipulation, and designed for long life (Downie Jr & Schudson, 2009). While consensus is mounting that professional journalism should be a public good, disagreement emerges as to the funding mechanism needed to sustain the institution. Some folks argue, as McChesney and Nichols (2011) do, that government funding models such as the Public Broadcasting Service (PBS) or National Public Radio (NPR) should become the pantheon. While liberals and Democrats would likely support such tax-based mechanisms, conservatives and Republicans would likely balk. Alternatively, as Mir (2020) notes, private funding through wealthy donors is another

The Cowbell Reform

option, though this approach has bias flaws that Mir discusses extensively. A newsroom dependent upon a benefactor inherits the incentives of that benefactor.

The most republican alternative is a structured balance between a public good and private financing. This balance is the recommendation of this book. Local communities should raise endowment funds that produce stable returns year after year. These endowments must operate behind a strong institutional wall that separates donors from newsroom decisions. Influence cannot flow through the funding structure. Local governments and wealthy benefactors should not control content. A newspaper that answers to political power or private fortune does not serve the public, but one that answers to a defined public mission serves the Republic.

Such papers require professional journalists who understand the discipline of verification. Their task is to report news, not to offer opinions, and not to become the story themselves. Journalism scholars have long argued that credibility depends on a clear separation between reporting and advocacy, along with editorial layers that slow the production cycle enough to secure factual accuracy (Kovach & Rosenstiel, 2021). Incentives must reflect that principle. Reporters should build careers around accuracy and depth rather than personal visibility. Citizens deserve information shaped by evidence rather than impulse.

Communities can rebuild this Fourth Branch. Endowment drives can secure capital sufficient for perpetual operation. Stable funding would allow editors to plan years ahead, not weeks. A reliable paper in each county or region would restore shared factual baselines. The informational center would slowly return, not as a nostalgic reconstruction of the past, but as a modern republican institution that protects deliberative democracy from the turbulence of digital acceleration. The goal is not a sentimental return to Walter Cronkite or Edward R. Murrow; nostalgia cannot rebuild a republic. The

More Republic, Less Cowbell

Republic needs durable institutions capable of stabilizing public judgment, and the Press has long served that republican purpose.

One historical example offers a useful guide. Joseph Pulitzer, whose own newspaper empire once trafficked in sensationalism, spent the final chapter of his life building the opposite: permanence. In 1904, he created a private endowment at Columbia University to establish a graduate school of journalism and to reward exemplary reporting through what became the Pulitzer Prizes (Morris, 2010).* That endowment continues to operate more than a century later, insulated from political control, donor pressure, and momentary passions. Pulitzer understood that public goods cannot survive on outrage or attention alone. Public goods require structure, discipline, and time.

That insight reaches beyond journalism. A newspaper sustained by a community endowment rather than a benefactor or a government budget stands a far better chance of becoming a republican institution rather than a partisan instrument. The same principle applies across the architecture of self-government. Durable institutions do not depend on perpetual virtue. Durable institutions depend on design. They channel energy, restrain excess, and outlast the personalities that momentarily inhabit them.

---

* Pulitzer remains one of the more paradoxical figures in American journalism. His early career helped fuel the sensationalism of the "yellow journalism" era, marked by bold headlines, fierce circulation battles, and accusations that his New York World blurred the line between news and spectacle. Critics charged that Pulitzer and William Randolph Hearst pushed news toward entertainment, especially during the Spanish–American War. Yet Pulitzer spent his later years advocating for ethical reporting, criticizing the very excesses he once deployed, and endowing Columbia University in 1904 to elevate journalism through professional training and annual prizes. Few figures have both contributed so much to sensationalism and invested so heavily in reform (Morris, 2010).

The Cowbell Reform

This chapter has traced what happens when those designs erode. The Chamber weakened when deliberation gave way to performance. The Pipeline fractured when party stewardship yielded to freelance campaigns. The Press faltered when permanence surrendered to velocity. None of these failures arose from malice. Each emerged from reforms that prized immediacy over durability and participation over structure. The result is a political system rich in passion and poor in restraint.

What now remains is to draw the lesson.

In Sum

The architects of the American Republic did not demand harmony from the citizenry. They demanded structure from government. They constructed a republican framework for democratic disagreement—not to tame or silence discord, but to direct conflict toward durable public ends. James Madison, Alexander Hamilton, and George Washington understood a truth that remains unchanged: democratic passion arrives quickly, while republican judgment requires time, distance, and craft. The Founders built institutions to absorb the first and sustain the second. Modern reforms—often justified by democratic instinct—have weakened those stabilizers. The nation gained immediacy and transparency, but surrendered much of the republican machinery that once converted democratic energy into governing authority.

The Chamber once provided that machinery. Committees supplied expertise, belonging, and structure. Members gained fluency in their jurisdictions, and committee chairs stewarded the legislative pace. That world produced tension and controversy, yet the same world also produced law. Leadership centralization, the rise of crisis calendars that force major decisions into last-minute, leadership-drafted packages, cameras in the Chamber, and the erosion of staff capacity have thinned those stabilizers across the last three decades. A legislature that lives under permanent visibility cannot negotiate, cannot reconsider, and cannot retreat from premature certainty. The Republic cannot thrive when the first branch behaves as a stage for theatrical combat rather than a workshop for republican craft.

Equally, the Pipeline that selects national legislators has shifted in equally consequential ways. Primaries once resembled caucuses of neighbors—small gatherings shaped by community memory and local trust. After 1968, reforms designed to democratize nominations unintentionally empowered factions rather than coalitions. Low-turnout contests, plurality victories, and front-loaded calendars placed extraordinary leverage in the hands of motivated minorities. A republic cannot sustain that dynamic without consequence. Nominees chosen by factions govern as factional representatives—polarization dominates and overtakes the Republic. A republic requires majority-backed candidates who can speak for a broad coalition and govern a country larger than one's home district.

Finally, the Press once formed the informational center between those structures and the People. Twentieth-century journalism, imperfect but resilient, supplied verification, context, and a shared factual baseline. That center has thinned as economic incentives shifted toward speed, outrage, and algorithmic escalation. Communities now rely on informational systems that accelerate passion faster than institutions can absorb that surge. No republic can survive when public judgment is shaped entirely by velocity.

A republic must slow, mediate, and filter. Democracy alone cannot perform those functions. The Chamber, the Pipeline, and the Press once provided that filtering capacity, and together these three institutions formed the skeleton of a functioning republic. Reconstructing the Fourth Branch—a professional press supported by independent endowments—completes the repair.

The Cowbell Reform

The reforms in this chapter—stronger committees, majority-producing primaries, and an endowment-backed press—restore the stabilizers the Founders considered indispensable. None of these reforms silence political passion. None retreat from democratic engagement. Each reform seeks to give democratic passion a structure, a pace, and a channel consistent with the scale of a continental republic. A society that governs 330 million people cannot operate as a continuous referendum. A republic of this size requires organized representation, tempered judgment, and institutions capable of holding the center when noise rises.

The final chapter now turns toward the reader. A republic does not renew itself by statute alone. Renewal begins with citizens who accept the burden of self-government—citizens who distinguish disagreement from enmity, persuasion from mobilization, and political opponents from existential threats. Self-government requires the defense of spaces where judgment forms away from the glare of instantaneous reaction. The Founders understood that a republic survives only when the People demand more of themselves than they indulge their passions.

Thus, the path forward does not require a new philosophy. The path forward requires a renewed commitment to an old one. Chapter 5 carries that call.

CHAPTER 5

The Citizen's Call

IN 1801, THE AMERICAN REPUBLIC faced a test that constitutional text alone could not resolve. The election of 1800 marked the first transfer of national power between rival political parties, and the rivalry ran deep. John Adams and Thomas Jefferson, once collaborators in independence, had come to represent competing visions of republican government.* Federalists warned

---

* The election of 1800 marked the first transfer of national power between organized political rivals in modern history. John Adams and Thomas Jefferson, once collaborators in independence, had become symbols of competing visions of republican government. Federalists warned that Jefferson's victory would dissolve constitutional order and invite popular excess, fears amplified through aligned newspapers. Republicans charged Adams with monarchical ambition, citing the Alien and Sedition Acts as evidence of creeping tyranny. The contest tested not only electoral machinery but constitutional restraint. Adams's decision to step aside without contest, despite deep personal bitterness and genuine fear for the Republic's future, established a precedent more fragile than Washington's voluntary retirement—and arguably more consequential (Wood, 2017).

The Citizen's Call

that Jefferson's victory would dissolve constitutional order and unleash mob rule. Republicans accused Adams of monarchical ambition and cited the Alien and Sedition Acts as evidence of creeping tyranny.* The campaign exhausted the young system without producing confidence or reconciliation. Adams lost.

What followed mattered more than the contest itself. Adams, the nation's first one-term president, did not contest the outcome. Adams did not summon supporters. Adams did not challenge the legitimacy of the process that removed authority from his hands. Adams departed the capital before dawn because the rules had held. No statute compelled submission. No enforcement mechanism guaranteed compliance. Constitutional continuity survived because restraint governed where defiance would have felt justified. The Republic endured not because passions cooled, but because the losing side accepted loss and allowed institutions to function under strain.

That transfer of power rivaled—and in some respects surpassed—George Washington's decision to step down after two terms. Washington relinquished authority at the height of prestige. Adams relinquished authority after defeat. Washington demonstrated that power could be surrendered voluntarily. Adams demonstrated that power could be surrendered under loss. The latter act carried greater institutional risk and established a precedent

---

* The term *Republicans* here refers to the Jeffersonian Republican Party of the 1790s—often called the Democratic-Republican Party—founded by Thomas Jefferson and James Madison in opposition to the Federalists. This party bears no organizational or ideological continuity with the modern Republican Party, which emerged in the 1850s. Party labels in the early republic reflected fluid coalitions rather than fixed institutional identities. See Christmas (2017).

no constitutional text could compel. Adams received little recognition for that choice, yet acceptance of defeat under lawful rules secured the Republic as surely as any founding moment.

This chapter begins from that premise. Self-government does not demand constant expression, maximal transparency, or perpetual mobilization. Republican self-government demands restraint when loss arrives and patience when institutions frustrate immediate desire. The call that follows offers no romance and promises no applause. The call is republican. Over the last half-century, American political reform moved in the opposite direction. The fracture examined throughout this book emerged not from excess disagreement, but from forgetting what restraint requires when power slips away.

More Cowbell?

Adams's response—to step away—was a republican response. Not passive. Not weak. Republican in the deepest sense of the word. Adams accepted the verdict of the people without inflaming them. He honored the process without worshiping the moment. He understood that the survival of the Republic mattered more than the validation of his pride. That decision deserves more than historical admiration. That decision deserves imitation.

Citizens face the same test, though at a smaller scale. Each election. Each controversy. Each viral moment. The question is simple and uncomfortable: does my response invite more cowbell, or more republic?

Consider the week Charlie Kirk was murdered on a college campus: grief competed with factional contempt, while a small fringe treated death as content and institutions rushed to punish speech before facts had settled. That pattern—the gunshot, the viral clip, the instant verdicts, the applause and the backlash—shows what happens when millions of small choices become one loud national reflex. That pattern—the gunshot, the viral clip, the instant verdicts, the applause and the backlash—captures the difference between democratic reaction and republican restraint.

When Congress retreats behind closed doors to hammer out a compromise, does the instinct demand transparency at all costs, or does it recognize that bargaining requires privacy to succeed? When a political party seeks to reform plurality-based primaries to blunt demagogic incentives, does the reflex cry "rigging," or does it acknowledge that rules shape outcomes, and that not every reform is a conspiracy against the People? When a viral clip surfaces of Alexandria Ocasio-Cortez or Jim Jordan angrily dressing down a witness, does the impulse amplify the outrage—click, share, perform—or does it pause long enough to ask whether spectacle is governing, or merely noise?

Democracy invites reaction. Republicanism requires restraint.

The republican citizen remembers Adams and takes a breath. The republican citizen slows the tempo of judgment. One less click. One less share. One less cowbell rung in righteous fury. The goal is not disengagement. The goal is deliberation. The goal is not disengagement. The goal is leaning in, but more slowly to give reason time to engage. Republican citizenship asks more of the mind than the emotions. It demands the discipline to hold two competing truths at once—to be of two minds—without collapsing disagreement into moral war.

Politics is not war by other means. Politics exists to prevent war by other means.

American history offers repeated warnings about what happens when democratic noise overwhelms republican structure. Shays's Rebellion was not dangerous because farmers protested. That moment was dangerous because the national government lacked the authority to respond. A weak central government may feel democratic, but it is not republican. It cannot secure order. It cannot mediate conflict. It cannot endure.

More Republic, Less Cowbell

On the eve of the Civil War, local majorities across the South invoked democratic self-rule to justify secession when the national majority turned against their cause. The logic sounded democratic. The result was catastrophic. A union held together only by convenience is democratic. A union held together by obligation is republican. Lincoln like Adams under the obligation.

In 1968, the Democratic Party responded to the noise of the convention floor by opening the nomination process in the name of participation. The reforms expanded voice, but they also weakened mediation. The unintended consequence was a primary system more vulnerable to celebrity, polarization, and demagoguery—more democracy, less republic.

The pattern continues in the digital age. The collapse of newspapers did not merely change how information travels. That collapse removed a republican filter. Viral videos thrive on emotional velocity. It rewards outrage, not judgment. It invites citizens to govern by reflex rather than reason. The cowbell never stops ringing because the platform profits from the noise.

The task of republican citizenship is to recognize this pattern and resist it.

More democracy does not automatically mean better self-government. Faster participation does not produce wiser outcomes. Volume does not equal legitimacy. The Republic depends on citizens willing to slow the pace of politics to the speed of deliberation—citizens who value durability over dominance, process over performance, and persuasion over applause.

Adams understood that truth when he walked away in silence. He chose continuity over catharsis. The Republic survived because enough citizens accepted the same discipline. The choice remains. Each generation rings the bell or lowers the mallet. The Republic does not ask for silence. It asks for restraint. One less cowbell. More republic.

The Citizen's Call

Structure Beats Virtue

Americans often tell the story of contested elections, like Adams–Jefferson as a morality play. One candidate is said to be gracious, another bitter. One noble, another selfish. Richard Nixon stepped aside in 1960. Al Gore went to court in 2000. The contrast invites judgment. The contrast misleads. The deeper story links Adams and Jefferson to Nixon and Kennedy, and Nixon again to Bush and Gore. In each case, the decisive factor was not personal virtue. The decisive factor was republican structure.

The election of 1800 nearly broke the young Republic. Adams lost. Jefferson won. The margin was narrow. The passions were real. Adams could have fought. He did not. His restraint is rightly admired, but admiration alone explains nothing. Adams stepped aside because the constitutional order still commanded loyalty across factions. Adams, steeped in constitutional governance, understood this order well. The system gave losing actors a future. The Republic mattered more than the moment.

The same logic governed 1960. The Kennedy–Nixon election was razor thin. Allegations of irregularities in Illinois and Texas were credible enough to justify legal action. Nixon chose not to pursue them. History remembers that choice as selflessness. History should remember it as rational. Nixon lost within a party-centered system that still buffered defeat. Political parties absorbed loss, preserved reputations, and deferred ambition rather than extinguishing a candidate's future. Losing did not exile a candidate from legitimacy. Nixon could afford to wait because the system gave him time. Eight years later, the same system returned him to the presidency.

By 2000, that architecture was gone. The Bush–Gore election unfolded in a candidate-centered system shaped by post-1968 reforms. Parties no longer mediated legitimacy. Candidates constructed personal coalitions, personal fundraising machines, and personal brands. Victory validated the candidate. Loss repudiated the candidate. Under those conditions, restraint no longer preserved future opportunity. Contestation did. Gore did not go to court because he lacked virtue. Gore went to court because the system offered no other place for legitimacy to land. Litigation replaced mediation. Courts replaced parties. The logic was structural, not moral.

This distinction matters because republics that depend on altruism do not survive.

Here, Ayn Rand enters the argument—not as a guide, but as a warning. A Russian-born novelist and philosopher, Rand emigrated to the United States in 1926, having witnessed the early consolidation of Soviet power firsthand. She became famous for her unapologetic rejection of altruism as a moral foundation, most notably in her seminal novel Atlas Shrugged (Rand, 2005), where she depicted a society collapsing under the weight of enforced self-sacrifice. Rand argued that systems built on expectations of virtue, generosity, or restraint eventually fail because they collide with durable human incentives. Her philosophy veered toward excess, but her critique of altruism contains a hard civic truth: hoping that political actors will consistently behave nobly is not a governing strategy. Hope is not a plan.

In many respects, Rand and James Madison represent different responses to the same problem. Rand, a staunch libertarian shaped by her escape from the early terrors of the Soviet experiment, placed little faith in government or bureaucratic authority. She is sometimes heralded as a queen of modern capitalism, and her work influenced a generation of free-market thinkers, including Milton Friedman (Burns, 2009; Friedman, 2016). Rand sought to construct an economic system that functioned precisely because it rejected altruism as an organizing principle.

Madison approached the same human reality from the opposite direction. Writing before the industrial revolution and long before the rise of modern capitalism, Madison nevertheless shared Rand's

The Citizen's Call

unsentimental view of human nature. He assumed ambition, self-interest, and faction as constants. Rather than attempting to reform human character, Madison sought to design a constitutional order that *channeled* those impulses. Republican government, in his formulation, did not depend on altruism. He relied on structure—on separation of powers, competing ambitions, and institutional delay—to approximate the social benefits that pure virtue could not reliably supply.

Both thinkers rejected the fantasy that good systems can be built on moral hope alone. Rand tried to solve the problem through markets. Madison tried to solve it through institutions. Their answers diverged sharply, but their diagnosis was shared: systems that depend on altruism eventually collapse under the weight of real human incentives. The American Founders understood this instinctively. Madison did not design a Constitution that required virtue (Ricks, 2020). Madison designed a Constitution that *assumed ambition*. The system worked not because leaders were good, but because incentives were aligned. Power checked power. Loss did not mean annihilation. Time remained available as a political resource.

That distinction matters because that viewpoint reframes how moments like January 6 should be understood. The riot at the Capitol was not, at its core, a sudden collapse of character—neither uniquely Donald Trump's nor uniquely the crowd's. That riot was the visible failure of a system that had been eroding for decades. The tragic event represents a chain of institutional breakdowns beginning in 1968, accelerating through the transformation of presidential primaries, and compounded by the hollowing of the House and the collapse of a mediating press. A nomination Pipeline that rewards plurality extremism, a legislative Chamber that performs outrage rather than deliberation, and a Press ecosystem that amplifies spectacle over judgment together produced a clumsy, dangerous, and ultimately embarrassing event—one now infamous in

American history. January 6 was not inevitable, but it was intelligible. The moment—not unique to either party—was what happens when ambition is no longer filtered, defeat is no longer survivable, and political legitimacy has nowhere to land except the street.

What I hope this book teaches is that when that structure weakens, appeals to character fill the gap—and fail. Calls for grace, unity, and restraint grow louder precisely when institutions stop rewarding them. Citizens scold candidates for fighting outcomes while voting systems, party rules, and media incentives punish concession. The moral lecture replaces the structural fix. The Republic pays the price. The lesson of Adams, Nixon, and even Gore is not about personal goodness. It is about republican design. Stable republics convert narrow defeat into future opportunity. Unstable systems turn every loss into an existential threat.

The call to citizens follows directly.

Do not demand better people. Demand better structure.

Seek reforms that do not rely on altruism, decency, or restraint as prerequisites. Seek reforms that *channel* ambition rather than deny it. Strengthen institutions that buffer loss, slow escalation, and preserve legitimacy across time. Rebuild party mediation. Reform primaries. Restore filters. Accept delay. Rebuild the Chamber, the Pipeline, and the Press.

Madison warned that factions, left unchecked, pursue advantage wherever opportunity appears. The answer was never to hope factions would behave better. The answer was to design a republic strong enough to survive them.

The Republic does not require saints. The Republic requires structure.

Madison, Rand, and Jesus

Speaking of saints, each democratic crisis eventually circles the same question: *Can a republic rely on altruism?* Not as a private virtue, but as a governing principle. Can a society of millions function if citizens and leaders consistently choose restraint, sacrifice, and the common good over appetite and advantage? Western civilization never answered that question with a single doctrine. It answered with three—each incomplete on its own, each indispensable in combination.

As we have seen throughout this book, the first answer is political. James Madison assumed that altruism could not be trusted at scale. The Constitution does not rely on moral hope. Our Founding document relies on structure. Ambition counters ambition. Power checks power. Delay tempers passion. Factions collide rather than dominate. Madison did not design a system for virtuous people. He designed one for human beings as they are. The Republic survives not because leaders behave altruistically, but because institutions restrain the damage when they do not.

The second answer is economic as we noted in the previous section. Ayn Rand rejected altruism altogether as a social operating principle. In her framework, systems function best when they do not depend on self-sacrifice. Markets coordinate effort through incentives, not virtue. Value emerges from voluntary exchange, not moral obligation. Where Madison constrained ambition, Rand liberated it. Prosperity does not require altruism. The market requires clarity, competition, and consent.

The third answer lies outside both politics and economics. Jesus of Nazareth placed his faith almost entirely in altruism itself. His teachings demand moral transformation rather than institutional design. Love enemies. Give freely. Expect nothing in return. The Sermon on the Mount offers no blueprint for governance and no theory of markets. His teachings speak instead to the individual conscience. Jesus himself acknowledged this separation when he warned his followers to render unto Caesar what belongs to Caesar, and unto God what belongs to God. His moral vision does not collapse into law or commerce. His divine wisdom stands apart from them—and above them.

Let me be clear. This scope of this book is not to make an argument for moral equivalence among Jesus, Rand, and Madison. If that takeaway is what one seizes alone, the point has been missed. These figures answer different questions, operate in different domains, and make fundamentally different claims. Jesus offers a moral command. Madison offers governing architecture. Rand offers an economic ethic. The comparison is structural, not ethical. My concern here is how societies function, not how souls are judged. Our American experiment has endured because we attempt to avoid collapsing these answers into one. America seeks to balance them—imperfect as we may be. Politics restrains power. Markets harness self-interest. Moral traditions cultivate virtue where institutions cannot reach. Each leg of the stool remains incomplete alone. Each fails when asked to substitute for the others.

Our current disorder reflects what happens when that balance is forgotten. Citizens ask politics to enforce virtue. They ask markets to deliver justice. They ask moral conviction to override institutional restraint. Each substitution fails. Each failure increases the noise. Each escalation erodes legitimacy.

The citizen's call is not to demand better angels from systems that were never designed to rely on them. Our call is to reclaim responsibility within the domain where altruism actually belongs: the individual. Institutions can restrain excess. Markets can coordinate effort. Only citizens can choose restraint when no rule compels us, honesty when deception pays, and patience when outrage is rewarded.

More republic does not mean less conviction. Clearer boundaries define conviction. Less cowbell does not mean silence. Discernment defines silence—knowing when noise corrodes judgment rather than sharpens judgment. A republic survives not because citizens act altruistically at all times—human beings are fallen and cannot meet that standard—but because enough citizens understand when altruism is required and when altruism must not be forced. Such judgment cannot be automated. Such judgment cannot be outsourced. Recalling Schwarzenegger, motivation fades; habit endures. Practice forms judgment.

That burden falls, as history shows repeatedly, on the citizen—us, *We the People*.

Responsibility without Scapegoats

A republic does not renew itself through legislation alone. Statutes can adjust formal rules, yet statutes do not alter behavior unless citizens reinforce the incentives those rules create. The reforms described in the previous chapter concern institutional repair rather than civic virtue. Such repair depends upon ordinary citizens shaping the environment in which representatives operate. The work rarely appears dramatic. The work involves restraint as much as action—reducing rewards for spectacle while restoring value to deliberation, patience, and procedural seriousness. Republican self-government asks for maintenance, not mobilization.

A revealing modern illustration emerged from a private effort to construct a Statue of Responsibility on the West Coast, envisioned as a deliberate counterweight to the Statue of Liberty that greets arrivals in New York Harbor. In his seminal work *Man's Search for Meaning* (1985), Viktor Frankl argued that freedom without responsibility will degenerate into arbitrariness and suggested that the Statue of Liberty on the Atlantic Coast be supplemented by a Statue of Responsibility on the Pacific Coast to reflect that balance. Contemporary efforts to realize that idea have progressed through non-profit campaigns and design proposals for a 300-foot monument, with involvement from figures such as Stephen Covey and sculptor Gary Lee Price, and ongoing site and funding discussions in Utah (Seariac, 2024). Liberty occupies a central place in the

American imagination. Liberty promises motion, release, and permission. Responsibility promises obligation, restraint, and continuity. A republic requires both. The absence of a monument to responsibility reflects a civic culture shaped toward rights rather than duties, toward expression rather than stewardship. The project seeks to correct that balance. Responsibility rarely inspires crowds, yet responsibility sustains institutions long after crowds disperse.

Citizens shape the legislative Chamber less through protest than through attention. Modern congressional behavior reflects constant observation by donors, activists, and digital audiences that reward visibility and punish compromise. Representatives respond rationally to those signals. Research on congressional behavior shows that increased visibility shifts incentives away from negotiation and toward performance, particularly under conditions of partisan polarization (Mann & Ornstein, 2006; Sinclair, 2014). Citizens who wish to strengthen the Chamber must weaken the incentives that transform lawmakers into performers. That process begins by refusing to treat politics as entertainment. Viral clips, outrage-driven fundraising appeals, and symbolic gestures thrive only when audiences respond. Withholding attention from theatrical conflict does not signal apathy. Withholding attention signals that performance no longer converts into civic capital. Citizens who instead reward committee work, oversight, and incremental legislation communicate a different expectation—one aligned with the Chamber's constitutional function.

Direct engagement still matters, yet the character of that engagement determines the result. Town halls, correspondence, and local meetings offer opportunities to reinforce institutional behavior rather than ideological posture. Questions about legislative process, committee jurisdiction, and negotiation strategy communicate seriousness more effectively than demands for maximalist positions. Expressions of support for difficult compromises—especially compromises that disappoint partisan allies—carry disproportionate influence precisely because such expressions remain rare. Research on partisan identity formation shows that public punishment of compromise intensifies polarization and discourages legislative bargaining (Mason, 2018). Citizens who accept the legitimacy of private deliberation protect the Chamber's capacity to govern. Absolute transparency, however appealing in theory, punishes revision and retreat. A citizen committed to republican repair resists demands for constant exposure and allows representatives the space required to bargain without performing for an audience. Republican citizenship rests on a quieter discipline: extending trust to a representative during service and withdrawing that trust through the ballot rather than through public humiliation, performative outrage, or the caustic lure of viral condemnation.

The nomination Pipeline requires even earlier discipline. Candidate behavior reflects the conditions under which selection occurs. Low-turnout primaries reward intensity rather than coalition-building, producing nominees accountable to narrow factions rather than governing majorities. Empirical work on primary electorates confirms that fear of ideologically extreme primary voters discourages compromise long before general elections occur (Anderson et al., 2020). Citizens who ignore the primary stage abandon the most consequential point of influence. Participation begins with voting, yet participation does not end there. Early engagement—before momentum hardens—allows persuasion to matter. Citizens who volunteer time, offer modest financial support, or provide local credibility during the early stages of a campaign influence which candidates survive long enough to compete seriously.

Evaluation criteria shape outcomes as much as participation. Citizens strengthen the Pipeline when support flows toward candidates who demonstrate an ability to assemble majorities across competing interests rather than candidates who excel at ideological signaling. Citizens should support the strongest governor in the room, not the loudest voice. Questions about governing strategy, coalition maintenance, and willingness to accept partial victories test readiness for office more effectively than questions about purity. Where institutional reform remains possible, advocacy for majority-producing mechanisms—runoffs, ranked-choice voting, or party rules that require broader consent—reinforces the principle that legitimacy precedes authority. Such mechanisms advantage no party permanently. Such mechanisms advantage candidates capable of governing.

The informational environment demands comparable restraint. Journalism did not weaken because citizens lost interest in truth. Journalism and the Press weakened because economic incentives rewarded speed over verification and outrage over context (Kovach & Rosenstiel, 2011; Mir, 2020). CNN and Fox News did not emerge because the People changed but because the business incentives of news making changed. Citizens retain leverage through subscription, donation, and attention. Supporting outlets that invest in reporting rather than reaction shifts incentives incrementally but meaningfully. Nonprofit and endowment-backed—not taxed-based—journalism offers a particularly important model, insulating verification from market volatility and partisan capture. Historical precedent supports this approach. Joseph Pulitzer's endowment of professional journalism demonstrated how private capital, disciplined by structure, can sustain a public good across generations (Morris, 2010).

Consumption habits also shape the informational commons. Sharing unverified information—even when emotionally satisfying—accelerates the erosion of shared factual ground. Restraint in circulation performs republican work. Silence, when verification remains absent, preserves space where judgment can form. Defending journalism as an institution likewise matters, even when individual failures provoke frustration. A republic cannot function when factual disagreement collapses into factional ownership of reality. Insisting upon verification as a professional norm sustains the possibility of shared judgment across disagreement (Abernathy, 2018).

None of these practices promise satisfaction. Republican citizenship does not offer emotional release or moral victory. Republican citizenship demands patience, repetition, and acceptance that outcomes often arrive incrementally and imperfectly. The Founders did not expect wisdom at each moment. The Founders expected citizens to protect institutions that compensate for human weakness. Renewal begins not with louder expression, but with steadier reinforcement of the structures that convert disagreement into judgment and conflict into law.

The Error We Repeated

American politics has not fractured because citizens have disagreed too fiercely, too loudly, or too often. Disagreement has defined the Republic since the Founding. Jefferson and Adams. Madison and Hamilton. Jackson and Clay. Lincoln and Douglas. Kennedy and Nixon. Trump and Clinton. Disagreement does not represent a failure of American politics. Disagreement represents a permanent feature of free societies ordered by law.

The fracture emerged from a quieter mistake. Over the last half-century, democratic pressure has been pushed directly into institutions designed to slow decisions, broaden perspective, and encourage compromise. The error was not malicious. The error was categorical. Democratic expression became confused with republican governance.

Democracy and republicanism serve distinct functions within the constitutional design. Democracy supplies energy and preference. Republicanism supplies process and restraint. The two stand in productive tension, balanced yet opposed. Votes register will; institutions translate will into law. The Framers treated democracy as an input—necessary, powerful, and volatile—while treating republican institutions as filters that impose delay, mediation, and coalition. Time, structure, and distance function as instruments of self-government. When democratic mechanisms migrate into spaces designed for republican process, immediacy overwhelms judgment and enthusiasm displaces deliberation. The result extends beyond institutional strain. The result manifests as civic breakdown—capitols overrun, debate displaced by force, and legitimacy openly contested.

Across the last half-century, reformers repeatedly misunderstood that architecture. Many reforms pursued honorable aims—fairness, inclusion, transparency, accountability—and promised to correct genuine abuses. Yet many reforms shared a common feature. Each shortened the distance between public passion and institutional action, removing layers of mediation in the name of democratic purity. Intentions remained sound. Institutional consequences compounded.

Institutions respond less to moral aspiration than to incentives and constraints. When reformers altered those constraints, institutions adapted predictably (Mann & Ornstein, 2006). Congress learned to perform rather than deliberate. The Chamber failed. Political parties shifted from coalition builders to ideological sorting mechanisms. The Pipeline failed. Journalism traded verification for velocity (Mir, 2020). The Press failed. Participation expanded as trust eroded. Input multiplied as outcomes diminished. Politics grew more democratic in appearance while becoming less republican in operation.

The mistake answered the wrong question. Democracy asks who decides. Republicanism asks how decisions endure. Democratic tools maximize participation. Republican tools maximize legitimacy across time. When democratic logic governs republican institutions, elections cease to function as endpoints and become permanent conditions. Campaigns bleed into governing. Governing collapses into messaging. Negotiation signals weakness. Delay appears illegitimate. Compromise appears corrupt. Visibility displaces judgment. Speed displaces persuasion. Citizens grow frustrated not because institutions resist democracy, but because institutions no longer convert democratic energy into governing outcomes. The democracy cowbells toll for thee.*

The pattern repeats across domains. Primary reforms after 1968 promised openness and delivered volatility. Procedural centralization after 1994 promised accountability and delivered performance. Twenty-first-century digital media promised voice and delivered fragmentation. Each reform followed the same arc: democratic access expanded while republican mediation declined. The system grew louder while growing weaker. More cowbell, less republic.

The crisis does not arise from disagreement itself. The crisis arises from placing disagreement where delay and insulation once governed. Federal courts restrict cameras to preserve testimony and judgment. Diplomatic negotiations unfold behind closed doors because public exposure hardens positions. Markets rely on rules and settlement periods rather than plebiscites. Each domain protects decision-making from immediate public pressure. Modern American politics removed those protections, exposing deliberation to permanent visibility and mistaking responsiveness for accountability. The result was not better governance, but diminished judgment.

---

* An allusion to John Donne's *Meditation XVII* (1624), commonly rendered as "never send to know for whom the bell tolls; it tolls for thee." The phrase is used here to emphasize that the erosion of republican restraint harms democracy itself rather than its perceived opponents. See Donne (1999).

More Republic, Less Cowbell

This diagnosis assigns no blame. Many reforms corrected genuine abuses. Yet correction without comprehension creates new failures. The American political crisis today reflects structural misalignment rather than civic decay. Citizens did not suddenly become unreasonable.

Moments such as January 6, the assassination of Charlie Kirk, and other episodes widely described as signs of national collapse—though deeply tragic—should be understood differently. Democracies periodically generate such moments, and the American record contains many (Gilje, 1999). These episodes do not arise because disagreement intensifies. These episodes arise when institutions fail to perform their mediating function—when deliberation thins, negotiation collapses, and democratic energy bypasses republican process. Disorder follows not because citizens grow louder, but because the structures designed to absorb disagreement no longer hold.

That distinction matters. Treating such moments as moral aberrations invites scapegoating. Treating such moments as institutional failures invites repair. A republic does not survive by demanding better behavior from citizens in moments of strain. A republic survives by maintaining the machinery that converts ordinary disagreement into durable outcomes even when passions rise. The American system has endured riots, assassinations, secession, economic collapse, and mass unrest not because citizens remained calm, but because institutions retained enough structure to outlast those storms.

The diagnosis therefore assigns responsibility without blame. Democratic energy remains necessary. Democratic participation remains legitimate. The failure lies not with democracy itself, but with the removal of the republican filters that once gave democracy shape and endurance. Repair does not require quieter citizens or weaker democracy. Repair requires rebuilding the Chamber, the

Pipeline, and the Press so that democratic energy once again encounters delay, mediation, and judgment before becoming law.

The remainder of this chapter turns toward that work—not as a program for moral renewal, but as a call to republican responsibility. Institutions cannot be sustained by passion alone. Institutions endure only when citizens accept restraint, tolerate delay, and permit process to do its work even when outcomes disappoint. The Republic does not ask for purity. The Republic asks for maintenance.

Representation at Human Scale

The most consequential reform described in this book concerns representation itself. The District Trustee proposal does not seek improvement through better rhetoric or purer motives. The proposal alters scale. Scale governs behavior. When representation exceeds the capacity for sustained human relationship, institutions drift toward abstraction, performance, and symbolic conflict. Modern congressional districts, now approaching three-quarters of a million residents, operate far beyond the limits of social maintenance. At that scale, representation relies almost entirely on money, media, and nationalized narratives rather than durable civic relationship (Mann & Ornstein, 2006). The District Trustee system restores representation to a human dimension without dismantling the national legislature.

Under this model, each congressional district elects not only a voting representative to Congress, but also a standing District Trustee—a non-voting officer charged with continuous advocacy for district interests. District Trustees operate at a scale closer to Madison's original design, maintaining durable relationships with constituents, local institutions, state officials, and fellow District Trustees across the country. The District Trustee does not legislate. The District Trustee represents—persistently, visibly, and locally. That distinction matters. Continuous representation restores social accountability to national politics by anchoring advocacy in lived community rather than episodic campaigns.

The consequences for gerrymandering follow directly. Gerrymandering thrives when political influence concentrates in a single electoral outcome and when representation disappears between elections. The District Trustee system diffuses that concentration. Even within distorted district boundaries, the presence of a standing advocate accountable to the entire population alters incentives. Legitimacy derives from ongoing service rather than partisan advantage. Political boundaries still shape elections, yet representation no longer vanishes during the long intervals between contests. Citizens regain access regardless of which party holds the congressional seat.

The District Trustee proposal also reshapes how pressure accumulates around fiscal crises, particularly budget standoffs and continuing resolutions. Modern shutdown politics depends upon distance. Negotiations occur under deadline, shielded by leadership control, while constituents experience disruption without meaningful access to the process. District Trustees change that dynamic by functioning as early-warning systems. As fiscal impasses approach, District Trustees aggregate district-level consequences before positions harden. Hospitals, schools, contractors, veterans' services, and state agencies gain a continuous channel into federal negotiation rather than a post-hoc appeal after damage begins. Pressure disperses across time rather than exploding at the deadline, restoring bargaining space and reducing incentives for theatrical brinkmanship (Bahal, 2025).

The proposal also introduces a consequential failure mode absent from the present system. When a budget impasse persists, District Trustees possess the authority to remove a House member from office. That removal mechanism—and the credible threat accompanying that authority—creates an incentive structure the modern Chamber lacks, particularly in matters of funding and fiscal governance. Under current arrangements, the dominant failure mode remains inaction. Shutdowns impose diffuse harm while political accountability remains attenuated. With District Trustees in place, that calculus changes. Fiscal paralysis carries personal and immediate consequence. Responsibility no longer dissipates across leadership layers or electoral cycles. Pressure returns to the representative charged with governing.

Beyond fiscal responsibility, the District Trustee role also reframes lobbying. Modern lobbying fills a vacuum created by scale. When elected representatives cannot sustain durable relationships with constituents, organized interests supply information, incentives, and pressure. District Trustees operate as public lobbyists— advocates whose sole client remains the people of a defined local community. That role does not eliminate private lobbying, yet that role restores balance. Information flows upward from lived experience rather than downward from national organizations. Representation becomes continuous rather than episodic, strengthening social maintenance across electoral cycles.

The primary power of the District Trustee derives not from formal legislative authority but from soft power. Soft power, in this context, refers to influence grounded in access, credibility, persistence, and relationship rather than in votes or procedural control. District Trustees convene local institutions, aggregate shared interests, and translate those interests into sustained presence within the governing ecosystem. District Trustees brief House members before crises form rather than after positions harden. District Trustees coordinate across districts when regional or national interests align. District Trustees shape agendas by determining which concerns remain visible over time rather than which controversies flare briefly and fade.

Such influence operates quietly. No single intervention commands attention. No single meeting resolves conflict. The cumulative effect matters. Repetition builds familiarity. Familiarity builds trust. Trust alters behavior. House members confronted regularly by a District Trustee representing hospitals, schools, veterans' services, small businesses, and state agencies encounter a different form of pressure than campaign advertising or social media outrage supplies. That pressure persists regardless of news cycles. That pressure reflects continuity rather than intensity.

For citizens, this design changes how influence operates. Political engagement shifts away from episodic mobilization and toward sustained relationship. The District Trustee becomes the daily face of federal representation—the official charged with listening, translating, and maintaining institutional memory. Citizens gain leverage not through volume, but through proximity. Governance regains texture. Representation regains scale. The Republic regains a structure capable of absorbing pressure without breaking.The proposal extends beyond structure into civic culture through an annual congressional meeting. An annual retreat hosted by a rotating state and organized jointly by Congress and District Trustees reintroduces physical proximity as a governing asset. The Founders understood the value of repeated contact, shared meals, and informal negotiation in sustaining cooperation across disagreement (Sinclair, 2014; Young, 1966). Modern Congress operates without those disciplines. The retreat exists neither for spectacle nor public performance. The retreat exists to rebuild familiarity across institutional layers— members, District Trustees, staff, and state officials—away from cameras, donors, and deadline theatrics. Cooperation emerges from repeated human contact rather than press releases.

The District Trustee system also rebuilds a governing bench—an element largely absent from modern legislative selection. Earlier American political institutions assumed apprenticeship. Legislators typically arrived in Congress after sustained service in state legislatures, committees, or executive roles that required coalition maintenance and procedural navigation (Hall, 1998; Hibbing, 2017). Contemporary politics reverses that sequence. Campaign skill

The Citizen's Call

substitutes for governing experience, and national office increasingly attracts candidates whose preparation occurred in media environments rather than institutional settings (Canon, 1990). The District Trustee role restores apprenticeship by design. Service as a District Trustee requires aggregation of competing interests, sustained negotiation across disagreement, and fluency in institutional process before legislative authority arrives. Research shows that legislators shaped by such experience demonstrate greater capacity for compromise and more effective participation once in office (Anderson et al., 2020; Harbridge, 2015). Ambition remains present. Structure disciplines ambition before power follows.

That bench alters incentives for both candidates and voters. Aspiring legislators gain a credible path to national office that rewards patience, competence, and service rather than ideological intensity or fundraising prowess. Voters gain observable evidence of governing behavior rather than promises delivered under campaign conditions. District Trustees build records measured not by messaging discipline but by sustained outcomes—resolved disputes, coordinated responses, and durable institutional relationships. When a District Trustee later seeks legislative office, constituents evaluate demonstrated capacity rather than rhetorical alignment.

The presence of such a bench also stabilizes legislative culture. Members entering Congress with prior experience in representation approach negotiation differently from members whose political lives unfolded entirely within campaign environments. Familiarity with compromise precedes exposure to power. Responsibility precedes authority. Over time, that pipeline replenishes the Chamber with legislators shaped by maintenance rather than mobilization, by continuity rather than confrontation. The Republic regains a class of leaders trained in governing before governing authority arrives.

For citizens, the implications remain direct and practical. The District Trustee becomes the most accessible point of federal representation. Constituents gain a standing advocate who remains visible between elections, operates locally, and maintains institutional memory across cycles. Civic engagement shifts from episodic outrage to continuous relationship. Citizens influence federal outcomes not by amplifying noise, but by participating in a structure designed to absorb pressure productively. Support for this reform does not require ideological alignment. Support requires recognition that representation must operate at a scale humans can sustain.

The gravity of the District Trustee proposal lies in what the proposal restores. Time returns to governance. Continuity returns to representation. Relationship returns to politics. Citizens who support this reform support a quieter republic—one capable of disagreement without collapse and pressure without panic. Such support rarely trends online. Such support sustains the Republic nonetheless.

Primary-System Reform

The final citizen's call will return us to the reforming the Pipeline. Modern polarization did not emerge from a sudden collapse of civic virtue. Polarization emerged from a quiet reengineering of political incentives. The transformation of the presidential primary system after 1968 altered how candidates are selected, how coalitions form, and how legitimacy is earned. Thought his reform mainly changed the presidential selection, the effect of the reform has filtered down to each level of our local, state, and federal elections. Few citizens recognize the magnitude of that change. Fewer still understand how a reform intended to democratize participation weakened the republican structure that once disciplined ambition.

As discussed throughout this book, the post-1968 primary reforms—most visibly associated with the McGovern–Fraser Commission—replaced party-mediated selection with voter-driven nomination contests (Shafer, 1983). Delegates became bound. Party gatekeepers lost authority. Informal coalition-building yielded to sequential state contests governed by plurality rules. Candidates no longer required majority support within a party to secure nomination momentum. Early wins sufficed. Volume substituted for breadth. Survival replaced synthesis. Motivation eclipsed governance as the defining trait of successful candidates.

This Pipeline shift did not mandate extremism. The shift unwittingly rewarded it. Plurality systems privilege intensity over breadth. Early contests magnify small differences. Media coverage converts narrow wins into perceived inevitability. Path dependence locks in outcomes before deliberation completes. These dynamics operate regardless of ideology. Incentives do not care about motives. Structures select behavior. The election of President Jimmy Carter, unknown at the time, embodied this shift, and most vividly demonstrated the perils for a little-known newcomer to national politics with little experience in legislative compromise was likely preordained to be a one-term president. Carter learned to be a great ex-president and became an international titan, but that ability was latent and emerged after his presidency. The Pipeline offered few clues and he was wholly unprepared to work with Congress, even in his own party. The Carter presidency was a small tilt towards polarization.

The causal chain resists clean falsification. No single reform explains polarization. Cultural change matters. Media change matters. Geography matters. Technology matters. The Popperian objection holds. No controlled experiment isolates the primary system as a solitary cause. Yet institutional analysis does not require monocausality. Institutional analysis asks a different question: whether a system amplifies known human tendencies or restrains them (Popper, 2005). The modern primary system amplifies factional sorting, ideological signaling, and negative partisanship. The historical record aligns with that prediction. The altruism and personal character of

Carter masked the perils the new primary system that he had discovered how to exploit. Later actors would find more demagogic means to supercharge the system.

Before 1968, parties absorbed conflict internally. Party leaders aggregated interests across regions, factions, and offices. That aggregation occurred before candidates reached the general electorate. The process was opaque. The process was imperfect. The derisive labels of political bosses and political machines hinted at corruption. Yet, the process was republican, if flawed too. Loss inside the party did not confer moral condemnation. Compromise remained survivable. Time functioned as a political resource as Nixon aptly demonstrated in his comeback bid after loosing the 1960 presidency to the Kennedy–Johnson machine.

After 1968, conflict moved outward. Primary contests became public trials rather than internal negotiations. Candidates performed for the most activated voters rather than the broadest coalition. Loss became delegitimization. Delay became obstruction. Compromise became betrayal. These outcomes reflect incentives, not character.

Reform must therefore target incentives rather than motives. Moral appeals cannot repair structural flaws. The primary system requires republican filters restored inside a democratic framework. Majoritarian selection mechanisms offer one such repair. Runoffs. Ranked-choice voting. Preference voting. Threshold requirements for nomination. Each mechanism forces coalition formation before victory. Each mechanism penalizes factional isolation. Each mechanism converts intensity into persuasion rather than dominance. Majoritarian rules within a party primary do not suppress participation. Majoritarian rules discipline ambition. Candidates must expand appeal. Candidates must reconcile factions. Candidates must earn legitimacy across time rather than capture momentum in sequence. These rules mirror the logic embedded in the Constitution itself.

Delay tempers passion. Aggregation precedes authority. Legitimacy emerges from breadth.

Yet procedural reform alone remains insufficient. The primary system also suffers from scale. National politics now demands coordination beyond human cognitive limits. Informal mediation has not disappeared. Informal mediation has gone underground. Money brokers. Media figures. Algorithmic amplification. Invisible hands still select candidates. Accountability vanished with visibility. This reality invites an uncomfortable but necessary comparison to historical political machines. Tammany Hall and other corrupt political machines functioned because local organization solved collective action problems that mass democracy could not. The failure of Tammany Hall lay not in mediation, but in corruption, opacity, and unaccountable power (Golway, 2014). Mediation itself remains unavoidable.

The District Trustee proposal embraces that reality without romanticism. District Trustees formalize local aggregation through lawful, transparent, and accountable means. District Trustees legitimize mediation rather than deny it. Local political figures already coordinate endorsements, fundraising, and turnout. District Trustees, activating as public agents, have incentives to perform many of the duties of local organization found with Tammany and political machines but with equally powerful incentives to avoid engaging in corruption and grift. The reform acknowledges that function and binds the function to geography, reputation, and responsibility.

The linkage of the District Trustee proposal to primary reform is indirect but restores one structural feature former machines provided: disciplined pre-primary aggregation. District Trustees filter ambition through accountable local intermediaries rather than anonymous activist surges. Under this model, primary competition begins after preferences have been aggregated locally. Candidates face structured intermediaries rather than unfiltered noise. Factions encounter negotiation early. Extremes confront boundaries before ballots print. The primary becomes coalition confirmation rather than factional audition.

This design does not resurrect bosses and Tweedism. This design replaces invisible power with visible authority. District Trustees are publically elected officials with reputations to uphold and other accountability incentives of elected officials. Corruption becomes prosecutable. Influence becomes contestable. Responsibility becomes traceable. The machine becomes public. That transformation aligns with republican principles rather than contradicting them. The District Trustees will not stand separate from reforms to political primaries but rather their tight coupling to local small-scale constituencies will bring empowerment to party reforms.

This design does not resurrect bosses and Tweedism. This design replaces invisible power with visible authority. District Trustees are publicly elected officials with reputations at stake and the accountability incentives that accompany office. Corruption becomes prosecutable. Influence becomes contestable. Responsibility becomes traceable. The machine becomes public. That transformation aligns with republican principles rather than contradicting them.

District Trustees will not stand apart from primary reform. They alter the incentive structure that governs nominations. John Aldrich argues in *Why Parties?* that political parties exist to solve collective action problems for ambitious politicians. Primaries, as currently structured, reward mobilization of intense minorities because turnout is low and districts are large. Candidates rationally appeal to activists rather than broad governing coalitions. The nomination system therefore selects for purity and amplification, not mediation.

A trustee layer anchored in smaller districts shifts that equilibrium. Candidates must persuade identifiable local officials whose own survival depends on broad reputational trust within compact constituencies. Trustees cannot hide inside national outrage cycles.

Their constituents know their record. Endorsing destabilizing figures carries immediate political cost.

The reform does not eliminate primaries. The reform re-embeds them in local accountability. Aldrich shows that parties respond to incentives. Change the structure, and party behavior changes with it. Republican stability requires visible intermediaries. Trustees restore that function.

Citizens often demand authenticity while rejecting mediation. No large republic survives such demands. Madison understood this tension. Ambition requires channels. Passion requires filters. Republican government fails when democracy bypasses structure rather than working through it. Primary reform remains politically difficult because the system's effects remain poorly understood. Few citizens connect nomination rules to governing outcomes. Fewer still recognize that democratic energy—such as the empowerment of District Trustees—must be converted before legitimacy can endure. The task of this generation is not to restore a vanished past. The task is to rebuild republican structure suited to democratic scale.

Participation alone does not preserve the Republic. Process does.

In Totum

The American republic has never been sustained by harmony. The historical record offers no such comfort. Conflict marked the early Union, shadowed its growth, and still defines public life. The Republic endured regardless. Endurance did not come from the disappearance of disagreement. Endurance came from a repeated return to republican restraint: the discipline to keep arguing after the vote, the patience to accept delay, and the maturity to treat loss as survivable rather than apocalyptic.

More Republic, Less Cowbell

That survival record should temper despair and arrogance. Despair imagines historical uniqueness, as though present disorder represents an unprecedented collapse. Arrogance imagines inevitability, as though survival requires no maintenance. Both instincts misread the American story. Earlier generations faced stresses no modern news cycle can replicate. Secession tore the nation in half. Economic collapse destabilized democratic faith. Global wars demanded mobilization at a continental scale. Political violence visited institutions and citizens alike. The Republic outlasted those storms because institutional structure reasserted authority—absorbing disagreement, imposing limits, and converting raw pressure into judgment. Recovery followed structure, not sentiment. We thus need more republican structure and less democratic cowbell.

This moment is not different. The failure of the Republic is only an option if we given in and become complacent.

Modern explanations often mistake symptoms for sources. Technology becomes the villain. Culture becomes the villain. Citizens become the villain. Such accounts comfort elites by shifting responsibility downward or outward. A republic designed to survive ambition, passion, and faction cannot indict those forces when institutional design falters. Madison never assumed virtuous citizens. Madison assumed interested citizens and designed a system capable of managing durable human impulses.

Refusing to blame the People establishes a necessary moral boundary. Citizens may argue loudly, organize aggressively, vote intensely, and still remain within the legitimate scope of self-government. The deeper danger arises when the mechanisms that once slowed decisions, broadened perspective, and compelled compromise weaken or vanish. Democratic energy must exist. Republican institutions are thus necessary to absorb that democratic energy. When that absorption fails, legitimacy erodes even as participation rises.

The Citizen's Call

Yet refusal to scapegoat citizens does not excuse citizens from responsibility. Self-government demands restraint as well as expression. Republican citizenship requires acceptance of loss when rules hold. Electoral loss tests republican character most severely, because restraint is hardest when victory disappears. Outrage gratifies immediately. Institutional repair frustrates consistently. Outrage accelerates. Repair slows. A republic cannot survive on emotional velocity alone. Stability requires repetition, delay, and the willingness to endure unsatisfying outcomes for the sake of durable order. Maintenance rarely feels righteous in the moment. Maintenance endures.

The citizen's call therefore begins with a simple internal question: does a given response ring another cowbell, or does that response strengthen a republic? Each click, share, and performative denunciation participates in an incentive system that rewards spectacle and punishes deliberation. Each disciplined refusal to amplify a cheap outrage interrupts that cycle. Silence, when evidence remains thin, becomes civic action. Patience, when instant judgment tempts the mind, becomes republican virtue. Those practices do not require sainthood. Those practices require habit.

Structure still matters more than moral lecture. The modern habit of treating political crises as morality plays misdirects attention. A stable system does not depend on altruism, decency, or restraint as prerequisites. A stable system channels ambition rather than denying ambition. The American design worked not because leaders were good, but because incentives aligned: power checked power, time remained available as a political resource, and loss did not mean annihilation. When that architecture weakens, appeals to character rush in to fill the gap, and those appeals predictably fail. The moral lecture replaces the structural fix. The Republic pays the price.

A parallel distinction clarifies the role of altruism. Western civilization never answered the altruism question with one doctrine.

More Republic, Less Cowbell

Western civilization answered with three, each suited to a different domain. Madison offered governing architecture built on the assumption that altruism cannot be trusted at scale. Rand offered an economic ethic grounded in voluntary exchange rather than enforced self-sacrifice. Jesus offered a moral command aimed at the individual conscience rather than the machinery of the state. A society fractures when citizens try to force one domain's answer onto the other domains: politics asked to enforce virtue, markets asked to deliver justice, moral conviction asked to override institutional restraint. Each substitution fails, and each failure increases the noise. The citizen's responsibility is not to collapse the three answers into one. The citizen's responsibility is to keep the boundaries intact, then practice responsibility where responsibility belongs—in the private conscience, in the habits of attention, in the discipline of judgment.

Repair, under that framework, begins with architecture, not attitude. Repair begins with the Chamber, the Pipeline, and the Press. Rebuilding legislative capacity and committee-centered work restores negotiation as craft rather than performance. Reforming nominations toward majority-producing rules restores coalition-building before power follows. Reconstructing an informational center restores verification and context as civic infrastructure rather than partisan luxury. None of these reforms silences political passion. None retreats from democratic engagement. Each reform gives democratic passion a structure, a pace, and a channel consistent with the scale of a continental republic. A society that governs hundreds of millions of citizens cannot operate as a continuous referendum. A republic of this size requires organized representation, tempered judgment, and institutions capable of holding the center when noise rises.

Representation at human scale belongs in the same category of repair. Modern districts operate far beyond the limits of sustained relationship, and scale pushes representation toward money,

The Citizen's Call

media, and abstraction. The District Trustee proposal confronts that problem directly by restoring a durable representational layer at a human dimension, building civic memory between elections, and creating a bench for future legislators trained in negotiation before power arrives. The design does not depend on better angels. The design changes incentives by changing scale, proximity, and accountability. That shift also alters how fiscal brinkmanship, lobbying pressure, and gerrymandered distortions play out over time, because continuous local advocacy reintroduces consequence where modern politics has learned to externalize harm.

The task before American citizens is therefore not the construction of a new republic. The task is the repair of republican guardrails weakened through sustained indifference to the Founding's design. Revolt promises clarity. Restoration myths promise return without cost. Both temptations evade the harder obligation of maintenance. Legitimacy does not reset with a single election. Leadership cannot substitute for structure. Trust does not return through shortcuts. Institutions recover only through deliberate repair, repeated over time, by citizens willing to defend process even when outcomes disappoint.

The Constitution provides no enforcement mechanism for republican restraint. Constitutional design presumes restraint. The extended republic functions only when citizens protect institutions that restrain one faction as readily as the opposing faction. That posture lacks drama. That posture preserves self-government.

This book has argued that American democracy suffers not from excessive disagreement, but from insufficient mediation. More republic, less cowbell. Repair does not require silencing voices or purifying motives. Repair requires rebuilding the structures that once transformed conflict into law. The Republic still holds. The work remains unfinished. The work now belongs to the citizen—We the People.

Acknowledgments

BEFORE OFFERING THANKS, I should offer a brief word about the way this book came together. This project unfolded through exploration rather than outline. Arguments emerged through reading, conversation, writing, revision, and occasional retreat. Ideas wandered. Some returned sharpened. Others did not return at all. The process required judgment—about what belonged in the main text, what belonged in the footnotes, and what belonged nowhere. If the book occasionally takes the long way around an idea, that reflects the path by which the idea arrived.

A word about the footnotes.* There are many. Some clarify arguments. Others trace intellectual side paths that proved too interesting to abandon but too distracting to place in the main narrative. Readers who enjoy such detours will find them waiting below the line. Readers who do not should feel free to skip them without penalty. The argument stands without them.

First and foremost, I thank my wife, Lisa, and my daughter, Grace.

---

* Yes, this paragraph also could have been a footnote. Footnotes exist because judgment about relevance is imperfect. This book makes no claim to exception.

Acknowledgments

Lisa deserves special recognition—not only for patience, but for restraint. Lisa and I do not share the same politics. She is a Democrat. I note that fact with a smile, not a sneer. Readers should not judge her too harshly for that fact. She listens thoughtfully, graciously, and often silently, even when disagreement is unmistakable. That listening reflects love. It may also reflect a measure of self-preservation. Either way, it has mattered more than she likely realizes. The arguments in this book were sharpened not by applause, but by the discipline of knowing when to stop talking and start thinking.

Grace has ventured off into her freshman year at the University of Chicago, and I could not be more proud. She graduated salutatorian from Bearden High School and delivered a remarkable commencement address—one I failed to record because my phone battery died at the worst possible moment. Such moments remain part of the parental craft that I continue to practice imperfectly. Grace has found her people and is pursuing her goals with confidence and joy. The University of Chicago mascot is the Phoenix, which feels appropriate. This book reflects the same hope I hold for her and for my family: life, liberty, and the pursuit of happiness—not as slogans, but as lived commitments.

I again thank the *Donuts for Democracy* discussion group. These Saturday morning conversations—though limited to a few weeks during the summer of 2025—served as a small republic: curious, challenging, good-humored, and serious in purpose. Many ideas in this book were tested, refined, and occasionally abandoned during those discussions. Thanks to Andy Andrew, Brian Walker, Chris Austin, and others who showed up consistently with open minds and sharp questions.

I also owe thanks to the West Knox and Karns Republican Clubs. With Grace entering college, time reopened for deeper civic engagement. Participation in these groups prompted further investigation into primary systems, party reforms, and the long institutional shadows cast by changes few remember but many feel. Conversations continued after meetings—often over dinner—where theory met practice. Martin Ammons, Kyle Nahrebne, Gary Loe, and others from West Knox deserve acknowledgment for the seriousness with which they engaged difficult questions and resisted easy answers.

I also thank the many friends and acquaintances who encountered early versions of these ideas as blog posts, short essays, and half-formed arguments scattered across social media. These encounters mattered. They revealed confusion. They exposed weak claims. They tested tone. Ideas improve when exposed to daylight rather than protected by certainty.

I must also acknowledge ChatGPT.

I approached artificial intelligence (AI) cautiously. For this book, AI served not as an author, but as a research partner. Like any junior assistant, it requires supervision. It must be questioned. Its work must be verified. It occasionally invents facts with confidence that would impress a first-year graduate student. Yet its value lies in speed and range. AI accelerates mundane research, allows rapid exploration of intellectual dead ends, and frees time for judgment rather than retrieval. Used carefully, the tool has made me more rigorous, not less.

I often think of the glass artist Dale Chihuly. After injuries ended his ability to work at the furnace, he did not abandon the craft. He reframed his role—from artisan to director, from dancer to choreographer—guiding the work even when other hands executed it. Tools and collaborators did not diminish the vision. They extended it. The same principle applies here. AI tools that reduce friction do not replace the work. They make the work more precise.

Finally, I thank the reader.

Thank you for reading—especially if disagreement accompanied the journey. Disagreement has improved my thinking more often than agreement. Mistakes instruct more reliably than success when

Acknowledgments

one remains open to correction. Folks who challenge ideas sharpen them. Folks who question conclusions strengthen them. If this book invites continued disagreement, conversation, or reconsideration, then it has succeeded as intended.

The Republic endures through such exchanges.

The invitation remains open—for more republic and less cowbell.

Further Reading

WHILE MANY BOOKS INFORMED the research and arguments in this volume, the works listed below extend its central claims beyond the page. These titles appear in the Works Cited section, yet merit repetition here for readers who wish to pursue the deeper structure of the argument—how republics endure conflict, why institutions matter more than intention, and where modern democratic systems have failed to mediate disagreement.

Some readers may recognize familiar authors from earlier work. The repetition is deliberate. The purpose has changed.

Structural Republicanism

The American Founders did not design a system to redeem human nature. They designed a system to survive it. These works examine the constitutional logic that assumes ambition, manages faction, and converts conflict into durability rather than collapse.

Ketcham, R. L. (1990). *James Madison: A biography*. University of Virginia Press.

Ricks, T. E. (2020). *First principles: What America's founders learned from the Greeks and Romans and how that shaped our country*. Harper Perennial.

Wood, G. S. (2017). *Friends divided: John Adams and Thomas Jefferson*. Penguin Press.

Rasmussen, D. C. (2021). *Fears of a setting sun: The disillusionment of America's founders*. Simon & Schuster.

The Chamber: Congress as an Institution

Democratic failure often emerges not from bad actors, but from hollowed structures. When institutional incentives reward spectacle over deliberation, even capable legislators struggle to govern. These works document how Congress lost its mediating function—and why restoring that function matters.

Mann, T. E., & Ornstein, N. J. (2006). *The Broken Branch: How Congress is failing America and how to get it back on track*. Oxford University Press.

Sinclair, B. (2016). *Unorthodox lawmaking: New legislative processes in the U.S. Congress* (5th ed.). CQ Press.

Golway, T. (2014). *Machine made: Tammany Hall and the creation of modern American politics*. W. W. Norton & Company.

The Pipeline: Parties, Primaries, and Selection Failure

Few structural reforms reshaped American politics as profoundly—and as quietly—as the post-1968 transformation of party nominations. Coalition-building gave way to sequential contests. Mediation gave way to momentum. These works explain how that shift altered incentives, rewarded extremity, and weakened democratic accountability.

Cohen, M., Karol, D., Noel, H., & Zaller, J. (2009). *The party decides: Presidential nominations before and after reform*. University of Chicago Press.

Rosenbluth, F., & Shapiro, I. (2018). *Responsible parties: Saving democracy from itself*. Yale University Press.

Shafer, B. E. (1983). *Quiet revolution: The struggle for the Democratic Party and the shaping of post-reform politics*. Russell Sage Foundation.

The Press: From Fourth Branch to Feedback Loop

A republic requires mediation. When journalism collapses into amplification, democratic noise overwhelms judgment. These works trace how economic pressure, technological change, and incentive misalignment transformed the press from gatekeeper to accelerant.

Benkler, Y., Faris, R., & Roberts, H. (2018). *Network propaganda: Manipulation, disinformation, and radicalization in American politics*. Oxford University Press.

Mir, A. (2020). *Post-journalism and the death of newspapers: The media after Trump*. Springer.

Postman, N. (2005). *Amusing ourselves to death: Public discourse in the age of show business*. Viking Penguin.

Faction, Collapse, and Democratic Stress

The American Republic was not born in tranquility. Disorder, protest, and institutional strain have always tested its capacity to

Further Reading

absorb dissent. These works examine how systems fail when mediation collapses—and what those failures reveal before the final break.

Gilje, P. A. (1999). *Rioting in America*. Indiana University Press.

Snyder, T. (2017). *On Tyranny: Twenty Lessons from the Twentieth Century*. Ten Speed Press.

Zubok, V. M. (2021). *Collapse: The fall of the Soviet Union*. Yale University Press.

Ganz, J. (2024). *When the clock broke: Con men, conspiracists, and how America cracked up in the early 1990s*. Farrar, Straus and Giroux.

Work Cited

Abernathy, P. M. (2018). *The Expanding News Desert*. Center for Innovation and Sustainability in Local Media, School of Media and ....

Adams, J. (1814). *Letter from John Adams to John Taylor*. University of Virginia Press. https://founders.archives.gov/documents/Adams/99-02-02-6371

Akerlof, G. A. (1970). The Market for "Lemons": Quality Uncertainty and the Market Mechanism. In *Uncertainty in Economics* (pp. 235-251). Elsevier.

Aldrich, J. H. (1995). *Why Parties?: The Origin and Transformation of Political Parties in America*. University of Chicago Press.

Altenmüller, M. S., Wingen, T., & Schulte, A. (2024). Explaining Polarized Trust in Scientists: A Political Stereotype-Approach. *Science Communication, 46*(1), 92-115.

Altman, M., & McDonald, M. (2010). The Promise and Perils of Computers in Redistricting. *Duke J. Const. L. & Pub. Pol'y, 5*, 69.

Alvarez, R. M., & Hall, T. E. (2010). Electronic Elections: The Perils and Promises of Digital Democracy.

Ambrose, S. E. (2014). *Eisenhower Volume Ii: The President*. Simon and Schuster.

Amer, M. L. (1993). *The Congressional Record; Content, History and Issues*. C. R. Service.

American National Election Studies. (2024). *Anes Guide to Public Opinion and Electoral Behavior: Feeling Thermometer Series (Own-Party, Rival-Party, and Affective Gap), 1980–2024*. (University of Michigan; Standford University. https://electionstudies.org

Work Cited

Anderson, S. E., Butler, D. M., & Harbridge-Yong, L. (2020). *Rejecting Compromise: Legislators' Fear of Primary Voters*. Cambridge University Press.

Axelrod, R., & Hamilton, W. D. (1981). The Evolution of Cooperation. *Science, 211*(4489), 1390-1396.

Bahal, S. L., Andrew; Fano, Arianna; Quakenbush, Caleb; Snyderman, Rachel. (2025). What to Know About Continuing Resolutions. https://bipartisanpolicy.org/explainer/what-to-know-about-continuing-resolutions/

Baier, B., & Whitney, C. (2021). *To Rescue the Republic: Ulysses S. Grant, the Fragile Union, and the Crisis of 1876*. HarperCollins.

Baldasty, G. J. (1992). *The Commercialization of News in the Nineteenth Century*. Univ of Wisconsin Press.

Balz, D. (1994a). After the Republican Sweep. Retrieved 1994-11-10, from https://www.washingtonpost.com/archive/politics/1994/11/10/after-the-republican-sweep/7d5ffc36-3904-40c9-809a-2c18cd12d53e/

Balz, D. (1994b). A Historic Republican Triumph: Gop Captures Congress. Retrieved 1994-11-09, from https://www.washingtonpost.com/archive/politics/1994/11/09/a-historic-republican-triumph-gop-captures-congress/f7e27522-df21-411b-ab47-18687f51906f/

Balz, D., & Johnson, H. (2010). *The Battle for America: The Story of an Extraordinary Election*. Penguin.

Banfield, E. C., & Wilson, J. Q. (1963). *City Politics*.

Barber, M. (2016). Donation Motivations: Testing Theories of Access and Ideology. *Political Research Quarterly, 69*(1), 148-159.

Barber, M. J., Canes-Wrone, B., & Thrower, S. (2017). Ideologically Sophisticated Donors: Which Candidates Do Individual Contributors Finance? *American Journal of Political Science, 61*(2), 271-288.

Beard, M. (2015). *Spqr: A History of Ancient Rome*. Liveright.

Beck, J. (2019). Two Boy Scouts Met in an Internment Camp, and Grew up to Work in Congress. https://www.theatlantic.com/family/archive/2019/05/congressmen-norm-mineta-alan-simpson-friendship-japanese-internment-camp/589603/

Bedford, S. (2023). Squad Goals: How Effective Have Aoc and Company Been at Legislating? https://www.washingtonexaminer.com/news/2583021/squad-goals-how-effective-have-aoc-and-company-been-at-legislating/

Benkler, Y., Faris, R., & Roberts, H. (2018). *Network Propaganda: Manipulation, Disinformation, and Radicalization in American Politics*. Oxford University Press.

Benoit, K. (2004). Models of Electoral System Change. *Electoral Studies, 23*(3), 363-389.

Berend, T. I. (2020). *A Century of Populist Demagogues: Eighteen European Portraits, 1918-2018*. Central European University Press Budapest.

Berger, V. L. (1912). *Berger's Broadsides*. Social-Democratic Publishing Company.

Bernstein, E. S. (2012). The Transparency Paradox: A Role for Privacy in Organizational Learning and Operational Control. *Administrative Science Quarterly, 57*(2), 181-216.

Berrang, A. G., Curtis. (2012). *National Primary Turnout Hits New Record Low: Summary Charts*.

Bice, A. (2021). Fauci: 'I'm Going to Be Saving Lives and They're Going to Be Lying'. *Politico*. https://www.politico.com/news/2021/11/28/fauci-lying-covid-research-cruz-523412

Bilder, M. S. (2015). *Madison's Hand: Revising the Constitutional Convention*. Harvard University Press.

Binder, S. (2014). Polarized We Govern? *Governing in a polarized age: Elections, parties, and political representation in America*.

Binder, S. A. (2004). *Stalemate: Causes and Consequences of Legislative Gridlock*. Rowman & Littlefield.

Binder, S. A., & Maltzman, F. (2009). *Advice and Dissent: The Struggle to Shape the Federal Judiciary*. Rowman & Littlefield.

The Birth of the Gerrymander. (2008). Massachusetts Historical Society. https://www.masshist.org/object-of-the-month/objects/the-birth-of-the-gerrymander-2008-09-01

Blumenthal, S. (1982). *The Permanent Campaign*. Simon & Shuster.

Bohn, R., & Short, J. E. (2012). Info Capacity: Measuring Consumer Information. *International Journal of Communication, 6*, 21.

Work Cited

Bonica, A. (2013). Ideology and Interests in the Political Marketplace. *American Journal of Political Science*, *57*(2), 294-311.

Borger, J. (2017). Donald Trump Blames Constitution for Chaos of His First 100 Days. Retrieved 2017-04-30, from http://www.theguardian.com/us-news/2017/apr/29/trump-blames-constitution-for-first-100-days-chaos-presidency

Bork, R. H. (2013). *Saving Justice: Watergate, the Saturday Night Massacre and Other Adventures of a Solicitor General*. Encounter Books.

Bork, R. J. (2019). *Supreme Revenge* [Interview]. PBS. https://www.pbs.org/wgbh/frontline/interview/robert-bork-jr/

Bowden, E., & Nelson, S. (2020). Covington Teen Nick Sandmann Speaks out on Being 'Defamed by the Media' during Rnc Speech. *NY Post*. https://nypost.com/2020/08/25/rnc-2020-nick-sandmann-speaks-about-being-defamed-by-media/

Bowen, D. (2011). The California Initiative Process at Its Centennial. *California Western Law Review*, *47*(2), 3.

Bowler, S., & Donovan, T. (2000). California's Experience with Direct Democracy. *Parliamentary Affairs*, *53*(4), 644-656.

Braga, A. A., Sousa, W. H., Coldren Jr, J. R., & Rodriguez, D. (2018). The Effects of Body-Worn Cameras on Police Activity and Police-Citizen Encounters: A Randomized Controlled Trial. *J. Crim. L. & Criminology*, *108*, 511.

Brinkley, D., & Lewis, E. (1999). *The Unfinished Presidency*. Blackstone Audio Books.

Brook, J. (2025). From Drones to Police Presence, Utah Campus Where Kirk Was Shot Lacked Key Public Safety Tools. https://www.ksl.com/article/51382833/from-drones-to-police-presence-utah-campus-where-kirk-was-shot-lacked-key-public-safety-tools

Brown, M., Bedayn, J., & Schoenbaum, H. (2025). University Where Charlie Kirk Was Shot Confronts Unwanted Infamy. Retrieved 2025-09-20, from https://apnews.com/article/utah-valley-university-charlie-kirk-fd5ca9b3b7338993970dd0a34dafb64b

Bundgaard, H., Bundgaard, J. S., Raaschou-Pedersen, D. E. T., von Buchwald, C., Todsen, T., Norsk, J. B., Pries-Heje, M. M., Vissing, C. R., Nielsen, P. B., & Winsløw, U. C. (2021).

Effectiveness of Adding a Mask Recommendation to Other Public Health Measures to Prevent Sars-Cov-2 Infection in Danish Mask Wearers: A Randomized Controlled Trial. *Annals of Internal Medicine, 174*(3), 335-343.

Burger, W. E. (1995). *It Is So Ordered: A Constitution Unfolds*. William Morrow & Company.

Burns, J. (2009). *Goddess of the Market: Ayn Rand and the American Right*. Oxford University Press.

Burt, R. S. (2003). The Social Structure of Competition. *Networks in the knowledge economy, 13*(2), 57-91.

Busch, A. (2005). *Reagan's Victory: The Presidential Election of 1980 and the Rise of the Right*. University Press of Kansas.

Bussewitz, C., & Grantham-Phillips, W. (2025). Workers Commenting on Kirk's Death Learn the Limits of Free Speech in and out of Their Jobs. Retrieved 2025-09-14, from https://apnews.com/article/charlie-kirk-workplace-speech-firing-29717a8612ccedebabc7cba29e7ef627

C-SPAN. (1987, July 1, 1987). *Robert Bork's America*.

C-SPAN. (2019a, October 23, 2019). *Facebook Ceo Mark Zuckerberg Testifies before House Committee*.

C-SPAN. (2019b, February 7, 2019). *House Oversight Committee Hearing on Campaign-Finance Reform*.

C-SPAN. (2019c, February 27, 2019). *Michael Cohen Testimony before the House Oversight Committee,*.

C-SPAN. (2023, July 12, 2023). *Fbi Oversight Hearing*.

C-SPAN. (2024a, June 4, 2024). *Department of Justice Oversight Hearing*.

C-SPAN. (2024b, April 11, 2024). *Rep. Jim Jordan Exchange with Fmr. Cbs Reporter Catherine Herridge*.

C-SPAN. (2025). *Our History*. https://www.c-span.org/about/history/

Cain, B. E., & Kousser, T. (2004). *Adapting to Term Limits: Recent Experiences and New Directions*. Public Policy Institute of California San Francisco, CA.

Campaign Finance Institute & Brookings Institution. (2019). *Vital Statistics on Congress: Table 3-1, "the Cost of Winning an Election, 1986–2018."* (Brookings Institution. https://www.brookings.edu/articles/vital-statistics-on-congress/

Work Cited

Canon, B. C., & Johnson, C. A. (1999). *Judicial Policies: Implementation and Impact*. CQ Press.

Canon, D. T. (1990). *Actors, Athletes, and Astronauts: Political Amateurs in the United States Congress*. University of Chicago Press.

Caro, R. A. (2002). *Master of the Senate: The Years of Lyndon Johnson Iii* (Vol. 3). Knopf.

Carter, J. (1995). *Keeping Faith: Memoirs of a President*. University of Arkansas Press.

Carter, J. (2003). Inaugural Address (January 20, 1977). *Religion and American cultures; 3*, 892-893.

Carville, J., & Begala, P. (2006). *Take It Back: Our Party, Our Country, Our Future*. Simon and Schuster.

Ceaser, J. (2017). Presidential Selection. In *The Presidency in the Constitutional Order* (pp. 234-282). Routledge.

Center for Effective Lawmaking. (2025). *Legislative Effectiveness Score*. University of Virginia; Vanderbilt University. https://thelawmakers.org/

Chen, J., & Rodden, J. (2013). Unintentional Gerrymandering: Political Geography and Electoral Bias in Legislatures. *Quarterly Journal of Political Science, 8*(3), 239-269.

Chernow, R. (2011). *Washington: A Life*. Penguin.

Chernow, R. (2016). *Alexander Hamilton*. Bloomsbury Publishing.

Christmas, B. S. (2017). *Washington's Nightmare: A Brief History of American Political Parties*. Self-published, CreateSpace.

Church Committee. (1976). *Intelligence Activities and the Rights of Americans: Final Report of the Select Committee to Study Governmental Operations with Respect to Intelligence Activities*. (S. Rep. No. 94-755). U.S. Government Printing Office.

Clay, J. (2019). More Cowbell! The History Behind Mississippi State's Maddening Tradition. Retrieved 2019-09-18, from https://www.kentucky.com/sports/spt-columns-blogs/john-clay/article235134937.html

Cohen, M., Karol, D., Noel, H., & Zaller, J. (2009). *The Party Decides: Presidential Nominations before and after Reform*. University of Chicago Press.

Collins, J. (2001). *Good to Great*. Random House.

Congressional Management Foundation. (2013). *Life in Congress: The Member Perspective*.

https://www.congressfoundation.org/projects/life-in-congress

Congressional Research Service. (2024). *Continuing Resolutions: Overview of Components and Recent Practices*. (CRS Report R46595).

Coppins, M. (2018). The Man Who Broke Politics. Retrieved 2018-10-15, from https://www.theatlantic.com/magazine/archive/2018/11/newt-gingrich-says-youre-welcome/570832/

Corsi, J. R. (2011). *Where's the Birth Certificate?: The Case That Barack Obama Is Not Eligible to Be President*. Wnd Books.

Cox, G. W., & McCubbins, M. D. (2005). *Setting the Agenda: Responsible Party Government in the Us House of Representatives*. Cambridge University Press.

Creitz, C. (2025). Dems Wanted to Draw Every Republican out of Maryland but Now Lambast Texas Redistricting. *Fox News*. https://www.foxnews.com/politics/dems-wanted-draw-every-republican-out-maryland-now-lambast-texas-redistricting

Crews, C. W. (2025). *Ten Thousand Commandments*. https://cei.org/studies/ten-thousand-commandments-2025/

Curry, J. M. (2022). *Legislating in the Dark: Information and Power in the House of Representatives*. University of Chicago Press.

Curry, J. M., & Lee, F. E. (2020). A Senate Majority Is Overrated. (We Checked.). *New York Times*. https://www.nytimes.com/2020/11/18/opinion/joe-biden-mitch-mcconnell-congress.html

Curry, J. M., & Lee, F. E. (2022). *The Limits of Party: Congress and Lawmaking in a Polarized Era*. University of Chicago Press.

Curtis, M. K. (1986). *No State Shall Abridge: The Fourteenth Amendment and the Bill of Rights*. Duke University Press.

Cutler, D. M., & Summers, L. H. (2020). The Covid-19 Pandemic and the $16 Trillion Virus. *Jama, 324*(15), 1495-1496.

Darwin, C. (1872). *The Descent of Man, and Selection in Relation to Sex* (Vol. 2). D. Appleton.

Davidson, R. H., Oleszek, W. J., Lee, F. E., & Schickler, E. (2019). *Congress and Its Members*. CQ Press.

Davis, C. M. (2014). Secret Sessions of the House and Senate: Authority, Confidentiality, and Frequency. https://www.congress.gov/crs-product/R42106

Work Cited

Davis, E., Escott, G., & Murphy, C. (2025). Employees and Students at These Colleges Have Been Punished for Comments on Charlie Kirk's Death. Retrieved 2025-09-22, from https://www.chronicle.com/article/employees-and-students-at-these-colleges-have-been-punished-for-comments-on-charlie-kirks-death

Dean, J. W. (2004). *Worse Than Watergate: The Secret Presidency of George W. Bush*. Hachette UK.

Deering, C. J., & Smith, S. S. (1997). *Committees in Congress*. Sage.

Derbyshire, S. W., & Bockmann, J. C. (2020). Reconsidering Fetal Pain. *Journal of Medical Ethics, 46*(1), 3-6.

DeRosa, M. B. (2021). Congressional Oversight of Us Intelligence Activities. In *National Security Intelligence and Ethics* (pp. 216-231). Routledge.

DeRose, C. (2020a). *The Fighting Bunch: The Battle of Athens and How World War Ii Veterans Won the Only Successful Armed Rebellion since the Revolution*. Macmillan.

DeRose, C. (2020b). 'Get the Hell out of Here and Get Something to Shoot With'. *Politico*. https://www.politico.com/news/magazine/2020/11/01/world-war-ii-veterans-rigged-election-433773

Desilver, D. (2021). Turnout Soared in 2020 as Nearly Two-Thirds of Eligible U.S. Voters Cast Ballots for President. https://www.pewresearch.org/short-reads/2021/01/28/turnout-soared-in-2020-as-nearly-two-thirds-of-eligible-u-s-voters-cast-ballots-for-president/

Desilver, D. (2025). Turnout Was High in the 2016 Primary Season, but Just Short of 2008 Record. https://www.pewresearch.org/short-reads/2016/06/10/turnout-was-high-in-the-2016-primary-season-but-just-short-of-2008-record/

Dicey, A. V., & Wade, E. C. S. (1982). *Introduction to the Study of the Law of the Constitution*. Liberty Fund.

Donaldson, G. A. (2014). *The Secret Coalition: Ike, Lbj, and the Search for a Middle Way in the 1950s*. Skyhorse.

Donne, J. (1999). Meditation Xvii. *Devotions upon emergent occasions, 1624*, 87.

Downie Jr, L., & Schudson, M. (2009). *The Reconstruction of American Journalism* (Vol. 20). Columbia University Graduate School of Journalism New York.

Draper, T. (1991). *A Very Thin Line: The Iran-Contra Affairs*. Hill and Wang.
Driesen, D. M. (2024). Donald Trump and the Collapse of Checks and Balances. *SMU L. Rev. F., 77*, 199.
Druckman, J. N. (2003). The Power of Television Images: The First Kennedy-Nixon Debate Revisited. *The Journal of Politics, 65*(2), 559-571.
Drutman, L. (2020). *Breaking the Two-Party Doom Loop: The Case for Multiparty Democracy in America*. Oxford University Press.
Dumbrell, J. (1995). *The Carter Presidency: A Re-Evaluation*. Manchester University Press.
Dunbar, R. (2010). *How Many Friends Does One Person Need? Dunbar's Number and Other Evolutionary Quirks*. Harvard University Press.
Dunbar, R. I. (1992). Neocortex Size as a Constraint on Group Size in Primates. *Journal of human evolution, 22*(6), 469-493.
Earman, C. D. (1992). *Boardinghouses, Parties and the Creation of a Political Society: Washington City, 1800-1830*. Louisiana State University and Agricultural & Mechanical College.
Earp, B. D. (2016). Science Cannot Determine Human Values. *Think, 15*(43), 17-23.
Edwards III, G. C. (2023). *Why the Electoral College Is Bad for America*. Cambridge University Press.
Elbeshbishi, S. (2021). Congress' Most Effective Lawmakers Aren't Generally Its Household Names | U.S. Senator Gary Peters of Michigan. https://www.peters.senate.gov/newsroom/in-the-news/usa-today-congress-most-effective-lawmakers-arent-generally-its-household-names
Ely, J. H. (1993). *War and Responsibility: Constitutional Lessons of Vietnam and Its Aftermath*. Princeton University Press.
Epsley-Jone, K., & Frenzel, C. (2025). *The Church Committee Hearings & the Fisa Court*. PBS. https://www.pbs.org/wgbh/pages/frontline/homefront/preemption/churchfisa.html
Epstein, L., & Segal, J. A. (2005). *Advice and Consent: The Politics of Judicial Appointments*. Oxford University Press.
Erikson, B. B., Gabriella. (2025). Democrats Protest Trump's Speech to Congress with Disruption, Exits and Solemn Signs. *Reuters.* https://www.reuters.com/world/us/democrats-

Work Cited

protest-trumps-speech-congress-with-disruption-exits-solemn-signs-2025-03-05/

Everett, B., & Levine, M. (2025). The Power of 10: Inside the 'Unlikely Partnership' That Sealed an Infrastructure Win. *Politico*. https://www.politico.com/news/2021/08/10/senate-infrastructure-bipartisan-partnership-502722

Fabry, M. (2016). Now You Know: Where Was the Original 'Smoke-Filled Room'? https://time.com/4324031/smoke-filled-room-history/

Farhi, P. (2020). Cnn Settles Libel Lawsuit with Covington Catholic Student. Retrieved 2020-01-08, from https://www.washingtonpost.com/lifestyle/style/cnn-settles-libel-lawsuit-with-covington-catholic-student/2020/01/07/f0b21842-319e-11ea-91fd-82d4e04a3fac_story.html

Farrand, M. (1911). *The Records of the Federal Convention of 1787* (Vol. 3). Yale University Press.

Feldman, N. (2017). *The Three Lives of James Madison: Genius, Partisan, President.* Random House.

Fenno, R. F. (1978). *Home Style: House Members in Their Districts.* Little, Brown.

Ferguson, M. (2025). Mtg Calls for "National Divorce" in Psychotic Post on Charlie Kirk. https://newrepublic.com/post/200465/marjorie-taylor-greene-national-divorce-charlie-kirk

Ferling, J. (2016). *Whirlwind: The American Revolution and the War That Won It.* Bloomsbury Publishing USA.

Ferrer, J. T. M. (2023). *2022 Primary Turnout Analysis.* https://bipartisanpolicy.org/report/2022-primary-turnout/

Fiorina, M. P., Abrams, S. J., & Pope, J. (2004). Culture War? The Myth of a Polarized America.

Fisher, L. (2013). *Presidential War Power: Revised.* University Press of Kansas.

Flynn, J. R. (1987). Massive Iq Gains in 14 Nations: What Iq Tests Really Measure. *Psychological bulletin*, *101*(2), 171.

Flynn, J. R. (2007). *What Is Intelligence?: Beyond the Flynn Effect.* Cambridge University Press.

Foner, E. (2005). *Reconstruction, America's Unfinished Revolution, 1863 - 1877.* Harper & Row.

Foner, E. (2019). *The Second Founding: How the Civil War and Reconstruction Remade the Constitution*. WW Norton & Company.

Forde, P. (2025). Mississippi State's Inspired Win Serves Notice: Starkville May Be Nation's Toughest Place to Play. https://sports.yahoo.com/how-raucous-12th-man-helped-mississippi-state-to-another-affirming-win-033042241-ncaaf.html

Fossedal, G. (2018). *Direct Democracy in Switzerland*. Routledge.

Fowler, J. H. (2006). Connecting the Congress: A Study of Cosponsorship Networks. *Political Analysis, 14*(4), 456-487.

Frank, R. H. (1985). The Demand for Unobservable and Other Nonpositional Goods. *The American Economic Review, 75*(1), 101-116.

Frankl, V. E. (1985). *Man's Search for Meaning*. Simon and Schuster.

Frantzich, S. E. S., John. (1996). *The C-Span Revolution*. University of Oklahoma Press.

Freeman, J. B. (2018). *The Field of Blood: Violence in Congress and the Road to Civil War*. Farrar, Straus and Giroux.

Friedman, M. (2016). Public and Private Charity: An Essay. In *Capitalism and Freedom*. Columbia University Press.

Fuoco, R. J. (1981). The Prejudicial Effects of Cameras in the Courtroom. *University of Richmond Law Review, 16*, 867.

Gamm, G. H. (1999). *Urban Exodus*. Harvard University Press.

Ganz, J. (2024). *When the Clock Broke: Con Men, Conspiracists, and How America Cracked up in the Early 1990s*. Farrar, Straus and Giroux.

Geiger, A. (2014). Political Polarization in the American Public. Retrieved 2014-06-12, from https://www.pewresearch.org/politics/2014/06/12/political-polarization-in-the-american-public/

Gennaro, G., & Ash, E. (2023). Televised Debates and Emotional Appeals in Politics: Evidence from C-Span. *Center for Law & Economics Working Paper Series, 2023*(01).

Gentner, D. (1983). Structure-Mapping: A Theoretical Framework for Analogy. *Cognitive science, 7*(2), 155-170.

Gentzkow, M. S., Jesse M.; Taddy, Matt. (2018). *Congressional Record for the 43rd-114th Congresses: Parsed Speeches and Phrase Counts* (https://data.stanford.edu/congress_text

Work Cited

Gerber, E. R. (2011). The Populist Paradox: Interest Group Influence and the Promise of Direct Legislation.

Gerstmann, E. (2025). The Level of Violent Imagery Directed against Covington High Boys Is Dangerous and Wrong. https://www.forbes.com/sites/evangerstmann/2019/01/24/the-level-of-violent-imagery-directed-against-covington-high-boys-is-dangerous-and-wrong/

Gibson, J. L., & Caldeira, G. A. (2009). Citizens, Courts, and Confirmations: Positivity Theory and the Judgments of the American People.

Gilje, P. A. (1999). *Rioting in America*. Indiana University Press.

Gingrich, N. (1994). Contract with America. In: U.S. House Republican Conference.

Gladwell, M. (2006). *The Tipping Point: How Little Things Can Make a Big Difference*. Little, Brown.

Goffman, E. (2023). The Presentation of Self in Everyday Life. In *Social Theory Re-Wired* (pp. 450-459). Routledge.

Goldin, M. (2025). Assassination of Charlie Kirk Prompts Flood of False and Misleading Claims Online. https://apnews.com/article/fact-check-charlie-kirk-shot-assassination-3354b7ba0d736c198b454f77b3744308

Goldman, S. (2004). Judicial Confirmation Wars: Ideology and the Battle for the Federal Courts. *U. Rich. L. Rev.*, *39*, 871.

Golway, T. (2014). *Machine Made: Tammany Hall and the Creation of Modern American Politics*. WW Norton & Company.

Goodwin, D. K. (1991). *Lyndon Johnson and the American Dream: The Most Revealing Portrait of a President and Presidential Power Ever Written*. Macmillan.

Goodwin, D. K. (2009). *Team of Rivals: The Political Genius of Abraham Lincoln*. Penguin UK.

Goolsbee, A., & Syverson, C. (2021). Fear, Lockdown, and Diversion: Comparing Drivers of Pandemic Economic Decline 2020. *Journal of public economics*, *193*, 104311.

Gorton, S. (2020). *Citizen Reporters: S.S. Mcclure, Ida Tarbell, and the Magazine That Rewrote America*. Ecco.

Gottman, J., & Silver, N. (2015). *The Seven Principles for Making Marriage Work: A Practical Guide from the Country's Foremost Relationship Expert*. Harmony.

Gould, S. J. (2011). *Rocks of Ages: Science and Religion in the Fullness of Life*. Ballantine Books.

Granovetter, M. S. (1973). The Strength of Weak Ties. *American journal of sociology, 78*(6), 1360-1380.

Green, J. C., Kellstedt, L. A., Smidt, C. E., Guth, J. L., Bullock, C. S., & Rozell, M. J. (2010). The New Politics of the Old South: An Introduction to Southern Politics.

Greenhouse, L. (2024). *Becoming Justice Blackmun: Harry Blackmun's Supreme Court Journey*. Macmillan.

Grossmann, M. (2014). *Artists of the Possible: Governing Networks and American Policy Change since 1945*. Oxford University Press.

Haberman, M. (2022). *Confidence Man: The Making of Donald Trump and the Breaking of America*. Penguin.

Hacker, J. S., & Pierson, P. (2005). *Off Center: The Republican Revolution and the Erosion of American Democracy*. Yale University Press.

Hall, R. L. (1998). *Participation in Congress*. Yale University Press.

Halperin, M., & Heilemann, J. (2013). *Double Down: Game Change 2012*. Penguin.

Hamilton, A., Madison, J., & Jay, J. (2015). *The Federalist Papers: A Collection of Essays Written in Favour of the New Constitution*. Coventry House Publishing.

Haney, C., Banks, C., & Zimbardo, P. (1973). Interpersonal Dynamics in a Simulated Prison. *The Sociology of Corrections (New York: Wiley, 1977)*, 65-92.

Harbridge, L. (2015). *Is Bipartisanship Dead?: Policy Agreement and Agenda-Setting in the House of Representatives*. Cambridge University Press.

Hasen, R. L. (2016). *Plutocrats United: Campaign Money, the Supreme Court, and the Distortion of American Elections*. Yale University Press.

Hatch, O. (2009). Goodbye to a Senate Giant, My Friend, My Colleague. *USA Today*, 11A-11A.

Hayek, F. A. (2011). *The Constitution of Liberty: The Definitive Edition* (Vol. 17). University of Chicago Press.

Heberlig, E. S., & Larson, B. A. (2012). *Congressional Parties, Institutional Ambition, and the Financing of Majority Control*. University of Michigan Press.

Henneberger, M. (2000). Drawing on Their Roots: Gore's Boyhood Divided between Tennessee Farm, D.C. Privilege. Retrieved 2000-06-08, from

Work Cited

https://www.deseret.com/2000/6/8/19511506/drawing-on-their-roots-gore-br-gore-s-boyhood-divided-between-tennessee-farm-d-c-privilege/

Hibbing, J. R. (2017). *Congressional Careers: Contours of Life in the Us House of Representatives*. UNC Press Books.

Hilbert, M., & López, P. (2011). The World's Technological Capacity to Store, Communicate, and Compute Information. *Science, 332*(6025), 60-65.

Hirano, S., Snyder, J., Ansolabehere, S., & Hansen, B. (2010). Primary Elections and Partisan Polarization in the Us Congress.

History.com. (2018). *1968 Democratic Convention—Protests, Yippies, Witnesses.* https://www.history.com/topics/1960s/1968-democratic-convention

Hofstadter, R. (1955). *The Age of Reform*. Knopf New York.

Hofstadter, R. (2012). *The Paranoid Style in American Politics*. Vintage.

Hong, R., & Murugan, S. (2025). School Board Battle: Rusd's Culture War. https://rocklinhsflash.net/7299/news/localnews/school-board-battle-rusds-culture-war/

Horbar, J. D., Badger, G. J., Carpenter, J. H., Fanaroff, A. A., Kilpatrick, S., LaCorte, M., Phibbs, R., Soll, R. F., & Network, M. o. t. V. O. (2002). Trends in Mortality and Morbidity for Very Low Birth Weight Infants, 1991–1999. *Pediatrics, 110*(1), 143-151.

Howe, D. W. (2007). *What Hath God Wrought: The Transformation of America, 1815-1848*. Oxford University Press.

Howell, W. G. (2015). *Thinking About the Presidency: The Primacy of Power*. Princeton University Press.

Howell, W. G., & Moe, T. M. (2020). *Presidents, Populism, and the Crisis of Democracy*. University of Chicago Press.

Hulse, C. (2009). In Lawmaker's Outburst, a Rare Breach of Protocol. *The New York Times*. https://www.nytimes.com/2009/09/10/us/politics/10wilson.html

Hutchinson, I. (2011). *Monopolizing Knowledge*. Lulu. com.

Issacharoff, S., Karlan, P. S., Pildes, R. H., Persily, N., & Tolson, F. (2022). *The Law of Democracy: Legal Structure of the Political Process*.

Issacharoff, S., & Pildes, R. H. (1998). Politics as Markets: Partisan Lockups of the Democratic Process. *Stanford law review*, 643-717.

Issue One. (2017). *The Price of Power: How Political Parties Squeeze Influential Lawmakers to Boost Their Campaign Coffers*. https://www.issueone.org/wp-content/uploads/2017/05/price-of-power-final.pdf

James, S. C. (2007). Timing and Sequence in Congressional Elections: Interstate Contagion and America's Nineteenth-Century Scheduling Regime. *Studies in American Political Development, 21*(2), 181-202.

Jamieson, K. H., & Birdsell, D. S. (1990). *Presidential Debates: The Challenge of Creating an Informed Electorate*. Oxford University Press.

Jasanoff, S. (2007). Technologies of Humility. *Nature, 450*(7166), 33-33.

Jefferson, T. (1789). *Thomas Jefferson to James Madison*. University of Virginia Press. https://founders.archives.gov/documents/Madison/01-12-02-0248

Jefferson, T. (1820). Letter from Thomas Jefferson to William Charles Jarvis. In W. C. Jarvis (Ed.). Monticello, Virginia.

Jefferson, T. (1826a). *Design for Tombstone and Inscription*. University of Virginia Press. https://founders.archives.gov/documents/Jefferson/98-01-02-6185

Jefferson, T. (1826b). *From Thomas Jefferson to James Madison*. University of Virginia Press. https://founders.archives.gov/documents/Jefferson/98-01-02-5912

Jefferson, T., Dooley, L., Ferroni, E., Al-Ansary, L. A., van Driel, M. L., Bawazeer, G. A., Jones, M. A., Hoffmann, T. C., Clark, J., & Beller, E. M. (2023). Physical Interventions to Interrupt or Reduce the Spread of Respiratory Viruses. *Cochrane Database of Systematic Reviews*(1).

Jenkinson, C. S. (2022). Why Does America Have Primaries? Retrieved May 29, 2022, from https://www.governing.com/context/why-does-america-have-primaries

Work Cited

Jensen, B., & Young, J. K. (2025). Is the United States Headed toward a Civil War? https://www.csis.org/analysis/united-states-headed-toward-civil-war

Jones, C. O. (2005). *The Presidency in a Separated System*. Rowman & Littlefield.

Kaiser, C. (2023). 'We May Have Lost the South': What Lbj Really Said About Democrats in 1964. Retrieved 2023-01-23, from https://www.theguardian.com/books/2023/jan/22/we-may-have-lost-the-south-lbj-democrats-civil-rights-act-1964-bill-moyers

Karabell, Z. (1998). The Rise and Fall of the Televised Political Convention. *Shorenstein Center Discussion Paper Series*.

Kennedy, E. M. (2009). *True Compass: A Memoir*. Twelve.

Kennedy, L. (2018). The 1994 Midterms: When Newt Gingrich Helped Republicans Win Big. https://www.history.com/articles/midterm-elections-1994-republican-revolution-gingrich-contract-with-america

Kerr, J., Panagopoulos, C., & Van Der Linden, S. (2021). Political Polarization on Covid-19 Pandemic Response in the United States. *Personality and Individual Differences, 179*.

Ketcham, R. L. (1990). *James Madison: A Biography*. University of Virginia Press.

Kettl, D. F. (2000). The Transformation of Governance: Globalization, Devolution, and the Role of Government. *Public Administration Review, 60*(6), 488-497.

Keyssar, A. (2000). *The Right to Vote: The Contested History of Democracy in the United States*. Basic Books.

Dover Area School District, (Dover, Pennsylvania 2005).

Klarman, M. J. (2004). *From Jim Crow to Civil Rights: The Supreme Court and the Struggle for Racial Equality*. Oxford University Press.

Klein, E. (2020). *Why We're Polarized*. Simon and Schuster.

Kokai, M. (2016). More Than One Snake in This Story. *The Carolina Journal*. https://www.carolinajournal.com/opinion/more-than-one-snake-in-this-story/

Kornberg, M. (2024). How Money Shapes Pathways to Power in Congress. https://www.brennancenter.org/our-work/analysis-opinion/how-money-shapes-pathways-power-congress

Kousser, T. (2005). *Term Limits and the Dismantling of State Legislative Professionalism*. Cambridge University Press.

Kovach, B., & Rosenstiel, T. (2011). *Blur: How to Know What's True in the Age of Information Overload*. Bloomsbury Publishing USA.

Kovach, B., & Rosenstiel, T. (2021). *The Elements of Journalism, Revised and Updated 4th Edition: What Newspeople Should Know and the Public Should Expect*. Crown.

Kramer, A. D., Guillory, J. E., & Hancock, J. T. (2014). Experimental Evidence of Massive-Scale Emotional Contagion through Social Networks. *Proceedings of the National Academy of Sciences, 111*(24), 8788-8790.

Kraus, S. (1977). *The Great Debates: Kennedy Vs. Nixon, 1960: A Reissue*. Indiana University Press.

Kraut, R. E., Fussell, S. R., Brennan, S. E., & Siegel, J. (2002). Understanding Effects of Proximity on Collaboration: Implications for Technologies To. *137*.

Kuhn, T. S., & Hacking, I. (1970). *The Structure of Scientific Revolutions* (Vol. 2). University of Chicago Press.

Kunda, Z. (1990). The Case for Motivated Reasoning. *Psychological bulletin, 108*(3), 480.

Kuntz, N. A. (1969). *The Electoral Commission of 1877*. Michigan State University.

La Raja, R., & Schaffner, B. (2015). *Campaign Finance and Political Polarization: When Purists Prevail*. University of Michigan Press.

Lacy, L. (2019). Curtailment of the National Security State: The Church Senate Committee of 1975–1976. Retrieved 2019-05-13, from https://www.boisestate.edu/sps-frankchurchinstitute/2019/05/13/curtailment-of-the-national-security-state-the-church-senate-committee-of-1975-1976/

Lakoff, G. (1993). The Contemporary Theory of Metaphor.

Lakoff, G. (2014). *The All New Don't Think of an Elephant!: Know Your Values and Frame the Debate*. Chelsea Green Publishing.

Landemore, H. (2020). Open Democracy: Reinventing Popular Rule for the Twenty-First Century.

Larson, E. J. (2008). *Summer for the Gods: The Scopes Trial and America's Continuing Debate over Science and Religion*. Basic Books.

Lebo, L. (2008). *The Devil in Dover: An Insider's Story of Dogma V. Darwin in Small-Town America*. The New Press.

Lee, B., Lee, K., & Hartmann, B. (2023). Transformation of Social Relationships in Covid-19 America: Remote Communication May Amplify Political Echo Chambers. *Science Advances*, *9*(51).

Lee, F. E. (2022). *Insecure Majorities: Congress and the Perpetual Campaign*. University of Chicago Press.

Leonard, N. E., Lipsitz, K., Bizyaeva, A., Franci, A., & Lelkes, Y. (2021). The Nonlinear Feedback Dynamics of Asymmetric Political Polarization. *Proceedings of the National Academy of Sciences*, *118*(50).

Leonhardt, D. (2022). Follow the Science? *The New York Times*. https://www.nytimes.com/2022/02/11/briefing/covid-cdc-follow-the-science.html

Lessig, L. (2018). *America, Compromised*. University of Chicago Press.

Lessl, T. M. (2007). The Culture of Science and the Rhetoric of Scientism: From Francis Bacon to the Darwin Fish. *Quarterly Journal of Speech*, *93*(2), 123-149.

Levine, M., & Everett, B. (2025). The Senate's Bipartisan Infrastructure Gang Saddles up for One Last Ride. *Politico*. https://www.politico.com/news/2021/08/03/senate-bipartisan-infrastructure-deal-502267

Levitsky, S., & Ziblatt, D. (2019). *How Democracies Die*. Crown.

Levy, D., & Nielsen, R. K. (2010). *The Changing Business of Journalism and Its Implications for Democracy*. Reuters Institute for the Study of Journalism, Department of Politics.

Lewis, J. B. P., Keith; Rosenthal, Howard; Boche, Adam; Rudkin, Aaron; Sonnet, Luke. (2025). *Voteview: Congressional Roll-Call Votes Database* (https://voteview.com

Liang, N., Grayson, S. J., Kussman, M. A., Mildner, J. N., & Tamir, D. I. (2024). In-Person and Virtual Social Interactions Improve Well-Being during the Covid-19 Pandemic. *Computers in Human Behavior Reports*, *15*.

Lijphart, A. (1994). *Electoral Systems and Party Systems: A Study of Twenty-Seven Democracies, 1945-1990*. Oxford University Press.

Lijphart, A. (1999). *Patterns of Democracy: Government Forms and Performance in Thirty-Six Countries*. Yale University Press.

Lim, K. (2018). A Friendship Born in One of America's Darkest Hours. *Sunday Morning*.

https://www.cbsnews.com/news/alan-simpson-norman-mineta-friendship-born-out-of-japanese-american-internment-camp/
Lincoln, A. (1860). *Cooper Union Address.*
Linz, J. J. (1990). The Perils of Presidentialism. *Journal of democracy, 1*(1), 51-69.
Liptak, A. (2010). Supreme Court Gets a Rare Rebuke, in Front of a Nation. *The New York Times.* https://www.nytimes.com/2010/01/29/us/politics/29scotus.html
Liptak, A. (2018). A Bitter Nominee, Questions of Neutrality, and a Damaged Supreme Court. *The New Yorker.* https://www.nytimes.com/2018/09/28/us/politics/kavanaugh-testimony-supreme-court.html
Little, B. (2020). How Ronald Reagan's 1976 Convention Battle Fueled His 1980 Landslide. https://www.history.com/articles/ronald-reagan-republican-contested-convention-1976-gerald-ford
Little, D. (1996). *1968: Hippies, Yippies, and the First Mayor Daley.* Chicago Tribune. https://www.chicagotribune.com/1996/07/26/1968-hippies-yippies-and-the-first-mayor-daley/
Lott, E. (2013). *Love & Theft: Blackface Minstrelsy and the American Working Class.* Oxford University Press.
Luria, S. (2003). National Domesticity in the Early Republic: Washington, D.C. *Common Place.* https://commonplace.online/article/national-domesticity-in-the-early-republic-washington-d-c/
Madison, J. (1785). Memorial and Remonstrance against Religious Assessments. *The Papers of James Madison, 8,* 295.
Madison, J. (1787). *James Madison to Edmund Pendleton.* University of Virginia Press. https://founders.archives.gov/documents/Madison/01-09-02-0151
Madison, J. (2016). The Federalist Papers. In *Democracy: A Reader* (pp. 52-57). Columbia University Press.
Madison, J. (c. 1786). Notes on Ancient and Modern Confederacies. In: Founders Online, National Archives.
Manin, B. (1997). *The Principles of Representative Government.* Cambridge University Press.

Work Cited

Mann, T. E., & Ornstein, N. J. (2006). *The Broken Branch: How Congress Is Failing America and How to Get It Back on Track.* Oxford University Press.

Mann, T. E., & Ornstein, N. J. (2016). *It's Even Worse Than It Looks: How the American Constitutional System Collided with the New Politics of Extremism.* Basic Books.

Mansbridge, J., Bohman, J., Chambers, S., Christiano, T., Fung, A., Parkinson, J., Thompson, D. F., & Warren, M. E. (2012). A Systemic Approach to Deliberative Democracy. *Deliberative systems: Deliberative democracy at the large scale,* 1-26.

Mansfield, H. C., & Winthrop, D. (2000). *Democracy in America, Alexis De Tocqueville.* University of Chicago Press.

Marder, N. S. (2012). The Conundrum of Cameras in the Courtroom. *Arizona State Law Journal, 44,* 1489.

Marino, M., Iacono, R., & Mollerstrom, J. (2024). (Mis-) Perceptions, Information, and Political Polarization: A Survey and a Systematic Literature Review. *European Journal of Political Economy, 85.*

Markovits, A. S., & Silverstein, M. (1988). *The Politics of Scandal: Power and Process in Liberal Democracies.* Holmes & Meier New York.

Mason, C. (2009). *Reading Appalachia from Left to Right: Conservatives and the 1974 Kanawha County Textbook Controversy.* Cornell University Press.

Mason, L. (2018). *Uncivil Agreement: How Politics Became Our Identity.* University of Chicago Press.

Matalin, M., & Carville, J. (1995). *All's Fair:" Love, War and Running for President".* Simon and Schuster.

Mayer, W. G., & Busch, A. E. (2003). *The Front-Loading Problem in Presidential Nominations.* Rowman & Littlefield.

Mayhew, D. R. (2004). *Congress: The Electoral Connection.* Yale university press.

Mayo, E. (2004). *The Human Problems of an Industrial Civilization.* Routledge.

Mbuqe, E. (2025). Secession in the Us: Could It Happen? *Syracuse University Today.* Retrieved 2025-10-02, from https://news.syr.edu/2025/10/02/secession-in-the-us-could-it-happen/

McCarty, N., Poole, K. T., & Rosenthal, H. (2016). *Polarized America: The Dance of Ideology and Unequal Riches*. MIT Press.

McCaskill, N. D. (2018). 'It's Almost Nasty': Dems Seek Crackdown on Sleeping in the Capitol. *Politico*. https://www.politico.com/story/2018/03/06/democrats-sleeping-capitol-crackdown-431969

McChesney, R. W., & Nichols, J. (2011). *The Death and Life of American Journalism: The Media Revolution That Will Begin the World Again*. Bold Type Books.

McCormick, R. P. (1982). *The Presidential Game: The Origins of American Presidential Politics*. Oxford University Press.

McGann, A. J., Smith, C. A., Latner, M., & Keena, A. (2016). *Gerrymandering in America: The House of Representatives, the Supreme Court, and the Future of Popular Sovereignty*. Cambridge University Press.

McLean, I., & McMillan, A. (2005). *State of the Union*. OUP Oxford.

Meacham, J. (2009). *American Lion: Andrew Jackson in the White House*. Random House Trade Paperbacks.

Memmott, M. (2010). If Alito Did Say 'Not True' About Obama's Claim, He May Have Had a Point. https://www.npr.org/sections/thetwo-way/2010/01/if_alito_did_say_not_true_abou.html

Milkis, S. M. (1995). What Politics Do Presidents Make? *Polity*, *27*(3), 485-496.

Milkoreit, M., & Smith, E. K. (2025). Rapidly Diverging Public Trust in Science in the United States. *Public Understanding of Science*, *34*(5), 616-627.

Millemann, M. (2017). Checks and Balances in the Age of Trump. *U. Md. LJ Race, Religion, Gender & Class*, *17*, 1.

Minozzi, W., & Caldeira, G. A. (2021). Congress and Community: Coresidence and Social Influence in the Us House of Representatives, 1801–1861. *American Political Science Review*, *115*(4), 1292-1307.

Mir, A. (2020). *Postjournalism and the Death of Newspapers. The Media after Trump: Manufacturing Anger and Polarization*.

Mir, A. (2023). The Viral Inquisitor; Social Media Have Unleashed a Culture of Instant Judging. *City Journal*.

Work Cited

Moe, T. M., & Howell, W. G. (1999). The Presidential Power of Unilateral Action. *Journal of Law, Economics, and Organization*, *15*(1), 132-179.

Moody, C. (2016). The Gop Convention's Unofficial Slogan: 'Lock Her Up'. *CNN.com*. https://www.cnn.com/2016/07/19/politics/hillary-clinton-republican-convention-chants/

Moore, K. L., Persaud, T. V. N., & Torchia, M. G. (2008). *The Developing Human: Clinically Oriented Embryology*. Elsevier Brasil.

Morozov, E. (2012). *The Net Delusion: The Dark Side of Internet Freedom*. PublicAffairs.

Morris, J. M. (2010). *Pulitzer: A Life in Politics, Print, and Power*. Harper New York.

Morris, J. S., & Francia, P. L. (2005). From Network News to Cable Commentary: The Evolution of Television Coverage of the Party Conventions. State of the Parties Conference,

Morris, R. B. (1988). *The Forging of the Union, 1781-1789*. Harpercollins Childrens Books.

Murray, A. S., & Birnbaum, J. H. (1988). *Showdown at Gucci Gulch*. Vintage.

Murray, C. A., & Cox, C. B. (1989). *Apollo, the Race to the Moon*. Simon and Schuster.

Nguyen, T. (2016). High-Profile Defections Threaten G.O.P. Plans to Stop Trump. *Vanity Fair*. https://www.vanityfair.com/news/2016/02/gop-politicians-support-trump

Noden, D. M. (2003). Human Embryology & Teratology. In: JSTOR.

Nord, M., Angiolillo, F., Good God, A., & Lindberg, S. I. (2025). State of the World 2024: 25 Years of Autocratization– Democracy Trumped? *Democratization*, *32*(4), 839-864.

Norrander, B. (2019). *The Imperfect Primary: Oddities, Biases, and Strengths of Us Presidential Nomination Politics*. Routledge.

O'Donnell, N. (2016). *Are Members of Congress Becoming Telemarketers?* 60 Minutes.

Office of the Federal Register. (2025). *Federal Register Annual Reports, 1940–2024*. National Archives and Records Administration Retrieved from https://www.federalregister.gov/reader-aids/office-of-the-federal-register-announcements/2015/05/federal-register-by-the-numbers

Olcaysoy Okten, I., Huang, T., & Oettingen, G. (2023). Updating False Beliefs: The Role of Misplaced Vs. Well-Placed Certainty. *Psychonomic Bulletin & Review, 30*(2), 712-721.

Olson, G. M., & Olson, J. S. (2000). Distance Matters. *Human–computer interaction, 15*(2-3), 139-178.

Oshinsky, D. M. (2019). *A Conspiracy So Immense: The World of Joe Mccarthy*. Free Press.

Outlook Staff. (2012). Getting Rid of Redistricting's Snakes, Earmuffs and Pterodactyls. *Washington Post*. https://www.washingtonpost.com/opinions/getting-rid-of-redistrictings-snakes-earmuffs-and-pterodactyls/2012/10/26/81ed183e-1dca-11e2-ba31-3083ca97c314_story.html

Padover, S. K. (1952). *Jefferson*. Penguin.

Page, D. L. (2024). *The Art of the Compromise: Returning American Democracy to Better Days*. Warped Minds Press.

Paine, A. B. (1912). *Mark Twain: A Biography; the Personal and Literary Life of Samuel Langhorne Clemens* (Vol. 1–3). Harper & Brothers.

Parker, A. M., Jonathan. (2013). Senate, 68 to 32, Passes Overhaul for Immigration. *The New York Times*. https://www.nytimes.com/2013/06/28/us/politics/immigration-bill-clears-final-hurdle-to-senate-approval.html

Paul, K. (2019). Ocasio-Cortez Stumps Zuckerberg with Questions on Far Right and Cambridge Analytica. Retrieved 2019-10-23, from http://www.theguardian.com/technology/2019/oct/23/mark-zuckerberg-alexandria-ocasio-cortez-facebook-cambridge-analytica

Penniman, N., & Potter, W. (2016). Op-Ed: Citizens United Is Only 15% of the Political Cash Problem. Retrieved 2016-03-08, from https://www.latimes.com/opinion/op-ed/la-oe-penniman-potter-political-campaign-finance-reform-20160308-story.html

Pentland, A. S. (2012). The New Science of Building Great Teams. *Harvard business review, 90*(4), 60-69.

Perman, M. (2001). *Struggle for Mastery: Disfranchisement in the South, 1888-1908*. Univ of North Carolina Press.

Work Cited

Perry, G. (2019). *The Lost Boys: Inside Muzafer Sherif's Robbers Cave Experiment*. Scribe Publications.
Pew Research Center. (2018). An Examination of the 2016 Electorate, Based on Validated Voters.
Pew Research Center. (2024). *Newspapers Fact Sheet* (https://www.pewresearch.org/journalism/fact-sheet/newspapers
Pildes, R. (2016). Two Myths About the Unruly American Primary System. Retrieved 2016-05-25, from https://web.archive.org/web/20160808144032/https://www.washingtonpost.com/news/monkey-cage/wp/2016/05/25/two-myths-about-the-unruly-american-primary-system/
Polanyi, M. (2012). *Personal Knowledge*. Routledge.
Polsby, N. W. (1968). The Institutionalization of the Us House of Representatives. *American Political Science Review, 62*(1), 144-168.
Polsby, N. W. (1983). *Consequences of Party Reform*. Oxford University Press.
Polsby, N. W., Wildavsky, A. B., & Hopkins, D. A. (2008). *Presidential Elections: Strategies and Structures of American Politics*. Bloomsbury Publishing PLC.
Popper, K. (2005). *The Logic of Scientific Discovery*. Routledge.
Porter, M. A., Mucha, P. J., Newman, M. E., & Warmbrand, C. M. (2005). A Network Analysis of Committees in the Us House of Representatives. *Proceedings of the National Academy of Sciences, 102*(20), 7057-7062.
Posner, E. A. (2024). *The Demagogue's Playbook: The Battle for American Democracy from the Founders to Trump*. Macmillan.
Posner, R. A. (1999). *An Affair of State: The Investigation, Impeachment, and Trial of President Clinton*. Harvard University Press.
Postman, N. (2005). *Amusing Ourselves to Death: Public Discourse in the Age of Show Business*. Penguin Books.
Putnam, R. D. (2000). *Bowling Alone: The Collapse and Revival of American Community*. Simon and Schuster.
Rabinowitz, H. (2024). 'I Will Not Be Intimidated': Attorney General Merrick Garland to Slam Attacks against Justice Department | Cnn Politics. Retrieved 2024-06-04, from

https://www.cnn.com/2024/06/04/politics/merrick-garland-justice-department-defense

Radicals: Thayer Flayed. (1927). *Time Magazine*. https://time.com/archive/6663921/radicals-thayer-flayed/

Rakove, J. N. (1998). Original Meanings: Politics and Ideas in the Making of the Constitution. *Journal of American Studies, 32*, 137-138.

Rakove, J. N. (2019). *The Beginnings of National Politics: An Interpretive History of the Continental Congress*. Johns Hopkins University Press.

Ramjee, D., Pollack, C. C., Charpignon, M.-L., Gupta, S., Rivera, J. M., El Hayek, G., Dunn, A. G., Desai, A. N., & Majumder, M. S. (2023). Evolving Face Mask Guidance during a Pandemic and Potential Harm to Public Perception: Infodemiology Study of Sentiment and Emotion on Twitter. *Journal of Medical Internet Research, 25*.

Rand, A. (2005). *Atlas Shrugged*. Penguin.

Ranney, A. (1975). *Curing the Mischiefs of Faction: Party Reform in America* (Vol. 3). Univ of California Press.

Rasmussen, D. C. (2021). *Fears of a Setting Sun: The Disillusionment of America's Founders*. Princeton University Press.

Rauch, J. E. (1994). Bureaucracy, Infrastructure, and Economic Growth: Evidence from Us Cities during the Progressive Era. In: National Bureau of Economic Research Cambridge, Mass.

Reagan, R. (1982). Remarks to the Reagan Administration Executive Forum. https://www.reaganlibrary.gov/archives/speech/remarks-reagan-administration-executive-forum-0

Reid, J. D., & Kurth, M. M. (1992). The Rise and Fall of Urban Political Patronage Machines. In *Strategic Factors in Nineteenth Century American Economic History: A Volume to Honor Robert W. Fogel* (pp. 427-445). University of Chicago Press.

Rekker, R. (2021). The Nature and Origins of Political Polarization over Science. *Public Understanding of Science, 30*(4), 352-368.

Remini, R. V. (2006). *The House: The History of the House of Representatives*.

Reuters. (2025). Reactions to the Fatal Shooting of Us Right-Wing Activist Charlie Kirk. Retrieved 2025-09-11, from https://www.reuters.com/world/us/reactions-fatal-shooting-us-right-wing-activist-charlie-kirk-2025-09-10/

Reynolds, G. H. (2006). *An Army of Davids: How Markets and Technology Empower Ordinary People to Beat Big Media, Big Government, and Other Goliaths.* Thomas Nelson Inc.

Richards, K. (2025). Marjorie Taylor Greene Is Calling for This Disturbing Change, and Experts Are Sounding the Alarm. Retrieved 2025-09-17, from https://www.huffpost.com/entry/marjorie-taylor-greene-america-change-experts_n_68c9ab78e4b0765c82509d22

Richards, L. L. (2014). *Shays's Rebellion: The American Revolution's Final Battle.* University of Pennsylvania Press.

Ricks, T. E. (2020). *First Principles: What America's Founders Learned from the Greeks and Romans and How That Shaped Our Country.* Harper Perennial.

Roberts-Miller, P. (2019). *Rhetoric and Demagoguery.* SIU Press.

Rohde, D. W. (1991). *Parties and Leaders in the Postreform House.* University of Chicago Press.

Roll, D. L. (2020). *George Marshall: Defender of the Republic.* Penguin.

Rosenberg, S. (2019). Democracy Devouring Itself: The Rise of the Incompetent Citizen and the Appeal of Right Wing Populism.

Rosenbluth, F., & Shapiro, I. (2018). *Responsible Parties: Saving Democracy from Itself.* Yale University Press.

Rosenthal, R. (1976). Experimenter Effects in Behavioral Research.

Ross, T. (2004). *Enlightened Democracy: The Case for the Electoral College.* World Ahead Publishing.

Ross, T. (2019). *Why We Need the Electoral College.* Gateway Editions.

Rottinghaus, B. (2015). *The Institutional Effects of Executive Scandals.* Cambridge University Press.

Rove, K. (2010). *Courage and Consequence: My Life as a Conservative in the Fight.* Simon and Schuster.

Rowland, T. (2022). The Us Has the Global Market Cornered on Scandal Suffixes. *Herald-Mail.*

Royal Institute of International Affairs. (1927). *The Chatham House Rule.* Chatham House. https://www.chathamhouse.org/about-us/chatham-house-rule

Russell, D. (2025). *Answer: Why All the Crazy Capital Letters?* SearchReSearch. https://searchresearch1.blogspot.com/2015/08/answer-why-all-crazy-capital-letters.html

Sabato, L. (1991). *Feeding Frenzy: How Attack Journalism Has Transformed American Politics.* Free Press.

Sandmann, N. (2019). Statement of Nick Sandmann, Covington Catholic High School Junior, Regarding Incident at the Lincoln Memorial. Retrieved 2019-01-21, from https://www.cnn.com/2019/01/20/us/covington-kentucky-student-statement

Sartori, G. (1997). *Comparative Constitutional Engineering: An Inquiry into Structures, Incentives, and Outcomes.* NYU Press.

Saturno, J. V. (2023). *Introduction to the Federal Budget Process.* (CRS R46240). Retrieved from https://www.congress.gov/crs-products

Scales, L. (2020). Why Chicago's 4th Congressional District—Those 'Earmuffs'—Are About Fairness and Not Gerrymandering. *Chicago Sun-Times.* https://chicago.suntimes.com/2020/3/11/21164850/illinois-4th-congressional-district-gerrymandering-voting-rights-act-census-liliana-scales

Schattschneider, E. (1942). *Party Government: American Government in Action.* Transaction Publishers.

Schick, A. (2008). *The Federal Budget: Politics, Policy, Process.* Brookings Institution Press.

Schlefer, J. (2025). American Democracy Might Be Stronger Than Donald Trump. *Politico.* https://www.politico.com/news/magazine/2025/09/19/american-democracy-resilience-00548910

Schmidt, C. (2018). The Rise and Fall of the No-Litmus-Test Rule - Iscotus Now. *ISCOTUS Now.* https://blogs.kentlaw.iit.edu/iscotus/rise-fall-no-litmus-test-norm/

Schrecker, E. (1998). *Many Are the Crimes: Mccarthyism in America.* Princeton University Press.

Schudson, M. (2008). *Why Democracies Need an Unlovable Press.* Polity.

Schultz, J. (2009). *The Chicago Conspiracy Trial: Revised Edition.* University of Chicago Press.

Work Cited

Schumer, C. E. (2014). End Partisan Primaries, Save America. *The New York Times*. https://www.nytimes.com/2014/07/22/opinion/charles-schumer-adopt-the-open-primary.html

Schwarzenegger, A. (2012). *Total Recall (Enhanced Edition): My Unbelievably True Life Story*. Simon and Schuster.

Seariac, H. (2024). 'Utah's Gift to the Nation' — Statue of Responsibility Inches Closer to Home in Utah. *DeseretNews*. https://www.deseret.com/utah/2024/05/22/statue-of-responsibility-in-utah/

Seimel, A. (2024). Elite Polarization—the Boon and Bane of Democracy: Evidence from Thirty Democracies. *Electoral Studies*, 90.

Shafer, B. E. (1983). *Quiet Revolution: Struggle for the Democratic Party and the Shaping of Post-Reform Politics*. Russell Sage Foundation.

Shafer, B. E., & Claggett, W. J. (1995). *The Two Majorities: The Issue Context of Modern American Politics*. Johns Hopkins University Press.

Sherif, M. (1988). *The Robbers Cave Experiment: Intergroup Conflict and Cooperation*. Wesleyan University Press.

Short, J., Williams, E., & Christie, B. (1976). *The Social Psychology of Telecommunications*. Wiley.

Siddique, H. (2011). Mob Rule: Iceland Crowdsources Its Next Constitution. Retrieved 2011-06-09, from http://www.theguardian.com/world/2011/jun/09/iceland-crowdsourcing-constitution-facebook

Sides, J., Tausanovitch, C., Vavreck, L., & Warshaw, C. (2020). On the Representativeness of Primary Electorates. *British Journal of Political Science*, 50(2), 677-685.

Simon, L. (2019). How the Republican Revolution Broke Congress. https://virginiapolitics.org/online/2019/1/16/how-the-republican-revolution-broke-congress

Sinclair, B. (1999). Transformational Leader or Faithful Agent? Principal-Agent Theory and House Majority Party Leadership. *Legislative Studies Quarterly*, 421-449.

Sinclair, B. (2014). *Party Wars: Polarization and the Politics of National Policy Making* (Vol. 10). University of Oklahoma Press.

Sinclair, B. (2016). *Unorthodox Lawmaking: New Legislative Processes in the Us Congress*. CQ Press.
Skowronek, S. (1997). *The Politics Presidents Make: Leadership from John Adams to Bill Clinton*. Harvard University Press.
Slotnick, E. E. (1983). The Paths to the Federal Bench: Gender, Race and Judicial Recruitment Variation. *Judicature, 67*, 371.
Smith, B. A. (2009). Unfree Speech: The Folly of Campaign Finance Reform.
Snowden, E. (2019). *Permanent Record: A Memoir of a Reluctant Whistleblower*. Macmillan.
Snyder, T. (2017). On Tyranny: Twenty Lessons from the Twentieth Century. In: Tim Duggan Books: New York.
Soave, R. (2019). The Media Wildly Mischaracterized That Video of Covington Catholic Students Confronting a Native American Veteran. Retrieved 2019-01-20, from https://reason.com/2019/01/20/covington-catholic-nathan-phillips-video/
Solove, D. J. (2007). *The Future of Reputation: Gossip, Rumor, and Privacy on the Internet*. Yale University Press.
Sorkin, A. (2020). *The Trial of the Chicago 7: The Screenplay*. Simon and Schuster.
Sprunt, B. (2020). Pandemic Revives Calls to Ban Lawmakers from Bunking in Their Offices. https://www.npr.org/2020/05/13/852359650/pandemic-revives-calls-to-ban-lawmakers-from-bunking-in-their-offices
Square, Z. P. (2024). What History Teaches Us About Demagogues Like the Donald. https://time.com/4375262/history-demagogues-donald-trump/
Stearns, C. B. (2016). *Life in the Marble Palace: In Praise of Folly*. FriesenPress.
Steger, W. (2013). Polls and Elections: Two Paradigms of Presidential Nominations. *Presidential Studies Quarterly, 43*(2), 377-387.
Steigrad, A. (2024). Fired Cbs News Reporter Catherine Herridge Accuses Network of 'Journalistic Rape' for Seizing Her Files at Capitol Hill Hearing. *NY Post*. https://nypost.com/2024/04/11/media/crossed-a-red-line-fired-cbs-news-reporter-catherine-herridge-speaks-out-over-seized-files-at-capitol-hill-hearing/

Work Cited

Steinbock, B. (2011). *Life before Birth: The Moral and Legal Status of Embryos and Fetuses*. Oxford University Press.

Stenmark, M. (2017). *Scientism: Science, Ethics and Religion*. Routledge.

Stoler, M. A. (2021). *George C. Marshall: Soldier-Statesman of the American Century*. Plunkett Lake Press.

Sunstein, C. R. (2019). *How Change Happens*. Mit Press.

Suzuki, J. (2015). *Constitutional Calculus: The Math of Justice and the Myth of Common Sense*. JHU Press.

Talev, M. (2023). Two Americas Index: 20% Favor a "National Divorce". Retrieved 2023-03-16, from https://www.axios.com/2023/03/16/two-americas-index-national-divorce

Tanenhaus, S. (1998). *Whittaker Chambers: A Biography*. Modern Library.

Taranto, J. R., David B. (2024). Why Samuel Alito Shuns the State of the Union. *Wall Street Journal*. https://www.wsj.com/opinion/why-samuel-alito-shuns-the-state-of-the-union-obama-supreme-court-polarization-6e1ed0a9

Teles, S. M. (2008). *The Rise of the Conservative Legal Movement: The Battle for Control of the Law*. Princeton University Press.

Thompson, J. B. (2013). *Political Scandal: Power and Visability in the Media Age*. John Wiley & Sons.

Thorning, M., & Racky, J. D. (2025). Congress' Staffing Problem Isn't Work Hours—It's Declining Capacity. Retrieved 2025-01-17, from https://bipartisanpolicy.org/article/congressional-staff-capacity/

Toobin, J. (2018). Brett Kavanaugh's Journey to Becoming a Supreme Court Nominee. *The New Yorker*. Retrieved 2018-07-10, from https://www.newyorker.com/news/daily-comment/brett-kavanaughs-journey-to-becoming-a-supreme-court-nominee

Torres-Spelliscy, C. (2017). Time Suck: How the Fundraising Treadmill Diminishes Effective Governance. *Seton Hall Legis. J.*, *42*, 271.

Trahan, L. H., Stuebing, K. K., Fletcher, J. M., & Hiscock, M. (2014). The Flynn Effect: A Meta-Analysis. *Psychological bulletin*, *140*(5), 1332.

Tufekci, Z. (2015). Algorithmic Harms Beyond Facebook and Google: Emergent Challenges of Computational Agency. *Colo. Tech. LJ, 13*, 203.

Tullock, G. (1971). The Paradox of Revolution. *Public Choice*, 89-99.

Turner, W. (1980). Reagan Says He Would Not Use Single-Issue Test to Pick Judges. *The New York Times*. https://www.nytimes.com/1980/10/02/archives/reagan-says-he-would-not-use-singleissue-test-to-pick-judges.html

Turque, B. (2000). *Inventing Al Gore*. Houghton Mifflin Harcourt.

Turtledove, A. (2018, 2018-11-04). *James C. Corman Congressional Matchbook*. Valley Relics Museum. https://valleyrelicsmuseum.org/uncategorized/james-c-corman-congressional-matchbook/

U.S. Bureau of Economic Analysis. (2025). *Table 1.1.5. Gross Domestic Product*.

U.S. House of Representatives, & Office of the Historian. Party Divisions of the House of Representatives, 1789–Present. https://history.house.gov/Institution/Party-Divisions/Party-Divisions/

U.S. Senate Historical Office. (1950). A Declaration of Conscience. https://www.senate.gov/about/powers-procedures/investigations/mccarthy-hearings/a-declaration-of-conscience.htm

University of Missouri. *The J-School Legacy*. https://journalism.missouri.edu/the-j-school/the-j-school-legacy/

Utah Valley University. (2025). *Welcoming You Back to Campus with Care*. https://www.uvu.edu/news/2025/welcoming-you-back-to-campus-with-care.html

Vargas, R. A. (2025). Utah Governor Calls on People to 'Stop Shooting Each Other' after Kirk Killing. Retrieved 2025-09-30, from https://www.theguardian.com/us-news/2025/sep/30/spencer-cox-charlie-kirk-killing

Varon, E. R. (2008). *Disunion!: The Coming of the American Civil War, 1789-1859*. University of North Carolina Press.

Waldman, M. (2022). Obama Was Right About Citizens United. https://www.brennancenter.org/our-work/analysis-opinion/obama-was-right-about-citizens-united

Wallach, P. A. (2023). *Why Congress*. Oxford University Press.

Work Cited

Walter, B. F. (2023). *How Civil Wars Start: And How to Stop Them*. Crown.
Warren, E. (1977). *The Memoirs of Earl Warren*.
Warren, M. A. (1973). On the Moral and Legal Status of Abortion. *The monist*, 43-61.
Washington, G. (1931). *The Writings of George Washington from the Original Manuscript Sources, 1745-1799* (Vol. 38). U.S. Government Printing Office.
Watson, B. (2007). *Sacco and Vanzetti: The Men, the Murders, and the Judgment of Mankind*. Penguin.
Watts, D. J. (2004). *Six Degrees: The Science of a Connected Age*. WW Norton & Company.
Watts, D. J., & Strogatz, S. H. (1998). Collective Dynamics of 'Small-World' networks. *Nature, 393*(6684), 440-442.
Westen, D. (2008). *The Political Brain: The Role of Emotion in Deciding the Fate of the Nation*. Public Affairs.
White, A. J. (2012). Bork Won. Retrieved 2012-10-01, from https://www.commentary.org/articles/adam-white/bork-won/
White, J. (2003). *False Alarm: Why the Greatest Threat to Social Security and Medicare Is the Campaign to "Save" Them*. JHU Press.
White, T. H. (1969). *1968*. Jonathan Cape.
Wilentz, S. (2006). *Rise of American Democracy: Jefferson to Lincoln*. WW Norton & Company.
Wilkerson, I. (2020). *Caste: The Origins of Our Discontents*. Random House.
Williams, W. (1914). The Journalist's Creed. In Missouri School of Journalism (Ed.).
Wilson, V. P. (2008). *Fair Game: How a Top Cia Agent Was Betrayed by Her Own Government*. Simon and Schuster.
Witcover, J. (1977). Marathon: The Pursuit of the Presidency, 1972-1976.
Wood, G. S. (2011). *The Creation of the American Republic, 1776-1787*. UNC Press Books.
Wood, G. S. (2017). *Friends Divided: John Adams and Thomas Jefferson*. Penguin.
Wright, S. J. (2016). Time to End Presidential Caucuses. *Fordham L. Rev., 85*, 1127.

Wyatt, T. (2019). Alexandria Ocasio-Cortez Delivers Ferocious Speech Dissecting Us Political Corruption. Retrieved 2019-02-08, from https://www.independent.co.uk/news/world/americas/us-politics/alexandria-ocasio-cortez-congress-speech-campaign-finance-corruption-election-aoc-a8769381.html

Yates, R. (1821). Secret Proceedings and Debates of the Convention Assembled at Philadelphia, in the Year 1787, for the Purpose of Forming the Constitution of the United States of America. 129–137. https://founders.archives.gov/documents/Hamilton/01-04-02-0098-0004

Youm, K. H. (2012). Cameras in the Courtroom in the Twenty-First Century: The Us Supreme Court Learning from Abroad. *Brigham Young University Law Review*.

Young, J. S. (1966). *The Washington Community, 1800-1828* (Vol. 69). Columbia University Press.

Zajonc, R. B. (1965). Social Facilitation: A Solution Is Suggested for an Old Unresolved Social Psychological Problem. *Science, 149*(3681), 269-274.

Zelizer, J. E. (2006). *On Capitol Hill: The Struggle to Reform Congress and Its Consequences, 1948-2000*. Cambridge University Press.

Zelizer, J. E. (2018). How Conservatives Won the Battle over the Courts. The Atlantic. https://www.theatlantic.com/ideas/archive/2018/07/how-conservatives-won-the-battle-over-the-courts/564533/

Zimbardo, P. G. (1973). On the Ethics of Intervention in Human Psychological Research: With Special Reference to the Stanford Prison Experiment.

Zorthian, J. (2015). How the O.J. Simpson Verdict Changed the Way We All Watch Tv. https://time.com/4059067/oj-simpson-verdict/

Zubok, V. M. (2021). *Collapse: The Fall of the Soviet Union*. Yale University Press.

Index

A

Adams, John
  fear of democracies, 27, 29–31
  first one-term president, 286
  monarchy charges, 285
  peaceful transfer of power, 285
  rivalry with Jefferson, 285
Adams–Jefferson election, 285, 290, 300
Akerlof. George, 242
Alito, Samuel, 59
altruism, 121, 291, 292, 293, 294, 295, 296, 293–96, 310, 315, 316
Amendments
  Fifteenth, 188
  First, 15, 247, 253
  Fourteenth, 170, 188, 198, 199, 200
  Fourth, 97
  Reconstruction, 188, 191, 198
  Thirteenth, 188
  Twelfth, 189
American Comeback Tour, The, 21
Americans
  Black, 102, 190, 192, 198, 199, 202
  enslaved, 187, 189, 190, 191, 192
  White, 41, 190, 192, 197, 198, 202
analogy, 131, 152, 153, 273
appointments, judicial, 73
Art of the Compromise, The, 146, 186, 212
Articles of Confederation, 159, 162, 168, 181, 182, 209, 216
Atlas Shrugged, 291
Axelrod, Robert, 121

B

Bacon, Kevin, 256
Battle of Michigan Avenue, the, 83
Begala, Paul, 26, 103
being primaried, 273, 274
Biden, Joe, 22, 57
Bilder, Mary Sarah, 158, 160
Black Americans, 102, 190, 192, 198, 199, 202
boardinghouse, 3, 5, 6, 8
Bork, Robert
  attacks by Kennedy, Ted, 102
  ideological tests, 101
  intellect, 100
  Kennedy on Bork's America, 101, 102
  litmus test, 101
  lynching of, 101
  nomination of, 100, 102, 103
  television, 101, 102
  to bork, 100, 104
  turning point, 148

Index

bork, to, 100, 101
Bowen, Debra, 165
Boyd, Lon V., 60
Brown v. Board of Education, 200, 201
Brown, Henry Billings, 199
Bryan, William Jennings, 43
budget reform
   District Trustee role, 267
   stablizing effects, 268–70
   supermajority, District Trustees, 268
Burger, Warren, 53
Bush, George W., 54, 98, 189, 191, 227
Bush–Gore election, 189, 190, 191, 290

C

C-3PO, 48
Caesar, 24, 51, 294
capitalization, 3, 30
Carter, Jimmy
   bypass traditional authority, 88
   campaign strategy, 81, 87, 88, 86–89
   celebrity over statesmanship, 89
   great ex-president, 310
   inauguration, 82
   inauguration walk, 88
   Jimmy who?, 82–86
   limited national experience, 310
   Naval Academy graduate, 87
   new primary rules, 79, 80, 82, 86, 87
   newcomer, 310
   nuclear engineer, 87
   obscurity, 82
   party realignment, 89
   peanut brigade, 81
   peanut farmer, 80
   presidency tilts toward polarization, 310
   smile full of teeth, 80
   strategy, 86
   wins Iowa, 81, 82, 85
Carter–Reagan election, 101
Carville, James, 26, 103
Chamber, the
   definition, 216
   needs, 228
   reform, 260–65, 266–70
   regular order, 228
   remain functional, 264
   shift, 227
   stop misguided reforms, 236
   term limits, 237
Chambers, Whittaker, 197
ChatGPT, 321
Chatham House, 232, 234
Cheney, Dick, 98
Chicago Seven trial, 133
Chicago, Burlington & Quincy Railroad Co. v. Chicago, 170
Church Committee, 97
Church, Frank, 97
CIA, 98
Citizens United v. FEC, 247, 248, 249, 253, 254
Civil Rights, 154, 184, 190, 197, 199, 204
Civil Rights Act of 1964, 110, 171, 201
Civil Rights Movement, 171, 199
civil war, a, 24, 25, 26, 75, 186, 193
Civil War, the, 33, 75, 111, 170, 186, 187, 189, 190, 191, 243, 289
Clinton, Bill, 98, 103
Clinton, Hillary, 95
CNN, 42, 45, 299
Cohen, Michael, 56
Compromise of 1877, 193
compromise, four-letter word, 12

Congressional districts, large single-member, 263–65
Constitutional Convention. *See* Philadelphia Convention
contempt
　factional, 6, 287
　for Congress, 130–33, 135
　in the Judiciary, 133
　injustice, 134
continuing resolutions, 67, 69, 70, 226, 305
Contract with America, 222
Cooper Union, 185
Covey, Stephen, 296
COVID, 46, 47, 50, 122
cowbell
　analogy, 153
　excessive use of, 1–318
　Mississippi State fans, 151
　noise maker, football, 151–53
Cox, Archibald, 102
Cox, Spence, 22
criminalization of politics, 98, 99, 291
crisis of 1876, 181, 189–92, 204
Crisis, Nullification, 33
Cronkite, Walter, 280
C-SPAN, 53, 54, 219, 226

D

Daley, Richard, 83
Darrow, Clarence, 43
Darwin, Charles, 242
Dayton, Tennessee, 43
Dean, Howard, 176
Declaration of Conscience, 195
demagogues
　definition, 28
　Federalist No. 10, 143
　Federalist No. 71, 28
　in America, 144
　Jackson, Andrew, 144
　Jefferson's thoughts on, 194

Long, Huey, 144
Madison's thoughts on, 194
McCarthy, Joseph, 144, 194–97
　role of news media, 147
　Trump, Donald, 144
democracy, definition, 155
Democratic control of the House, 222
Democratic National Convention, 1968, 83, 133, 239
Democratic Party, 39, 84, 95, 289
Democratic-Republican Party, 39, 286
Dickinson, John, 209
direct democracy, definition, 156
District Trustee. *See* Public Trustee of the District
divorce
　couples arguing, 130
　national, 25–27
Donaldson, Sam, 60
Donne, John, 302
Dover, Pennsylvania, 44
drain the swamp, 89, 127
Druckman, James, 233
Dunbar, Robin, 66, 256, 257
Dunbar's Number, 256

E

Eisenhower, Dwight D., 195, 196, 201
election
　Adams–Jefferson, 285, 290, 300
　Bush–Gore, 189, 190, 191, 290
　Carter–Reagan, 101
　Hayes–Tilden, 189
　Kennedy–Nixon, 189, 233, 290, 300

Index

Trump–Clinton, 300
Election Day, 36, 252
Electoral College, 189, 237
enslaved Americans, 187, 189, 190, 191, 192
Ethics in Government Act, 99

F

Facebook, 56, 125, 278
face-to-face interaction, 122
Faubus, Orval, 201
Fauci, Anthony, 46
Federalist No. 1, 143
Federalist No. 10
  demagogues, 143
  enlarge the sphere, 66, 91, 183, 244
  inevitability of faction, 39
  pure democracy, 172
  small republics, 237
  violence of faction, 22
  well-constructed union, 154
Federalist No. 51, 184
Federalist No. 52, 114
Federalist No. 53, 114
Federalist No. 55, 173
Federalist No. 63, 143, 146, 197
Federalist No. 71, 28
Federalist No. 78, 58
Federalists, the party, 173, 285, 286
Flynn Effect, 179
footnotes, abused by author, 1–318
Ford, Gerald, 61, 62
Four Horsemen of Calumny, 195
Fourth Branch, 8, 15, 277, 279, 280, 283, 325
Fox News, 45, 299
Frankl, Viktor, 296
Franklin, Benjamin, 2
Fraser, Donald M., 84
freelance political actor, 270

Friedman, Milton, 291

G

Gang of Eight, 234
gangs, bipartisan, 234
Garfield, James, 62
Garland, Merrick, 56
-gate scandals, 99
Gerry, Elbridge, 64
gerrymandering, 64, 263, 305, 317
Gingrich Revolution, 105, 106, 113, 124, 129, 223
Gingrich, Newt
  conflict with O'Neill, Tip, 54
  Contract with America, 222
  C-SPAN, 54
  leadership of, 222
  reforms in 1994, 222
  revolution of, 105, 106, 113, 124, 129, 222, 223
  style on House floor, 55, 57, 223
  television in Congress, 54
Gitlow v. New York, 170
God, 49, 51, 294
Gore, Al, 120, 290, 291, 293
Gottman, John, 130
Green, Al, 59
Greene, Marjorie Taylor, 4, 25

H

Hague, Frank, 83
Hamilton, Alexander
  elitist warning, 173
  nationalist, 182
  on demagogues, 27, 28–29, 143
  on the judiciary, 105
  on the People, 29
  rivalry with Madison, 300
  Shays's Rebellion, 209
Hamilton, William, 121

Harding, Warren, 62
Hayes, Rutherford B., 189, 191
Hayes–Tilden election, 189
Herridge, Catherine, 57
Hoffman, Julius, 133
Humphrey, Hubert, 83

I

impeachment, 98, 99, 267, 268
institutional containment, 195
Iran–Contra affair, 98

J

Jackson, Andrew
  demagogue, 144
  democratization, 39, 142
  founding Democratic Party, 39
  on nullification, 187
  party press, 149
  People's President, the, 144
Jacksonian era, 40
January 6, 292, 303
Jefferson, Thomas
  books for Madison, 159
  concern over his legacy, 31
  doubt in the Republic, 27, 31
  founding Democratic-
    Republican Party, 39
  gravestone enscription, 31
  on demagogues, 194
  on enlightened citizens, 174
  rivalry with Adams, 285
  transfer of power, 285
Jesus of Nazerath, 294–95
Jim Crow, 181
  caricature, 192
  courts dismantling, 198–202
  era, 191–93
  institutional, 198
Johnson, Hiram, 164
Johnson, Lyndon, 97, 110, 119, 125, 201

Jordan, Jim, 55, 56, 57, 288

K

Kanawha County, West Virginia, 44
Katz v. United States, 97
Kennedy, John F.
  allegations of voter fraud, 290
  Church Committee findings, 97
  first televised debate, 233
  television, calm poise, 54
  wiretapping MLK, 97
Kennedy, Robert, 84
Kennedy, Ted, 101, 102, 103, 125, 148
Kennedy–Nixon election, 189, 233, 290, 300
Kenney, Ted, 102
King, Martin Luther, 97
Kingfish, the, 144
Kirk, Charlie
  aftermath, 32
  American Comeback Tour, The, 21
  assassination, 20–22, 29, 287, 303
  celebratory reactions to death of, 22–23
  Cox, Spence, 22
  misinformation surrounding death of, 23
  violence of faction, 22
Koppel, Ted, 62

L

Lamb, Brian, 53
last battle of the Second World War, the, 44
Lewinsky, Monica, 98
litmus test, 101
lock her up!, 178

Index

Long, Huey, 144, 149

M

Madison, James
  altruism, 291, 294
  assumptions, 266, 267, 292, 294, 314
  best informed man, 182
  books from Jefferson, 159
  college student, 20
  enlarge the sphere, 244
  Father of the Constitution, 12, 158
  fears of, 171, 204, 213
  federal negative, 170, 171, 169–71, 188, 200
  filters, 13, 34, 42, 262
  founding Democratic-Republican Party, 39
  friend of Jefferson, 31
  insights, 12–13
  nationalist, 182
  Notes on Ancient and Modern Confederacies, 160
  Notes on the Constitutional Convention, 158
  on demagogues, 194
  on democracies, 34
  on factions, 22, 225, 230, 237
  on Nullification Crisis, 33
  on political parties, 39
  on political violence, 24
  on Socrates, 173
  pragmatist, 20
  republican architecture, 12–13, 206, 221, 224, 230, 292, 295
  rivalry with Hamilton, 300
  seat of government, 210
  studies of Ancient democracies, 159
  violence of faction, 22
  well-constructed Union, 154
  Witherspoon's student, 20
MAGA, 21, 40, 41
MAGA hat kid, 40–43
marriage, 130
Marshall, George C., 194
Marshall, Thurgood, 199
matchbooks, campaign swag, 61
McCarthy, Joseph, 194–97
  censure of, 196
  congressional hearings, 103
  demagogue, 144
  echo of, to bork, 103
  fear tactic, 103
  rebuke of, 196
  role of ex-Soviet spy, 197
  role of Nixon, 196
  television, 144, 149
McCarthyism, 103, 154, 181, 194–97, 197, 204
McGovern, George, 84
McGovern–Fraser Commission, 84, 88, 93, 239, 250, 309
Melian Dialogue, 185
Millennium Falcon, 48
Mineta, Norm, 125
Mississippi State fans, 151
MoMo, 60
Monkey Trial, 43
motivated reasoning, 41, 75
Moyers, Bill, 201
Moynihan, Daniel Patrick, 101, 125
Murrow, Edward R., 280

N

NAACP, 199
nationalists, 182
negative, federal, 169, 170, 171, 169–71, 188, 199, 200
neocortex, 256
newspapers, death of, 9, 145, 146

Nixon, Richard
  Church Committee findings, 97
  comeback, 311
  containing McCarthyism, 195
  defeats Humphrey in 1968, 84
  fallout from, 99–100
  first televised debate, 233
  first to get caught, 97
  institutional containment, 195
  judicial appointments, 73
  nobility of, 189, 290, 293
  partisan misuse of government, 98
  permanent investigation, the, 99
  reforms after, 89
  resignation, 97
  Saturday Night Massacre, 102
  television, shadowed fatigue, 54
nullification, 33, 187, 217
Nullification Crisis, 33, 187

O

O'Neill, Tip, 54
Obama, Barack
  birtherism, 98
  Nobel Peace laureate, 58
  on Kirk assassination, 22
  scolding Supreme Court, 58
  You lie! incident, 58, 132
Ocasio-Cortez, Alexandria, 4, 55, 56, 57, 58, 273, 288
one another, Biblical phrase, 4, 6, 49, 119, 120, 121, 131, 263, 268

P

party conventions,
  tranformation of, 63
party realignment, 89, 110, 201
Peacock Effect, 242, 244
peanut brigade, 81
People's President, the, 144
Permanent Campaign, 113, 115, 246, 248, 250, 254, 276
permanent investigation, the, 89, 99
Philadelphia Convention, 158, 159, 160, 167, 168, 169, 173, 183, 184, 199
Pipeline, the
  constituent–donor financing, 248
  definition, 8, 207, 216
  governs ambition, 15, 18
  legislature inherits from, 245
  party control, 252
  party governance, 253
  Permanent Campaign, 246–54
  political calendar, 251
  reform, 211, 248, 251, 254, 260–65
  reform, majoritarian, 239–41
  selects preformers, 240
  shift, 8
Plame, Valerie, 98
Plessy v. Ferguson, 199
polarization, 1, 11, 12, 24, 46, 80, 92, 96, 107, 112, 113, 126, 143, 148, 149, 205, 212, 214, 215, 218, 222, 238, 240, 272, 283, 289, 297, 298, 309, 310
political machine, 44, 273, 312, 313
political theater, television, 59
politics of scandal, 98
portmanteau, 64
Press, the

Index

collapse, 278
death of newspapers, 9, 145, 146
definition, 216
Fourth Branch, the, 15
necessary for, 15, 18
on Carter Campaign, 81
post-journalism, 177
protection, 15
reform, 282
Viral Editor, 278
watchdog function, 98
Watergate, 98
Price, Gary Lee, 296
primaries, low-turnout, 9, 216, 273
Prisoner's Dilemma, 121
Public Trustee of the District
30,000:1 ratio, 260
choice of term trustee, 266
district size limits, 265
District Trustee (shorthand), 260
fiduciary authority (budget failure), 266–67
gerrymandering, 263
national annual convention, 261
no legislative authority, 261
opposing parties, 261
preserve large, single-member districts, 263–65
reside in home district, 261
stablizing effects (budget reform), 268–70
supermajority vote, 269
Tammany Hall connection, 262–63
Pulitzer, Joseph, 281, 299

R

Rand, Ayn, 291–92
Rather, Dan, 61
Reagan Revolution, 88

Reagan, Ronald
coronation, 60
drain the swamp, 128
Iran–Contra affair, 98
judicial appointments, 73
nomination of Bork, 102
party nomination, 60, 61
primary with Gerald Ford, 61
revolution of, 88
Reagan–Ford primary, 61
Reconstruction era, 170, 184, 188, 189, 190, 191, 192, 202
Red Scare, 194
reform
Chamber, the, 260–65, 266–70
consituent–donor financing, 248
District Trustee, 260–65
gerrymandering, 263
Pipeline, the, 248, 251, 254, 260–65
political calendar, 251
post-1968, 95, 166, 212, 239, 240, 241, 250, 270–72, 283, 290, 302, 309
Press, the, 282
primary synchronization, 251
shorter nomination windows, 251
single Election Day, 252
regular order, 220, 227, 228
republic
comparison to democracy, 155–57
definition, 156–57
if you can keep it, 2
well-constructed, 154
Republican Party, 61, 105, 111, 201
Republican Revolution. *See* Gingrich Revolution
Residence Clause, 210
revolution, digital, 142–43
Reynolds, Glenn, 176

368

Richardson, Elliot, 102
Rickover, Hyman G., 87
Robbers Cave experiment, 121
Rocklin, California, 44
Roe v. Wade, 101, 247
Rove, Karl, 104, 227
Ruckelshaus, William, 102

S

salamander, 64
Sandmann, Nick, 40
Saturday Night Live, 74
Saturday Night Massacre, 102
scandals, presidential, 98, 99
Schwarzenegger, Arnold, 272, 296
Scopes Trial, 43, 44
Scopes, John, 43
Secession, 184, 185, 204, 314
Shays's Rebellion, 168, 181, 182, 184, 185, 186, 288
Sherif, Muzafer, 121
Simpson, Alan, 125
Simpson, O.J., 53, 54, 134, 235
six degrees of Kevin Bacon, 259
Smith, Margaret Chase, 195
Snowden, Edward, 42
Solo, Han, 48
Southern Manifesto, 200
spy, ex-Soviet spy, 197
Statue of Liberty, 296
Statue of Responsibility, 296
strategy, fifty-percent-plus-one, 227
suicide pact, not, 253

T

Tammany Hall
  Boss Tweed, 36, 271
  corruption, 36, 312
  District Trustee, 262
  durability, 37
  history, 38

informal representation, 37
moral stain, 37
outside constitutional legitimacy, 38
political machine, 37, 90, 273, 312
Tax Reform Act of 1986, 225
television
  appeal of Spencer Cox, 22
  Army–McCarthy hearings, 196
  Bork, Robert, 102
  C-SPAN, 53
  entertainment incentives, 220
  first televised debate, 54, 233
  Gingrich in Congress, 54
  Kennedy–Nixon debate, 233
  MAGA hat kid, 40
  McCarthy, Joseph, 144
  party conventions, 61
  political theater, 53–59
  psychology experiment, 234
  Republican National Convention, 60
  scream of Howard Dean, 176
  scrutiny of Bork, 101
Tilden, Samuel J., 189, 190
Tit for Tat, 121
Tocqueville, Alexis de, 30
Trump, Donal
  mastered social media, 149
Trump, Donald
  Bible in-hand photo, 55
  conflict with party, 95, 273
  demagogue, 144
  drain the swamp, 89
  House Democrats protest, 59
  mastered social media, 144
  People's President, the, 144
  polarization, 205–6
  transformed federal judiciary, 73

Index

Trump–Clinton election, 300
trustee, 266
Tweed, William M. (Boss), 36, 272
tyranny, 1, 11, 15, 28, 29, 159, 169, 200, 213, 285, 286

V

Vance, J.D., 22
violence of faction, 22
Viral Editor, 142, 143, 148, 205, 278
Vote for My Uncle, T-shirts, 60
Voting Rights Act of 1965, 171, 201, 202

W

Walken, Christopher, 74
Walter, Barbara, 26
Warren, Earl, 200
Washington, George, 40
   fears of, 34–36, 172
   nationalist, 182
   on Congressional representation, 65
   on factions, 27
   only intervention in Philadelphia, 65, 255
   secrecy in Philadelphia, 52, 183
   step down from power, 286
Watergate, 53, 68, 82, 89, 96, 97, 98, 99, 102, 148
Watkins, Athur V., 196
Watt, Mel, 63
Watts Bar Nuclear Plant, 44
We the People, 11, 254, 296, 318
Welch, Joseph, 196
White Americans, 41, 190, 192, 197, 198, 202
White House, 46, 82, 89, 93, 224
White Southerners. *See* White Americans
Wilson, Joe, 58, 132
Witherspoon, John, 20

Z

Zuckerberg, Mark, 56

ABOUT THE AUTHOR

David Lon Page, Ph.D., is a Research Scientist with a doctorate in Electrical Engineering from the University of Tennessee. His day job and professional work focus on applied research in computer vision. Outside that work, he has maintained a lifelong interest in American politics. He began volunteering on campaigns at the age of ten and has since remained an engaged observer of civic life, party politics, and the structural mechanics of democratic governance.

David lives in Knoxville, Tennessee, with his wife, Lisa. Their daughter, Grace, is away at college, a development rendering the household officially empty-nested and noticeably poorer. *The Art of the Compromise* is his first full-length nonfiction book on American politics, and this second book continues that project.

www.ingramcontent.com/pod-product-compliance
Lightning Source LLC
LaVergne TN
LVHW020426070526
838199LV00004B/303